BATH

TOWN AND CITY HISTORIES
HISTORICAL EDITOR: STEPHEN CONSTANTINE

BATH
A NEW HISTORY

Graham Davis
and Penny Bonsall

KEELEUNIVERSITYPRESS

First published in 1996
by Keele University Press
Keele University, Staffordshire, England

© Graham Davis and Penny Bonsall

Composed by
Keele University Press
and printed by Hartnolls
in Bodmin, England

ISBN 1 85331 028 X

Contents

Historical Editor's Foreword

The books in this series are designed and written with a broad readership in mind: local people interested to know how the character of their town has been shaped by major historical forces and the energies of their predecessors; newcomers and visitors curious to acquire a historical introduction to their new surroundings; general readers wishing to see how the sweeps of national and international history have manifested themselves in particular urban communities; and the scholar seeking to understand urbanization by comparing and contrasting local experiences.

We live, most of us, in intensely urban environments. These are the products largely of the last two centuries of historical development, although the roots of many towns, of course, go back deep into the past. In recent years there has been considerable historical research of a high standard into this urban history. Narrative and descriptive accounts of the history of towns and cities can now be replaced by studies such as the TOWN AND CITY HISTORIES which investigate, analyse and, above all, explain the economic, political and cultural processes and consequences of urbanization.

Writers for this series consider the changing economic foundations of their town or city and the way in which change has affected its physical shape, built environment, employment opportunities and urban character. The nature and interests of those who wield power locally and the structure and functions of local government in different periods are also examined, since locally exercised authority could determine much about the fortunes and quality of urban life. Particular emphasis is placed on the changing life experiences of ordinary men, women and children – their homes, education, occupations, social relations, living standards and leisure activities. Towns and cities control and respond to the values, aspirations and actions of their residents. The books in this series therefore explore social behaviour as well as the economic and political history of those who lived in, and helped to make, the towns and cities of today.

To Louie Stride and the people of Bath

Acknowledgements

Our debts are many and extend over a long period. Firstly, a word of appreciation for Professor Angus Buchanan of the University of Bath. He supervised the doctoral thesis out of which the book evolved, and he has always given his support and encouragement over many years. A posthumous debt is owed to Professor R. S. Neale of the University of New England, New South Wales, a pioneer in the social history of Bath who led the way for others to follow who, in turn, have offered their own interpretations.

Our enthusiasm for the study of Bath history has been shared with our own students at Bath College of Higher Education and with extra-mural students at Bristol University and some of those have engaged in their own research which is drawn on in the book. In particular, we are grateful to Alex Kolaczkowski for permission to draw on her doctoral thesis, at the University of Bath, on the politics of civic improvement in Victorian Bath.

Inevitably, much is owed to the advice and help received in local libraries and archives. Our thanks go to Colin Johnstone and his staff at the Guildhall Archives, to the staff of the Bath Library, the University library and the Newton Park Library at Bath College of Higher Education. Special thanks are due to Dr John Robb, head of geography, for his unstinting advice and expertise in preparing the maps. Finally, a heartfelt debt of gratitude to Dr Stephen Constantine, the series editor, for his meticulous and tireless attention to detail, and to Jill Palmer, the humanities faculty secretary at Newton Park, who processed the text of the book with incredible good humour.

The material drawn on and the emphasis in the writing of this book is different from the content of most of the published histories of Bath. In this new social history, deliberate weight is given to the lives of ordinary citizens and to the history of the modern, post-Georgian city. Indeed, five of the eight chapters are devoted to the nineteenth and twentieth centuries. It is also argued that it is possible to comprehend the history of Bath in terms of a tension between image and reality and that a process of camouflage disguised less attractive features in the interests of a dominant image that changed over time according to historic circumstances. That was as true of the past as it is of today. The commercial exploitation of the city's history to serve the needs of the tourist industry continues to overemphasize its most saleable assets: the Roman and Georgian periods, the famous visitors, the elegant architecture and the 'heroic' contribution of Ralph Allen, 'Beau Nash' and John Wood.

This book sets out to redress the balance of heritage history with a social history that reconstructs the experience of the people of Bath. Hence the dedication to Louie Stride, a poor, hungry child of Edwardian Bath, who wrote her own remarkable story, *Memoirs of a Street Urchin*, and to the people of Bath.

List of Tables

List of Maps

List of Illustrations

Chapter 1

The Origins and Early History of Bath to 1700

The cite of Bath is sette both yn a fruiteful and pleasant botom, the which is environed on every side with great hills, out of the which cum many springes of pure water that be conveyed by dyverse ways to serve the cite.

Leland's Itinerary, 1540.[1]

Bath lies in its 'pleasant botom' at the southern end of the Cotswolds, within the boundaries of the historic county of Somerset. The city underwent many changes of image and function from its early origins to the end of the seventeenth century. From Roman spa, Saxon monastic town and Norman cathedral city, it developed into a regional market and woollen centre in the Middle Ages, to become the national health resort of the sixteenth and seventeenth centuries. The impact and consequences of its rapid expansion in the Georgian period, of relative decline from the later 1700s and subsequent changes in the nineteenth and twentieth centuries need to be set within the context of its earlier history. The growth and development of Bath from its origins to the end of the seventeenth century are the subject of this chapter.[2]

Roman spa, cathedral city and woollen centre

The city is sited on a river crossing, and the earliest walled settlements were located on a peninsula of land within the north–south and east–west reaches of the meander of the River Avon. The river was significant for Bath's history not only in determining early settlement, but also for its later importance in developing trade with the nearby port of Bristol, and with London and other parts of the country after the building of canals. The economy of Bath was closely associated with the rural hinterland. As the town grew, it developed a regional market function and attracted migrants from the surrounding counties of Somerset, Wiltshire and Gloucestershire. The Somerset coalfield, in the north-eastern part of the county, extended on its eastern limits to villages within a few miles of Bath, which was an important market for the output of the local collieries, from the early eighteenth century onward.[3]

The river valley in which Bath is located is spectacularly deep to the east of Bathampton Down, but it broadens out downstream from the city. The valley and its surrounding green hills were to provide an attractive setting for the 'Queen of Spas', but air tends to stagnate at the bottom of the valley, where it creates a moist and somewhat enervating atmosphere. 'Balmy Bath' and its mild winters were promoted as one of its advantages in the eighteenth century and beyond, but not all of the city's visitors appreciated the local climate. Alexander Pope described Bath as a 'sulphurous pit', and Mrs Piozzi (a friend of Dr Johnson) described the lower town as being like a 'stew-pot'.[4]

River crossings were commonplace sites for early settlement, but at Bath, as elsewhere, the local geology shaped future growth and development. Bath benefited from three natural resources: the hot springs on which its fame primarily rests, the stone with which much of it was built, and the presence of fuller's earth clay. The hot springs rise out of a clay ridge in a bend of the Avon valley to emerge at the rate of a quarter of a million gallons a day, at a temperature of around 40°C. Bath stone caps the hills around the city, but working has been confined to the southern areas and was not extensive before the eighteenth century. The stone is mined rather than quarried, a process which has left the Combe Down area honeycombed by underground workings. When it is first used, Bath stone is almost white but its surface tends to rot as a result of weathering and its affinity for soot (which forms a hard black scale on the exposed stone) proved to be another disadvantage. Anne Eliot, the heroine of Jane Austen's *Persuasion* (1818), dreaded 'the possible heats of September in all the white glare of Bath',[5] but by the later nineteenth century much of the city was grey or soot-blackened. Bath's third natural resource, fuller's earth, was mined to the south of the city until recent times. It was used to remove grease from woollen cloth, and its local occurrence contributed to the growth of the regional textile industry in medieval times, when cloth-making for more than domestic use began. The presence and exploitation of the hot springs gave 'both name and fame to the place', as Daniel Defoe noted, but in suggesting that the city would have been 'insignificant' without the existence of the baths, Defoe made the commonplace error of accepting that the history of Bath is encapsulated within its dominant image.[6] In reality, all three of its natural resources contributed to the growth and development of the city, and the issues explored in this study reveal a more complex history than the usual emphasis on Bath as a spa resort indicates.

Nonetheless, no account of Bath's origins would be complete without some reference to the traditional explanation of the discovery of the healing powers of the hot springs by the legendary Bladud, a princely figure ostracized on account of his leprosy and reduced to the lowly role of swineherd. His swine were also diseased, but their sores healed after they wallowed in the waters. Bladud, following their example, immersed himself in the spring and he too was cured. This mythical origin of Bath was widely known as early as the twelfth century, but there is also archaeological evidence of human activity in the Bath region in prehistoric ages. Artifacts from the neolithic period (4000–2000 BC) and the early Bronze Age (2000–1500 BC) have been found at various sites, and tumuli or burial mounds have been identified on Lansdown, at Bathampton Down and on Charmy Down. A defended settlement dating from the Iron Age (800 BC–AD 500) has also been identified, at Bathampton. We may assume that some of these early settlers made use of the waters, for excavations carried out in the 1970s around the main spring (beneath the present King's Bath) revealed a wall of the Iron Age period.

The coming of the Romans in AD 43 heralded the development of the spa as the chief settlement of its kind in Roman Britain. The marshy ground around the springs was drained in successive phases of activity, and within a walled area of about twenty-four acres the Romans erected a complex of buildings, including the baths and a temple to Sulis-Minerva, who was an amalgamation of the Celtic deity Sul and the Roman goddess Minerva. It was the Romans who gave the city its first recorded name, Aquae Sulis. The settlement was not a large one (substantially smaller than the nearby Roman city of Cirencester, in Gloucestershire, for example) but its importance as a religious shrine and spa attracted pilgrims from throughout Romano-Britain and across Europe. Under Roman rule the prosperity of Aquae Sulis was largely dependent on its religious and spa functions but, as in later ages, its character and economy were more varied than its image suggests. The city also provided a local market for the sale or exchange of commodities, and small-scale manufacturing (such as glass-working and the marking of pewter vessels) was carried on within the walled city and at Lansdown.

Between the collapse of the Roman empire in the early fifth century AD and the arrival of the Saxons, little is known of the city's history. It is likely that the walled area was continuously occupied, but that the baths, the temple and many of the other buildings fell into ruin. However, in AD 577 Saxon forces triumphed at the battle of Dyrham, and Bath thereafter came under Saxon rule. Over the next two centuries it developed into a major Christian religious centre. King Osric established a convent there in 676, and in 757 King Offa made a grant of lands to the monastery of St Peter, on which the Saxon abbey was built. This was one of the greatest churches in England, of such prestige that it was chosen as the site for the coronation in 973 of the first king of all England, King Edgar.

The Norman conquest of England in 1066 did not immediately disturb the religious élite who dominated Saxon Bath, and the monastic authorities

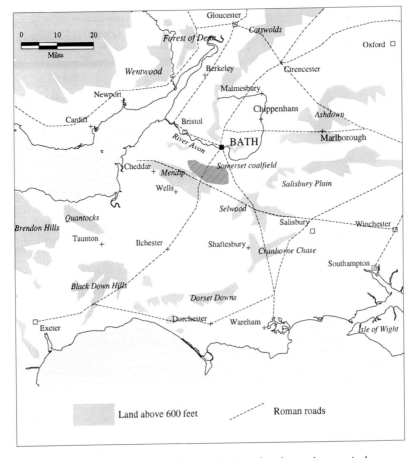

Map 1 Location map of Bath in the medieval and early modern periods

retained their lands and property. However, by the time of the Domesday
survey in 1087 the Saxon mint and some local estates had become royal
possessions. These royal estates and the strategic importance of the city's
location on a river crossing attracted the unwelcome attention of armed
insurrectionists in 1088, when Bath was burned and pillaged in a short-
lived rebellion against the accession to the throne of William Rufus. The
city was virtually destroyed by the rebels, but once William Rufus had
secured his accession he appointed John de Villula of Tours as Bishop of
Wells, and granted him the abbey at Bath with all its lands and properties. John of Tours was evidently an ambitious and enterprising man,
who had plans for the development of Bath. In 1091 he moved the see
of the Somerset bishopric from Wells to Bath, and instigated several
major building projects. The greatest of these was the construction of a

new abbey church, of such an immense size that the whole of the present-day abbey would have fitted into its nave. Abbey cloisters, a chapter house and prior's lodgings were also planned, and John of Tours established a collegiate school in Bath at which the medieval scholar Abelard was educated. The great cathedral church was unfinished at the time of John of Tours' death in 1122, but the church owned and ran the baths at this time, as well as several lodging houses. John of Tours' efforts to develop Bath are an early example of the tendency of the city's ruling élite to look to the past for present prosperity. What he created was a Christian version of Aquae Sulis, which had flourished as a combined spa and religious centre. As a result, from Norman times to the end of the fifteenth century, Bath was best known as a monastic city, controlled by the ecclesiastical authorities, and its prosperity was closely linked to the appeal of its curative waters and to increasing pilgrimage to the city.

Nonetheless, medieval Bath had other functions. Beneath the dominant image of a healing and holy city lay different realities. Although the connection between the church and the town would always have been close, Bath was, in addition, a local and regional market, its economy ever more dependent on the wool trade and the cloth industry. Its population in the late 1300s has been estimated, on the basis of poll tax returns, at between 1,000 and 1,100,[7] and most of these inhabitants were working people whose livelihoods did not depend on the spa. These returns provide no evidence of occupations related to the baths and, furthermore, it seems that even the monks were occupied primarily in spinning and weaving and the final preparation of cloth for the market. The monastery certainly bought in raw wool, and its property included a fulling-mill on the banks of the Avon. It therefore seems that the economy of Bath was not based mainly on those features for which it was best known at the time, the waters and the religious foundation: most of the skilled workers in Bath were engaged in the wool trade. Labourers and servants predominated among the 328 individuals listed in the late fourteenth-century poll-tax return, but workers in the textile industry accounted for the majority of the 106 craftsmen and tradesmen. Moreover, the economic life of Bath did not exist in isolation from the surrounding region. In addition to commerce and trade at the markets, coal came into the city from Radstock, and much of the cloth woven in the nearby industrial village of Twerton (Twiverton-on-Avon) was finished in Bath. One of the city's dyers, Ralph Hunt, complained to the authorities in 1405 about the theft of ten yards of blue cloth, which had been stolen from the rack on which he had left it stretched on tenterhooks to dry.[8]

For much of the fourteenth and fifteenth centuries Bath existed as a small, moderately prosperous, wool town, despite the decline of its priory and its diminishing importance as a religious centre. The economy continued to develop and the corporate powers of the townspeople increased. The number of monks in the Bath priory fell to twenty-one by the end of the fourteenth century, partly as a consequence of the Black Death plague in the 1340s and 1360s. When Bishop Oliver King visited the priory in 1499 he found it poorly maintained and undisciplined: there was feasting in the refectory, the monks were idle, and women were often seen at 'unseemly times' in the monastery precinct.[9] Bath was gradually superseded by Wells as a focus of religious life (after the Somerset bishopric was made a joint see in the late thirteenth century) and the Norman abbey degenerated into a ruinous state. Bishop King decreed that this must be rectified, and ordered that the running costs of the priory and the convent be reduced to pay for repairs. It was, however, virtually a new abbey that began to be erected on the site – a building that was still incomplete in 1535.

Religious pilgrims and the sick in search of cure still contributed to the local economy at the end of the fifteenth century, but Bath's prosperity rested fundamentally on the wool trade, on its weekly cattle and produce market, and on its three annual fairs. Chaucer's *Wife of Bath* was representative of the town's inhabitants in her occupation, if not in her enthusiasm for taking husbands. Her skill at weaving was such that 'Of clooth-making she hadde swiche an haunt, she passed hem of Ypres and of Gaunt.'[10]

It was between 1500 and 1700, centuries of political conflict and social upheaval in England, that power and authority came to be vested wholly in the corporate body. The dissolution of the monasteries in the 1530s was of particular significance for the city's future. The cathedral monastery at Bath was dissolved in 1539 and its estates surrendered to the crown. The still unfinished abbey was offered to the city authorities for use as a parish church but, perhaps because of the money needed to complete it, the offer was initially declined. However, some thirty years later the citizens petitioned for the renovation of the existing abbey buildings, and in the early 1570s it was reconsecrated to SS Peter and Paul the parish church. Meanwhile, under letters patent of 1552, the property of the priory had been transferred to the mayor and citizens of Bath. Thereafter the corporation controlled all the city's major assets and owned four-fifths of the property within its walls. The city had become a borough under a charter of 1189, but in 1590 Elizabeth I granted Bath a new charter of incorporation, under which all the powers previously held by the bishops and the prior were vested in the civic authority.

The political constitution of the city rested on the 1590 charter until the Reform Act of 1832 and the Municipal Corporations Act of 1835. Power was concentrated in a small élite: the corporation was made up of a mayor, no fewer than four or more than ten aldermen, and twenty common councillors. New councillors were chosen by the existing body from the 'freemen', who otherwise had no say in the corporation's actions,

1. The west front of the Abbey Church, begun in 1499 by Bishop Oliver King. The Abbey was restored twice in the nineteenth century. The west front was restored in the 1890s and again in the 1990s. (Authors' collection)

but who shared in the monopoly of trade in the city up to 1765 and also in the revenue from the Freemen's Common. The mayor and aldermen were elected by the common councillors. As the governing body and the owner of much property within the city, the corporation was intimately involved in the growth and development of Bath. It derived most of its income from its property, which included the city wall, the guildhall and the market place, much of the area within the city limits, and the baths themselves.[11] These changes influenced some aspects of economic and political life for centuries to come. For example, the corporation's owner-ship of property and land, and the careful management of its assets in the eighteenth century, gave it an assured income which continued to benefit the residents of Bath right down to the twentieth century, in the form of low rates.

National events in the seventeenth century also impinged on Bath, although their effects proved to be less significant for its future than the earlier dissolution of the monastery. During the Civil War (1642–6) Bath, like the rest of the nation, was divided in its sympathies. Its citi-zens were mainly royalists, but parliamentarians formed the majority on the council. However, the impact of the Civil War and its aftermath were less disruptive in Bath than in many other places, for there was no marked dislocation of economic life or extensive damage to property.

Bath itself never came under siege from either side, although in July 1643 the king's Cornish army attacked parliamentary forces holding Lansdown. The battle ended indecisively, with the parliamentarians making a tactical withdrawal to the city, which they briefly occupied. The royalists won a decisive victory shortly afterwards, in an engagement at Roundway Down near Devizes in Wiltshire, and Bath came under royalist control from 1643 to 1645.[12] Political life in the city was inevitably strained, but no purges of either group on the council took place, and by the time Oliver Cromwell died (September 1658) both royalists and parliamentarians were ready to forget their differences. Hope that a lasting political settlement would create a stable climate in which trade would improve led to growing enthusiasm for the restoration of the monarchy. Bath was the first city in the country to proclaim Charles II as king, on 12 May 1660, and it was also the first to offer him a loyal address. Later, in the Monmouth Rebellion of 1685, Bath was staunchly behind James II.[13] Areas on the outskirts of the city were used as assembly grounds for the regular army, but the most dramatic episode of the 'pitchfork rebellion' in Bath was the public execution of six Somerset men, who were sentenced to death by the notorious Judge Jeffreys. The county sheriff thoughtfully reminded the city authorities 'to provide an axe and a cleaver for the quartering the said rebels', who were butchered in the brutal manner of the times.[14]

Meanwhile, perhaps sustained by the desire for political stability, the local economy grew, but the balance of its constituent parts altered. During the sixteenth and early seventeenth centuries, the city had grown slowly from an estimated population of 1,200 in 1524 to around 1,500 in 1641. Its cloth trade, however, was in decline. This was not unique to Bath, for rural competition (beginning in the fifteenth century and accelerating thereafter) was undermining the economic base of a number of textile towns, such as York, Canterbury, Gloucester and Salisbury. In Bath, the effects of this change were apparent by 1530, when John Leland noted in his *Itinerary* that the place 'hath somewhat decayed'. Nearly a century later, in 1622, the mayor complained 'we are a very little poor City, our Clothmen much decayed, and many of their workmen amongst us relieved by the city'. Nearby cloth towns, such as Bradford on Avon (Wiltshire) and Frome (Somerset), retained their staple industry, partly by increasing specialization, and they benefited from the general revival of the trade after the Restoration. But within the city limits of Bath the textile industry continued to decline. It has been said that at this time there were fifty broad looms in the parish of St Michael (outside the walls but within the city limits) and an equal number proportionately within the walls, but that the freemen's monopoly of trade within the city limits, and the regulations enforced by their companies, encouraged 'unfree' weavers to move out beyond Bath's boundaries to south of the river.[15] If this was the case, then attempts by the corporation to protect the local economy by defending freemen's rights actually contributed to the decline of trade within the city. Another possible explanation for change has been suggested by Sylvia McIntyre, who argues that if Bathonians did not take advantage of the regional revival in the cloth trade it may have been because they had an alternative: rather than competing with west country cloth towns or the mercantile power of Bristol, Bath could flourish by specializing as a health and leisure resort. By the late seventeenth century the city had changed its primary role from that of a manufacturing centre to a watering place. In the 1680s Celia Fiennes commented that 'the town and all its accomodations is adapted to the batheing and drinking of the waters and nothing else'.[16]

The revival of the spa

The hot springs had attracted people to Bath since Roman times, but the visitors were of relatively little demonstrable economic importance, until a fortuitous interest in the curative properties of mineral waters encouraged greater numbers to visit the spa at a time when the cloth trade was declining. In the late sixteenth century there was a spate of writings on the benefits to health of bathing in spring waters. Bath, as the possessor of one of the only two English mineral waters of note (the other being Buxton, in Derbyshire) was given much publicity in books such as that written by Dr William Turner in 1557. In his account of the spas of Germany, Italy and England, Turner specifically recommended the curative powers of the waters at Bath. It was medical fashion that made the spa 'resorted unto so greatly ... the pilgrimage of health to all saints', as the Bath physician Sir John Harrington described it in the 1590s, but the fashion that popularized spa treatments was not solely to Bath's advantage. It encouraged a search for new sources, and a multitude of springs with medicinal properties was discovered to rival Bath, although the heat and volume of its waters remained unique. These attributes, however, seemed less advantageous from the late sixteenth century, when medical opinion began to promote the idea of drinking mineral waters rather than bathing in them. Fortunately for the local economy, at Bath the warm water came to be drunk also as a preparation for bathing. The growing enthusiasm for cold bathing in the seventeenth century was another threat to Bath, but medical writers such as the local practitioner Dr Thomas Guidott defended the hot baths successfully, and the spa continued to attract the sick.[17]

Ownership and control of the baths by the corporation was clearly an advantage in developing the resort, but it seems to have been largely as a result of the influence of physicians and apothecaries that the governing body adopted a more entrepreneurial spirit towards the spa. Some of the medical fraternity, attracted to Bath by the growing opportunities it provided for their professions, became a part of the political élite, and many others also had vested interests in the health function of the city, for example as lodging-house keepers. Sir John Harrington and Dr Oliver (inventor of the Bath Oliver biscuit, as part of his patients' dietary regime) are but two examples of medical practitioners who were absorbed into the élite and who used their influence as councillors to persuade the corporation to develop facilities for the visitors. Oliver published a pamphlet in 1705, in which he argued the medical case for drinking the hot Bath waters all year round. This would extend the season beyond a short period in the summer, which made Bath in 1676 a place 'where all the people live all the winter (like Nightingales) upon the stock of their summer fat'. The lack of shelter near the baths was likely to deter invalids from drinking the waters out of the conventional season, as Dr Oliver indirectly acknowledged in his assertion that catching a cold was 'one of the worst accidents that could happen to anybody in the course of drinking Bath waters'. However, his pamphlet and his arguments in council were supported by another local physician, Dr Bettenson, who donated £100 towards the cost of overcoming this problem, and in 1705 the corporation decided to build a pump room on the north side of the King's Bath.[18] Through their writings, the medical fraternity 'puffed' or advertised not only the waters, but also the accommodation available to visitors. As early as the 1620s, Dr Thomas Venner drew attention to the convenient lodgings around the baths. By the beginning of the seventeenth century, a dozen hotel inns and many lodging houses had been established in the city. The admittedly incomplete Hearth Tax records for 1664 reveal that Bath had a comparatively high ratio of 4.04 hearths per householder, and this reflected its specialization as a resort. In some cases, no doubt, individuals paid for hearths in several houses, but many of the more substantial taxpayers (with 10–29 hearths or, in three cases, 30–37 hearths) were the owners of inns or lodging houses. The medical fraternity often kept lodgings for their patients, and the surviving Hearth Tax returns record three 'Doctors of Physick', who paid tax for a total of 24 hearths in 1664.[19]

The success of Bath as a spa depended on more than the natural resources of the springs and local willingness to exploit their commercial potential. Many other English towns were becoming social centres for local gentry and the 'middling' classes in the seventeenth century, but the spas differed from other urban centres because, as Sylvia McIntyre points out, they catered primarily for people who had little connection with the town itself, other than as a place of amusement. Attracting the healthy, wealthy and fashionable social élite was therefore as important – perhaps more so – than attracting the sick. Royal visits from Elizabeth I in 1574 and 1591, and from the early Stuart kings in 1613, 1615, 1628 and 1634, brought the glamour of the court to Bath and raised its status as a place of fashionable resort. Three years after the Restoration, Charles II took his wife Catherine to the spa in the hope of conceiving a legitimate heir, for by then the waters were being promoted as a cure for infertility as well as dropsy, gout, skin diseases, numerous general ailments and the pox. Even though no pregnancy occurred, Catherine made a second visit to Bath as queen dowager in 1686. In the following year, the wife of James II (Mary of Modena) came to bathe in the Cross Bath. Her visit was more successful than Catherine's had proved, for Mary was soon reported to be with child. This was a marvellous publicity coup for the Bath waters. It received widespread public attention in the Glorious Revolution of 1688: a Catholic succession, it seemed, had been secured by the efficacy of the Bath waters – but Mary of Modena's pregnancy also prompted a Protestant uprising. However, what really set the seal of royal approval on Bath was the patronage of the future Queen Anne, who came in search of a cure for her gout and dropsy in the 1680s and again in 1692. As reigning queen, she made further visits to the city in the early eighteenth century. To the delight of the corporation, her frequent presence, with her court and entourage, confirmed the appeal of Bath as an exclusive resort for 'the quality'. The value of royal patronage to Bath's embryonic tourist trade had already been clearly recognized and exploited by the corporation. Celebrations were organized to publicize royal visits, and to encourage royal guests to return, while royal patronage was advertised through such civic improvements as the new Queen's Bath (1618), which had been named in honour of Anne of Denmark, queen consort to James I.

In addition to exploiting royal connections, the corporation and individual entrepreneurs began to provide entertainments for visitors. By the mid-seventeenth century a few tree-lined walks had been laid out in the old abbey gardens, and there were bowling greens and a real-tennis court for more energetic physical exercise. Theatrical performances took place occasionally, either in the Guildhall or in the courtyards of the larger inns. As late as 1683, however, the Somerset justices still preferred to hold the assize court at Wells, because Bath 'had not so good accommodation for entertainments',[20] and there were no organized social activities on the scale of those to come in the eighteenth century.

Another aspect of the positive strategy adopted to promote the spa and resort functions of Bath was the perceived need to raise and maintain its social tone. Royal visits brought the nobility and upper classes crowding into the city, but if 'the quality' were to be attracted to Bath on a regular basis then a suitable ambience of fashionable elegance was necessary. Achieving this in a city which was also a magnet for various 'undesirables' provoked an alternative or negative strategy from the authorities. Bath had been notable for its many religious and charitable foundations from the twelfth century onward. The largest of these foundations was the St John the Baptist hospital for the sick and poor,

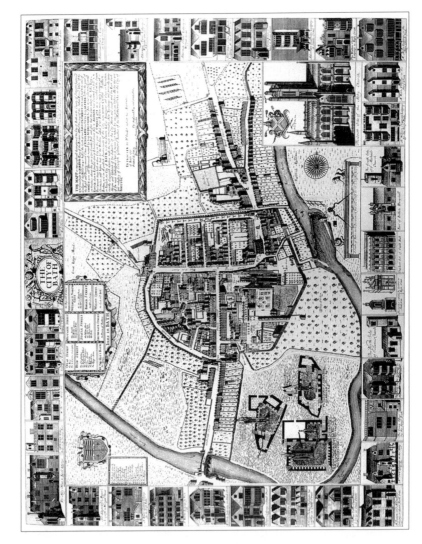

Map 2 Gilmore's map of Bath, 1694. Before the period of rapid growth in the eighteenth century, Bath remained predominantly a walled city, with modest extensions from Northgate into Walcot and from Southgate to the bridge across the River Avon. The open spaces, the Abbey Garden and the Old Bowling Green, occupied part of the site of the Norman cathedral priory. Note also the gabled lodgings decorating the border of the map.

established in 1174 but given over to the corporation in 1552. The existence of such charitable institutions, plus the presence of wealthy visitors, attracted numerous poverty-stricken invalids to the city in search of a cure at the baths, and also brought beggars and vagrants looking for hand-outs to relieve their destitution. The authorities were concerned about the effects of the influx of such undesirables, but showed little understanding of its causes. By the early 1570s the corporation had concluded that so many poor and diseased people were flocking to Bath that only an Act of Parliament could protect the city's interests. The mayor therefore petitioned for an Act granting the corporation powers to ensure that: 'no diseased or impotent poor person living on alms ... shall resort or repair from their dwelling place to the said city of Bath and to the baths there for the ease of their grief unless such person be not only licensed so to do by two Justices of the Peace in the county where such person doth dwell but also provided for by the inhabitants [of their own parish].'[21] The subsequent Act of 1572 transferred the cost of supporting poor patients from the city of Bath to the parish of their origin. It also gave power to the authorities to control the numbers of undesirables entering the city. Under the terms of the Act, any sick or poor person arriving at the gates without a licence could be turned away, or treated as a vagabond and taken into custody for punishment. Attempts to restrict the numbers of the poor therefore coincided with the vigorous promotion of the spa. The need to make provision for more middle- and upper-class visitors coming to take the waters was given priority over the interests of the lower social orders. St John's Hospital, once the haven of only the poor sick, was enlarged by the corporation in the later sixteenth century to provide letting accommodation, as was the abbey house, which had formerly been the prior's lodging.

At the end of the seventeenth century Bath still remained a walled medieval city, with narrow streets and cramped buildings dominated by the abbey church, a reminder of its monastic past. With a population of around 3,000 it was still essentially a small market and wool town. However, the spa was attracting ever-growing numbers of visitors. The city had always been of more than local importance, but its most dramatic transformation lay ahead in the eighteenth century.

Chapter 2

The Resort of Frivolity
and Fashion, 1700–1820

Bath's role in the life of the nation was never to be greater or more flamboyant than it was between 1700 and the 1790s, when the city was the premier resort of frivolity and fashion.[1] In the course of the eighteenth century the enduring image of Georgian Bath was created, as a place where terraces and squares formed an elegant setting for the pleasures of the nobility and the gentry. Yet, even in its heyday, other realities underlay the dominant image. In spite of increasing specialization as a leisure resort, the city nonetheless retained a mixed economy. Moreover, although 'the quality' flocked to the spa, Bath was not exclusively attractive to the wealthy and distinguished. Other less welcome visitors from the impoverished underclass were also drawn to the city. Rural migrants came too, in search of work, while the permanent resident population included substantial numbers of the labouring classes and the lower orders of society.

Furthermore, the prevailing image of Georgian Bath to some extent obscured the dynamics of socio-economic changes, which were taking place even as that image was emerging. By the later 1700s Bath was far less fashionable than it had been in earlier decades. The social composition of the visiting company broadened, with fewer aristocrats and more members of the middle classes arriving for the season. An increasing number of the wealthy middle and upper classes chose to settle permanently in Bath, beginning the process that was to shape its later dominant image as a place of genteel residence. Simultaneously, incipient industrialization was underway – albeit on a small scale – and this also foreshadowed developments in the decades beyond 1820.

The building of Bath

Building in Bath in the early eighteenth century was at much the same level of activity as in the country as a whole, and the capital sums involved were relatively small in comparison with later investment. Harrisons'

Assembly Rooms, for example, were built for £1,000 in 1708. The boom really took off in the late 1720s, and reached peaks of activity in the periods 1726–32, 1753–8, 1762–71 and 1785–92. In general these periods coincided with the availability of 'cheap money', when interest rates were low, but two improvements in local transport acted as an additional stimulus to the first phase of building, by reducing the costs of materials.

The first of these was the Avon Navigation scheme to canalize and deepen the river between Bristol and Bath in order to lower the costs of transporting goods from the port to the city. Work began on the project in 1725. It was not completed until 1729, but the first barge reached Bath in December 1727, with a cargo made up chiefly of timber and lead for the building industry. The scheme also contributed to the development of Bath by providing an alternative means of access to the city at a time when the state of the roads made overland travel an uncomfortable and sometimes dangerous matter. In May 1728 the Princess Amelia (one of George II's daughters) completed her journey from London to Bath by boarding a barge, decorated in her honour, at Bristol. By 1740 there were two regular passenger boats daily each way between the port and the city of Bath.[2]

The second improvement was undertaken and financed by Ralph Allen (1693–1764) of Prior Park, one of the key figures in the development of Bath. As a shareholder in the Avon Navigation and the owner of the stone quarries at Combe Down, Allen had a strong vested interest in the growth and trade of the city. In the early 1730s he constructed a tramway almost two miles long (at a cost of £10,000) from his quarries down to the Dolemeads area beside the river. This cut the cost of stone on site in Bath and also made it economically viable for Allen to develop a small export trade. Between 1731 and 1733 some 1,800 tons of Bath stone were shipped out on the Avon Navigation.[3]

The cost of building Georgian Bath has been estimated by R. S. Neale as being in the region of three million pounds. This is a crude figure, but it suggests a surprisingly large scale of investment in speculative building at a time when the country was beginning to industrialize. The key entrepreneurs in the first half of the eighteenth century were the Duke of Chandos and the architect-developer John Wood (1704–54), while William Johnstone Pulteney was a comparable figure in the later phase of development. The corporation itself took no direct part in speculative building before the 1750s, but 'craftsmen undertakers' played a significant and sometimes underestimated role in development.[4] With the building of Pulteney Bridge (1769–74) a new town was opened up on the Bathwick estate to the eastern side of the city, with Great Pulteney Street as its centre piece, leading majestically to Sydney Gardens. These developments to the north and east of the old medieval city were to dictate further building of squares, crescents and villa residences. Lansdown

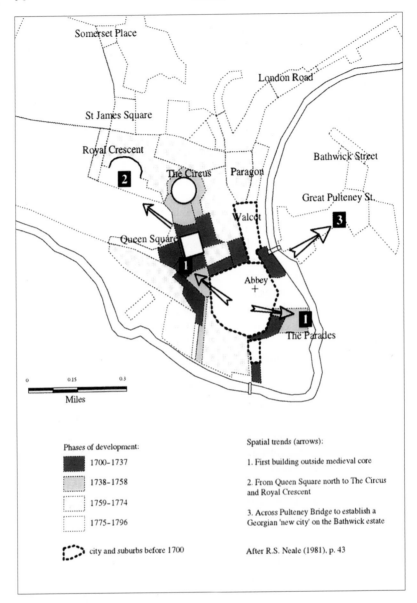

Map 3　Bath, the Georgian city

and Bathwick became the wealthiest suburbs in Bath, a process that began in the eighteenth century and matured into the nineteenth century.

The Duke of Chandos is the outstanding example of how outside money was used in developing Bath. He was at the centre of a web of national and international credit. He had made separate princely fortunes out of the lucrative post of Paymaster-General during the War of the Spanish Succession and from the South Sea Bubble affair. His interest in property development in Bath was inspired by dissatisfaction with his lodgings, and with the general standard of provision for visitors, when he stayed at St John's Hospital in the spring of 1726. Over the summer he negotiated through an agent, the Quaker banker Richard Marchant, for the site of St John's Hospital, which was owned by the corporation. By October, he had acquired life-hold leases, at a cost of £3,250. In January 1727 he contracted with John Wood, and the first stage of development was underway. It was financed largely by merchants, bankers and discount houses in London. An estimated 66 per cent of traceable investment came from the capital city.[5] Money was raised by means of bills of exchange, promissory notes and annuities, but the entire project was underpinned by the personal wealth of Chandos and the network of provincial, national and international credit on which he could draw.

Credit was also essential to John Wood's career as an architect-developer on his own account. For the development of Queen Square, Wood acquired a five-acre site on the Barton Farm estate owned by the London surgeon Dr Robert Gay and his descendants. Having negotiated a ninety-nine year lease at an annual rent of £137, Wood then granted seventy-five underleases (worth over £350 in total annual ground rent) to masons, carpenters and others, who used them as security to raise mortgages and finance the building of houses to John Wood's designs.

According to Neale, John Wood was not merely an architect who worked only with 'perfect harmony and the most delightful proportion', but one who believed that classical architecture came from God's command. Whether his vision of Bath was inspired by the Britannic myth which identified the ancient city as the metropolitan seat of the Druids, or by the idea of a new Rome, his buildings were designed to be uplifting to the onlooker, and so arranged as to provide the space and setting for civilized urban living. For instance, the north side of Queen Square (1728–35) was built in the Corinthian order, and, symbolizing Nature in all her springlike glory, commands the enclosed space with all the 'grandeur of a palace'. By contrast, the Parades (1740–8) provided open spaces on the outside of the buildings for promenading and social intercourse, seen as a distinguishing feature of urban society. John Wood designed, and his son completed, the King's Circus (1754–69) as two perfect circles, with the outer circle divided into three segments, representing the idea of the Trinity, and the three orders of columns

2. The north side of Queen Square, built by John Wood the Elder (1728–34).
The building of Queen Square played a pivotal role in the development of
Bath to the north of the medieval city (see Map 3). (Guildhall Archives, Bath)

placed above each other, symbolising 'virginal beauty, elegance, and attitude'.[6] If inspiration was Wood's intention in designing the King's Circus, he failed to convince the critics at the time. Tobias Smollett has his character, Matthew Bramble, discuss it as 'a pretty bauble, contrived for shew',[7] whilst an anonymous writer in 1779 described it, cruelly, as 'a handsome Wedgwood plate', a vulgar symbol of conspicuous consumption.[8] The King's Circus led, via Brock Street, to the Royal Crescent, built by John Wood the Younger between 1767 and 1775, and this provided a grand climax to the series of Palladian buildings designed by the Woods, father and son. The triumphal sweep of the Royal Crescent, with its 114 Ionic columns, broad, flagstoned promenade and gently sloping foreground, commanded a magnificent site. It signalled a move away from the formal garden design that marked John Wood the Elder's work in Queen Square and was probably influenced by the taming of nature inherent in the work of the landscape gardener, 'Capability Brown', who was at work at Kelston and Newton St Loe near Bath at the time.

The key figure in the development of Bath in the 1780s and early 1790s, William Johnstone Pulteney, was in somewhat different circumstances from those of either Chandos or Wood. The second son of a Scottish landowner, he was an Edinburgh lawyer and a partner in a Dumfries bank. He took the name Pulteney on marrying into that family. Like Chandos, Pulteney was an immensely wealthy man but he was constrained by the fact that the Bathwick estate, which his wife had inherited in 1767, was entailed. The estate had not been fully exploited because of the lack of a bridge between Bathwick and Walcot. If it was to be developed, Pulteney needed to convince the trustees that this was a sound investment. He evidently did so, for by 1769 a scheme for a bridge over the Avon had gained both their approval and also the support of the corporation. Under the necessary Act of Parliament (1769), the trustees were given collective powers to grant building leases and water rights to the corporation, to allow it to build a reservoir in Bathwick, and to extend the powers of the Bath magistrates to the area. They were also empowered to raise a £3,000 mortgage on the estate to pay for the bridge, but Pulteney used his own resources to provide short-term funds to speed up its construction. The building of Bathwick new town was financed in much the same way as that of Queen Square, described above, but Pulteney also drew on his private wealth to supply some mortgage money at the outset of development.

The emergence of new financial institutions in the eighteenth century made a significant contribution to the building boom of 1785–92. By this time easy credit was available in Bath as well as from London banks. The first bank in the city was founded in 1768, and five more were established between 1775 and 1790. They were a popular amenity with visitors, who could now draw up in their carriages in Milsom Street to cash a bank draft, rather than travelling to the resort carrying large sums of money over roads frequented by highwaymen. The banks also provided investment for the regional cloth industry and for the local coalmines, and they played a crucial part in the success of small developers with little capital, such as the architect John Eveleigh. When he developed Grosvenor Place (1791–2), most of the investment came from mortgages raised at Bath banks.

The corporation was cautious about involving itself in speculation and borrowing before the 1750s, but it acquired powers of compulsory purchase in 1711 in connection with the Avon Navigation scheme, and these powers were extended in 1766 to facilitate the redevelopment of the markets. As a result, the civic body remained a major landowner, and by the 1750s revenue from property rents was being augmented by the sale of leases. Eventually, the authorities found the confidence to undertake development themselves. In 1755 Bladud Buildings were begun and the success of this venture in raising revenue brought about a change of attitude. The corporation was arguably over-cautious before 1750, after which it did too little, too late. It was frequently castigated for its caution and lack of imagination towards developing and improving the city ('Narrow minds will ever have narrow views', as Smollett wrote of it in 1752), but, in its defence, Sylvia McIntyre has pointed out that it was not obvious in the first part of the century that Bath's popularity would

3. The King's Circus, planned by John Wood the Elder and built by John Wood the Younger (1754–70), Thomas Malton, 1784. (Victoria Art Gallery, Bath)

last.[9] Outright opposition to all improvements would have been against the interests of most members of the corporation, but the costs involved deterred them from undertaking major projects. The corporate revenue was not large – an average of £375 per annum in the 1690s and £531 in the 1700s. It rose to £965 in the 1720s and to £1,565 in the 1740s, but evidence from the chamberlain's accounts shows that expenses rose equally, or more rapidly. Moreover, income from the spa itself was not substantial. The pumps and baths brought in a maximum of £230 per annum up to 1750, but most of that sum was absorbed by the costs of maintenance and repairs.[10] Yet, between 1755 and the early 1790s, the corporation's enthusiasm for development matched that of private entrepreneurs. During that period, sites were cleared for a new town hall and markets, corporation land outside the walls was given over to speculative building, and part of the city walls was demolished to assist this development. Improvements were made to the Pump Room and the baths, and the decayed city centre was redeveloped to give better access between corporation-owned facilities in the lower town and the rapidly growing upper town. All these activities were financed by borrowing. Interest charges accounted for a growing proportion of municipal expenditure, rising from an average of 5 per cent over the years from 1700 to 1771, to 24 per cent of total expenditure by the late 1790s.[11]

Relationships and connections between aristocrats, entrepreneurs and the local political élite involved in building clearly existed. John Wood

4. The Royal Crescent, built by John Wood the Younger (1767–75), Thomas Malton, 1777. (Victoria Art Gallery, Bath)

had worked for the Duke of Chandos before coming to Bath in 1726. Wood had an uneasy relationship with the corporation, which never employed him as an architect, but his first employment in the city as a subcontractor on the Avon Navigation is said to have resulted from the influence of Ralph Allen. Allen arrived in Bath at the age of nineteen in 1712, where he made a fortune from his career in the postal service, and subsequently purchased the stone quarries as well as investing in many local enterprises. He quickly established himself as one of the most prominent businessmen in Bath, and was soon absorbed into the political élite. In March 1725 he was made an honorary freeman. Four months later, he was elected as a council member and he went on to be Mayor of Bath several times.[12]

Many members of the corporation, including physicians, surgeons, clothiers, plumbers and glaziers, were also private developers. So too, however, were many skilled tradesmen, who had no role in the governing body. It was 'craftsmen undertakers' who built most of Bath's new housing in the period from 1730 to the beginning of the nineteenth century. Of the 37 houses erected in Milsom Street in about 1764, and of the 60 or so built in St James Parade after 1767, 20 and 46, respectively, were put up by craftsmen in the building trade. The necessary capital was supplied, it seems, by long-term loans, and it is likely that craftsmen of different trades took adjoining plots in order to pool their skills. This may have been the case in the construction of Bennett Street

Table 1 Occupations of members of the corporation of Bath, twenty-year intervals, 1700–1800

1700: 26 members

1 tailor
1 mercer
1? clothier
14 unidentified

2 saddlers
2 vintners
1 attorney
13 of the 26 owned or
    had owned lodgings or inns

1720: 28 members

1 clothier
4 vintners
1 barber
1 baker
1 distiller
4 apothecaries
7 unidentified
3 of the 28 may have owned lodgings or inns

1 mercer and quarry-owner
1 linen draper and mercer
2 saddlers
2 maltsters
1 milliner
1 glazier
1 shopkeeper

1740: 30 members

1 linen draper
1 saddler
2 maltsters
1 shopkeeper
1? attorney
1 ironmonger or tallow chandler
1 postal contractor and quarry-owner
3 unidentified

1 woollen draper
6 vintners
1 baker
1 upholder
1 'gent'
6 apothecaries (1 also 'gent')
3 plumbers and glaziers

1760: 30 members

3 surgeons
1 ironmonger
1 tallow chandler
1 linen and woollen draper and wholesaler
2 plumbers and glaziers (also builders)
8 apothecaries (1 'gent', 1 'esq.')
1 carpenter and joiner
1 wine cooper and land developer
1 postal contractor and quarry-owner
1 unidentified

1 vintner
2 attorneys
1 silk weaver
1 postmaster
1 bookseller
1 'esq.'
1 saddler
1? baker
1 carrier

1780: 30 members

2 linen drapers	1 silk weaver
1 hosier and hatter	1 laceman
1 bookseller	1 saddler
5 apothecaries (2 'gents')	2 physicians
2 bankers (both originally apothecaries)	3 attorneys
1 mailcoach contractor, theatre owner, etc.	1 carrier
3 unidentified	6 surgeons

1800: 30 members

1 linen draper	1 saddler
1 brewer	1 wine merchant
7 apothecaries	5 surgeons
4 doctors of physick (1 knight)	3 esquires
1 surgeon and/or physician	2 bankers
1 chemist and druggist	1 theatre-owner
2 unidentified (possibly apothecaries)	

Source: Sylvia McIntyre, 'Bath: The Rise of a Resort Town, 1660–1800', p. 224, in Peter Clark (ed.), *Country Towns in Pre-Industrial England* (Leicester, 1981).

around 1774: the identifiable builders included six carpenters, four masons, two plasterers and a tiler, who between them supplied all the necessary skills, except those of plumber, glazier and painter. Moreover, craftsmen-builders usually retained newly-built houses for letting either to seasonal visitors or leisured residents (who were disinclined to buy and thus tie up their capital), or to Bath's less well-off inhabitants. This provided opportunities for the accumulation of capital and for further entrepreneurial activities, as the career of John Hensley indicates. Hensley, a carpenter in the late 1760s, operated as a timber merchant and coach-builder and one of the more prominent 'undertakers' or developers until his death in 1802. His estate (auctioned in 1803) included thirty-seven dwellings, of which eleven were in fashionable terraces and twenty were court tenements. Of these properties, thirty-four were sold for £11,010 and the remainder were valued at about £750 in total.[13]

Political power in Bath was in the hands of businessmen, shopkeepers, tradesmen and commercial interests. A distinctive feature of local administration in Bath during the eighteenth century and beyond was the relative lack of participation by the resident social élite in the political life of the city. As Table 1 illustrates, the corporation included many men of apparently humble occupational backgrounds.

Participation in the governance of Bath was, however, determined by those who already held power, since the city was run by a self-perpetuating oligarchy. The ruling group elected its officers from amongst its own members. Aldermen (a minimum of four and a maximum of ten) and common councillors held office for life. Vacancies were filled by nominations from the council, which usually selected men who had purchased the freedom of the city. The corporation (which also sent two Members to Parliament) controlled the freemen, who had rights to practise trades and to share in the income from the commons. Freedom could be achieved by servitude (which entailed serving an apprenticeship within the city limits) or by purchase, the price of which was increased from just over £10 in 1733 to £75 in 1801. The mayor, nine aldermen and twenty councillors formed the governing group, which kept tight control of business within the city. The advantages to an ambitious man of being a member of this group are exemplified by the career of Thomas Warr Attwood, who clearly used his position for self-advancement. He was a partner in the Bladud Bank, and served on the council committee set up to supervise the building of the new Guildhall in the 1760s. Although described as a plumber and glazier by trade, he managed to secure for himself the position of city architect. He then succeeded, despite some opposition to his plans and estimates, to win the contract for building the Guildhall. The pursuit of vested interests and the practice of nepotism were marked features of local government in eighteenth-century Bath, as they were in many other places.

The resident social élite, largely excluded from the political life of Bath, played only a minor part in the city's development. The leisured and professional classes were mainly confined to the role of lessees, but even in this role they were out-numbered by tradesmen, and their significance declined over time. These classes accounted for 36 per cent of lessees for the Parades (1740–9), but at most only 20 per cent of those for corporation developments in 1761 and 1781; a similar picture can be seen in Bathwick between 1788 and 1792.[14]

Conflicts of interest arose between various parties within the city during the building of Bath. The corporation clashed with William Johnstone Pulteney over his belated decision to build shops on Pulteney Bridge. His influence and power were sufficient to allow him to override the objections of the corporation, but another part of his plan for the Bathwick estate was defeated by local interest groups. Before Pulteney Bridge was completed, he proposed a second one across the Avon at Bathford. He intended to put in a new turnpike, which would have diverted London traffic from the existing one running through Walcot, across the Bathwick estate and into the city over Pulteney Bridge. This would have raised land values in Bathwick to the benefit of the Pulteney estate, but it was strongly opposed by the corporation and by the trustees of the existing Bath Turnpike (established in 1707), who included several council members and some developers. Pulteney's scheme came to nothing, for his opponents triumphed when it was first raised in 1771 and did so again in 1774.

The structure of investment in the Bath Turnpike reveals only limited involvement by the its trustees, whereas the role of the small urban saver became increasingly important.[15] Investments of £500 or less, and in the range of over £500 but less than £1,000, made up a significant portion of the value of total holdings in the company in the period between 1785 and 1805. Much of this investment was local, and from the later eighteenth century tradesmen and artisans appear occasionally as contributors. Women were particularly important in the 1770s, when they provided 46 per cent of the capital then raised, and they were drawn from all classes. Among the gentlewomen and the widows and daughters of professional men, lodging-house keepers and even a few servants also featured as investors. When the turnpike trustees themselves were in conflict with the corporation in the 1780s, they were therefore defending the interests of a group far broader than any local élite. News spread that one of the powers being sought under the proposed Improvement Act in 1789 would allow the corporation to raise money by imposing an extra half-toll on the Bath Turnpike, to be used as security for borrowing £25,000. Local landowners, colliery owners, coal hauliers and citizens joined the trustees in opposition to the proposal. The corporation gained the powers it sought, but the Act embodied exemptions and provisos designed to ensure that visitors to the city – rather than residents or tradesmen – would pay the extra toll, and thereby finance the development of facilities for their benefit and that of Bath's economy.

As a result of the 'rage for building', lodgings for visitors became cheaper, and improved in quality and comfort. However, physical expansion was closely associated with social segregation in eighteenth-century Bath, and what was considered to be a 'good address' changed over time. The northern half of Avon Street (built in the 1730s as part of the first phase of development outside the city walls) was designed to provide fashionable lodgings, but within a generation the area lost its wealthy clientele to the new developments north of Queen Square. The area between the abbey and the River Avon, in a low-lying part of the city frequently inundated by flood water, gradually came to be one of small-scale industry and working-class housing. Topography mirrored social class differences. As Lady Nelson observed when writing to her husband from New King Street in the spring of 1797, in Bath it was the case that 'the higher you go, the dearer'.[16] By this time it had become fashionable to rent a house for the season, rather than lodgings, but while annual rents were £90 in New King Street, they were £160 in Gay Street. The weekly cost of hiring a room fell from 10s. (50p) in 1700 to half that price by the 1740s, when John Wood estimated that the city could accommodate 12,000 visitors.

The fashionable company

The number of visitors that actually went to Bath in any one year is difficult to establish. Estimates range from 8,000 at a season in the early eighteenth century to Wood's claim of accommodation for some 12,000 by the 1740s. The visiting company listed in the *Bath Journal* from its origins in 1744, gives some indication of the numbers of sufficient 'quality' to merit inclusion. These rose from 510 in 1746 to 2,525 in 1760, 3,091 in 1780 and 5,341 in 1801. This growth in numbers was encouraged by Bath becoming more accessible between the late seventeenth century and 1800, as transport facilities and roads improved. The number of weekly services from London to Bath (a distance of some 107 miles) was between 32 and 46 from 1740 to 1777, but had increased to 147 by 1800. Moreover, the journey time from London by road (which was over 60 hours before 1680) fell from 36 hours in 1750 to little more than 10 hours by the late 1790s. The summer season gradually evolved into two short seasons in autumn and spring, but in 1762 the master of ceremonies estimated that it had extended to six full months. Evidence from the *Bath Guides* indicates that, from 1780, the expensive season for lodgings lasted for nine months, from September to May. Improvements to lodgings and public facilities, in addition to Bath's growing popularity, probably account for this change. Indeed, as early as 1739 the poet Alexander Pope 'drank Bristol Hotwell water in Bath, because he wanted the comforts available there in winter'.[17]

The season at Bath became an integral part of the annual social round of the nation's aristocracy and lesser nobility, but as the premier resort in England the city attracted an increasingly extensive range of visitors. The cultural élite of the Georgian period, for example, was also attracted to Bath. Among the litany of famous names associated with the city are those of the novelists Fielding, Smollett and Jane Austen, the painter Gainsborough, and the actors David Garrick and Sarah Siddons. Moreover, as the city grew in size and prestige, the social composition of its visitors broadened to include many modest clients from the middling gentry, and the rising professional and commercial middle classes. Among these less-distinguished visitors was a boat-owner from Langport, Somerset, who stayed for three months from September 1796. His wife tried the waters at the Hot Bath once and the couple went to prayers at the abbey several times, as well as making one attendance at Lady Huntingdon's proprietary chapel. They made no visits to the Pump Room or to any functions at the Assembly Rooms.[18] The entertainments and pleasures on offer in Bath were vital to its success as a spa. In general it was the lure of fashionable frivolity that brought in the visitors, even though some, like the Langport boat-owner and his wife, did not participate fully in the social round. By the 1720s, according to Defoe, bathing was 'made more a sport and diversion, than a physical prescription for health'.[19] Simply to be in Bath for the season, 'Where gaming and grace, Each other embrace, Dissipation and piety meet',[20] to see and be seen as part of 'the company', was the underlying motive for most visits, whatever the ostensible reason. At least two-thirds of those who came to take the waters did so, in the opinion of one commentator in 1776, 'entirely from the influence of fashion and to alleviate an insurmountable itch for pleasure'.[21]

Yet the social tone had changed considerably by the mid-eighteenth century. The city had been transformed from a riotous, brawling place into one that was at least superficially decorous, where social life was governed by rigid conventions. This transformation is commonly ascribed to Richard 'Beau' Nash (1676–1761), who imposed a strict code of behaviour on 'the quality' who thronged the spa. Nash came to Bath in 1705. An educated man who had, however, already failed in more than one career, he had a passion for gambling and a reputation as a talented organizer of social events. His known connection with court life and the social scene in London were, no doubt, useful assets when he came to Bath as little more than a penniless adventurer. Contemporaries and some historians credit Nash with enormous influence on the development of Bath, and even portray him as the primary instigator of most of the improvements made to the spa, but his role has been greatly exaggerated. Even his 'appointment' as master of ceremonies in 1705, a part of the Beau Nash legend, is not documented in the corporation records, and he was probably chosen informally by the company to fulfil this function.[22] Nonetheless, as 'King of Bath', Beau Nash set the social tone of the spa by imposing – through sheer force of personality – his rule of conduct on the visitors. Duelling and the carrying of swords in the city were discountenanced, men in riding boots and women wearing white aprons (the emblem of prostitution) were banned from assemblies. Nash's code of manners was published and posted up in various public places. It also appeared in the *Bath Guides*, until long after his death in 1761.

Diversions and entertainments abounded in Bath. Visitors of distinction were listed in the local papers and greeted on arrival by the master of ceremonies. Bell-ringing and music from the town band were part of the welcome, despite complaints from the sick, but, like everything in Bath, they had their price, from half a guinea (52p) upwards, according to social rank. A visit to the Pump Room and baths was part of the daily round, if not to bathe then to enjoy the spectacle of the quality and trade folk 'jostling each other without ceremony'.[23] The Lower Rooms (originally Harrisons' Assembly Rooms, opened in 1708) and Upper Rooms (1778) included card rooms, tea rooms, and ballrooms for the twice-weekly balls which were funded by subscription tickets. These were formal events in the early evening, followed, after a tea break, by country dancing with no distinction of social rank. Nash's code decreed that balls ended promptly at eleven o'clock. Theatrical performances and musical events provided alternative evening entertainments. Days were whiled away by strolling along the streets or in the pleasure gardens, shopping or merely window shopping, browsing in the libraries or dropping into a coffee house. Every taste was catered for in Bath: beneath the veneer of elegant refinement and strict codes of public behaviour, there lay a sordid world of gambling, pornography and vice.[24]

Gamblers and card sharpers flocked to Bath in the early eighteenth century. Even Beau Nash's income derived from his luck at the tables, for he received no salary as master of ceremonies. Public concern about the nationwide craze led to various Acts of Parliament to suppress private lotteries and games of chance. New games were invented to evade the Act of 1739 and, as they in their turn were made illegal, the prohibition on games involving numbers was circumvented by substituting letters for figures as, for example, in the game 'Even or Odd'. Nash promptly bought up all rights in the game, after taking professional advice as to its legality. E and O, as it was known, was introduced at Bath and Tunbridge Wells, with Nash taking a share of the profits from both spas. He was cheated of some of his share, or so he believed, and sued his partners for £20,000. Nash lost the case, and his reputation: his vested interest in organized gambling had not previously been common knowledge, and his amateur status was destroyed by the revelation. Beau Nash lived on until 1761 in relative poverty, no longer the darling of 'the quality', but the butt of jokes among the visitors. Meanwhile, E and O and all games of chance were prohibited by a 1745 Act of Parliament. As a result, gaming was banned from the assembly rooms, and keepers of illegal gaming houses in the city were prosecuted. Inevitably, this simply drove gambling underground. As late as 1790 a visitor commented that there was virtually no other place in the world where gaming was carried on to such a pitch as it was at Bath.

Part of the proliferation of obscene writing in the first half of the eighteenth century was made up of the pornography that was available in Bath. The most notable example is Thomas Stretzers' *A New Description of Merryland*. Merryland, a 'Paradise of Pleasure, and Garden of Delight' was the female body, its physical form and sexual attractions described in the manner of a serious work of topography. It was brought out in 1740 by James Leake, Bath's leading printer and bookseller. Within two years it had gone into a tenth edition and become the book of the season, gleefully discussed by mixed company over the coffee cups and card tables. It is highly likely that similar books were available from some of the ten bookshops and libraries in the city at the end of the century. Indeed, Georgian Bath was 'suffused with sex' according to the historian R. S. Neale. It certainly provided opportunities for romantic flirtations and illicit sexual encounters, as well as functioning as a marriage market. Brothels and bawdy houses, street walkers and casual prostitutes

5. 'The King's Bath', by Thomas Rowlandson, *The Comforts of Bath*, 1798.
(Victoria Art Gallery, Bath)

were commonplace, long before Smollett's reference in 1771 to 'the nymphs of Avon Street', a pointer to the infamous red-light district that Avon Street became.

So many of the visitors to Bath left some record of their impressions that innumerable perspectives compete for attention. Alexander Pope enjoyed the amusements of the place in 1714, whereas Horace Walpole disliked the company at Bath in the 1760s. The artist William Landor loved the city, but Jane Austen, who visited and lived there at times (and who is closely associated with Bath in her novels *Northanger Abbey* and *Persuasion*), is said to have hated the place. Many writers, however, shared an urge to mock Bath's pretensions by poking fun at its image and satirizing its proclaimed fashionability and elegance. One of the most caustic literary representations of Bath is in Smollett's *The Expedition of Humphry Clinker* (1771). Smollett's landowner from Wales, Matthew Bramble, found nothing but disappointment in Bath. His naïve young niece Lydia saw the corrupting city as 'an earthly paradise', but Bramble was critical of the architecture, horrified at the sight of ulcerated bodies in the baths, and uncertain whether 'the patients in the Pump-room don't swallow the scourings of the bathers'. As for the company, Bramble declared Bath to be a place where 'a very inconsiderable proportion of genteel people are lost in a mob of impudent plebians'. To his horror, one of the 'distinguished' visitors welcomed by bell-ringing was 'Mr Bullock, an eminent cow-keeper of Tottenham'. Bramble's nephew described the social mix at Bath to a friend in the following terms:

Yesterday morning, at the Pump-room, I saw a broken-winded Wapping landlady squeeze through a circle of peers, to salute her brandy-merchant, who stood by the window, propped upon crutches; and a paralytic attorney of Shoe-lane, in shuffling up to the bar, kicked the shins of the chancellor of England, while his lordship, in a cut bob, drank a glass of water at the pump.[25]

By the 1770s such chaos of the social orders in Bath deterred many of the quality from visiting. Over the second half of the eighteenth century Bath slowly ceased to be a centre for élite fashionable groups, although it continued to attract growing numbers of middling-gentry visitors, and those of the professional and commercial middle classes, whose presence somewhat lowered the social tone. Those of the nobility and upper classes who did visit became more status-conscious and showed a preference for select private parties rather than the vulgar throng of evening assemblies. The growth of the city and the rise in its popularity had increased social segregation and altered the forms of social life. The master of ceremonies could no longer meet all the visiting company, and public entertainments were being replaced by private events among various 'sets' or cliques. Other spas – smaller, more exclusive and often cheaper – were now competing with Bath. Leamington Spa and Tunbridge Wells were attracting visitors, and Cheltenham (where the population rose from 3,076 in 1801 to 13,396 in 1821) was a well-established rival. Moreover, a change in medical opinion in favour of sea-bathing encouraged the development of seaside resorts.

Royal patronage is often seen as crucial to the growth of Brighton, visited by the Prince of Wales from 1783, and of Weymouth, where the king was a visitor from 1789. Their visits (as in the case of Bath in the late seventeenth and early eighteenth centuries) were not actually a cause of the development of these resorts, but an indication of the powerful influence of medical fashion. Just as Bath benefited earlier from the medical enthusiasm for inland spa waters, so Brighton and other coastal resorts gained economically from the new trend for sea-bathing. By 1801 Brighton was the largest resort in Britain, with a population of 7,339. The number of recorded visitors to the town in 1760 was 400, and this had risen to over 4,300 by 1794. Smaller resorts closer to Bath were also developing. As early as 1788 Ilfracombe, for example, was reported to be 'remarkably full of genteel company … from most parts of the country'.[26] Furthermore, the influence of the Romantic movement developed the fashion of visiting mountains and moorland, while, after the end of the Napoleonic Wars, in 1815, European tours also competed with the attractions of Bath. Yet it was the sheer size of Bath that effectively destroyed its reputation as an exclusive resort of the quality.

The number of houses in the city increased by 45 per cent between 1780 and 1793. Market forces had earlier led to the speculative building

6. A view from Terrace Walk towards North Parade, John Nixon, 1795.
(Victoria Art Gallery, Bath)

7. A doctor in
conversation with a
lady in the Pump Room,
John Nixon, 1803.
(Victoria Art Gallery,
Bath)

boom of 1710–20, in response to the demand for lodgings, but the even more active period of construction took place in 1780–93, after Bath had passed its social peak as a fashionable resort. By 1793, war with France had broken out and the last phase of development ended abruptly. The resulting economic uncertainty led to a general loss of confidence that culminated in a financial crash. Two of Bath's banks went broke, several entrepreneurs and members of the corporation were made bankrupt, and buildings stood unfinished as funds ran out. Receipts for the half-toll on visitors using the turnpike roads into the city reached their highest level in 1792, then dropped sharply between mid-1793 and mid-1795. There was no sustained recovery until the early 1820s, although the building industry recovered somewhat around 1805, and, for a lucky few, individual fortunes revived. The builder John Pinch, made bankrupt in 1800, was active as an architect-developer by 1807. A new theatre was built at Beauford Square in 1804–5, and housing was put up at New Sydney Place (1807–8), Park Street (1808), Cavendish Place (1808–17) and Sion Hill Place (1817–20). Several churches were also built, including St Mary's at Bathwick (1814–20), which was designed by John Pinch.

The opening decades of the nineteenth century foreshadowed the city's Victorian role as a place of genteel residence. What attracted people to Bath was no longer the social glamour of its heyday, but more mundane things, such as the cost of living. This was what brought the Eliot family of Jane Austen's *Persuasion* (1818) to Bath in 1814. When Sir Walter Eliot's spendthrift ways forced him to retrench by letting his country residence, Bath was chosen as the most appropriate place for a prolonged visit because 'he might there be important at comparatively little expense'.[27] The period from 1700 to 1820 had, therefore witnessed Bath's rise to become the premier resort of fashion, followed by its decline into staid respectability. It was 'discovered' and enjoyed by a wealthy élite, who then tired of it, as their presence, and the development stimulated by their demand, increased its popularity and size so much that it lost its defining exclusivity as a resort of 'the quality'.

The enduring image of Bath, promoted even in many modern guide books, offers a celebratory and heroic perspective on the Georgian city. It is seen as the embodiment of the highest aspirations of its age for an ordered and gracious society, and its creation is often ascribed to the individual talents of Ralph Allen, Beau Nash and John Wood. In reality, it was the product of market forces and the fashions of the time, and what it became was open to harsh critical and satirical commentaries from writers such as Smollett and Austen. Our understanding of its image needs to be informed not only by the gracious world portrayed by Gainsborough and Reynolds, but also by the savage caricatures of Rowlandson and Gilray. As Neale has called it, Bath was a 'valley of pleasure' for some, a 'sink of iniquity' for others.[28]

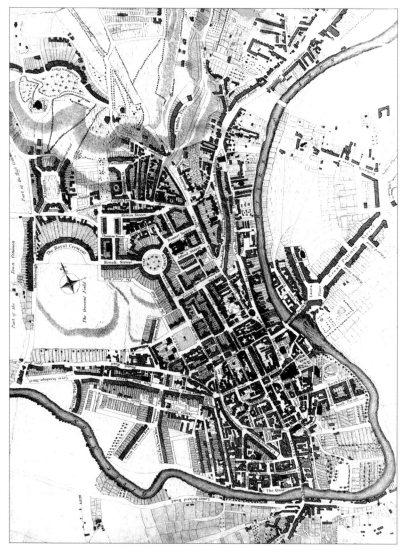

Map 4 City plan of Bath, c.1820. The medieval core of the city is plainly discernible on this map, which records the full extent of the eighteenth-century expansion of the city. Note the development of the Bathwick estate, through Great Pulteney Street to Sydney Place. Also featured are the further developments to the north of the Royal Crescent and the Circus: St James's Square (1790–93), Portland Place (1768), Lansdown Crescent (1789–93) and Camden Crescent (1788).

Although the spa was indeed the pre-eminent resort of frivolity and fashion for most of the period from 1700 to 1820, the emphasis often given to its appeal for 'the quality' and the cultural élite obscures other aspects of the reality of its history. There is, for example, no place in the present-day image of Georgian Bath for the other extreme of the social order – the thieves, prostitutes, pickpockets and beggars, whose presence constantly threatened to undermine the notion of the city as a centre of elegant refinement. Moreover, the importance of its leisure function can be overemphasized, thereby distorting our understanding of its increasingly variegated economy. Yet the 'dregs' of society and the labouring classes also played their part in the life of Britain's premier resort, and its prosperity was not dependent solely on visitors.

Chapter 3

The Lower Orders
in Bath, 1700–1820

The labouring poor made up the least visible component in Bath's contemporary image.[1] For well into the nineteenth century and indeed beyond, Bath was predominantly perceived as a place without industry or extensive trade. Far more conspicuous was the undesirable 'company', whose arrival in the city was invariably heralded by the annual influx of wealthy visitors. An assortment of rogues, vagabonds and petty criminals also came for the season, and for specific events such as the Bath races. Their presence could not be ignored – indeed, the city was notorious for its beggars. The nursery rhyme 'Hark, hark, the dogs do bark, the beggars are coming to town' (dated about 1790) records the response to their arrival, and they were a subject of common complaint when it was customary to pen a few lines in celebration of a visit to the city:

> I always have heard that the provident mayor
> Had a terrific rod to make beggars beware;
> But I find to my cost, they infest ev'ry street –
> First a boy with one eye, – then a man without feet,
>
> Who cleverly stumps upon two pattern rings, –
> One bellows, one whimpers, one snuffles, one sings;
>
> From Holloway's garrets and cellars they swarm;
> But I pause, – on this subject I'm growing too warm.[2]

Beggars, rogues and vagabonds

The old Elizabethan Act of 1572 that had been intended to regulate the presence of the sick and poor was never more than partially effective, and, after it lapsed in 1714, they came to Bath in ever-growing numbers, in search of a cure for their ailments or alms from the city's charities and visitors. Charitable benevolence was a part of Bath's self-image, but the

49

authorities were always uneasy about the threat to social order posed by the underclass. They were also continuously concerned about the possibly damaging effect that the notorious beggars of Bath might have on the city's trade and reputation. Their attitudes and policies were based on the perceived need 'to discriminate real objects of charity from vagrants and other imposters who crowd both the church and the town to the annoyance of the gentry residing here and who ought to be, by the care of the magistracy, expelled and punished'.[3]

A mixture of humanitarianism and enlightened self-interest therefore inspired the charitable activities of Bath's wealthy residents. Beau Nash, Ralph Allen, John Wood, numerous apothecaries and physicians, and many other members of the local élite became involved with a project to build a hospital for 'poor lepers, cripples and other indigent persons resorting to Bath for cure, well recommended and not otherwise provided for'.[4] The city became 'the hospital of the nation' and managed thereby to impose some control on the poor sick, while also contributing significantly to maintaining the health of the national workforce. Founded in 1738 as the Bath General Hospital (now the Royal National Hospital for Rheumatic Diseases), it was unique at the time in admitting patients from all parts of the country. Its specialism in the treatment of rheumatism and arthritis grew out of the proven effectiveness of hydrotherapy in cases of paralysis. Admission to Bath General Hospital was tightly controlled. Only those deemed likely to benefit from the waters, and who had been recommended by a 'responsible person' as being worthy of charity, were allowed entry. This policy went some way towards ensuring a suitably deferential attitude on the part of the patients, and it also benefited the reputation of the hospital. A careful selection of suitable cases for treatment guaranteed a satisfactory level of 'cures', providing evidence of the efficacy of the Bath waters.

Between 1790 and 1811 fourteen new charitable organizations were founded in the city. These included the Stranger's Friend Society (1790) and the Society for the Relief of Lying-in Women (1792). In 1805 the most important charity for the poor in Bath was founded. It was the creation of the social élite of Bath and became financed by the same group. Its original, and revealing, title was 'The Society for the Suppression of Common Vagrants and Imposters, the relief of Occasional Distress, and the Encouragement of the Industrious Poor.' Later in the nineteenth century its title was changed to the Monmouth Street Mendicity Society. It was a forerunner, in its policy of discriminating charity and case-study approach, of the famous Charity Organisation Society, which was founded nationally some sixty years later.

Contemporaries did not fully understand the economic basis of mendicity, but their fear of 'imposters' reflected their outrage at the threat to the social hierarchy that profitable begging posed. The Monmouth Street Society employed anecdotal evidence in its annual reports to support the claim that beggars represented a mass of trickery posing as genuine poverty. The case of a black beggar was cited in the 1812 report. When the man was arrested for assaulting a woman during a quarrel over sharing their takings, he was found to have collected 8*s*. (40p) from passers-by in only a few hours. The underlying question was who would work for the employing classes if a man could get as much from a day's begging as he could from a week of honest work. Yet the belief that most of the vagrants and beggars in Bath were imposters was not actually borne out by the society's own figures. Only about a third of the cases investigated could be classed as fraudulent. Those who applied for relief included the resident poor, but also men on the tramp looking for work, the wives of soldiers on active service, and the continual flow of emigrants from Ireland *en route* to London from Bristol. The numbers helped by the society probably account for a large proportion of the total passing through Bath, but by no means all. In 1817, a year of acute economic depression, 5,062 travellers received some sort of aid.

The labouring poor

The city attracted numerous immigrants from its rural hinterland and beyond. An analysis of the places of origin of over 350 applicants for poor relief in the years between 1763 and 1824 shows that only a minority – less than 20 per cent – were born in Bath.[5] The counties of Somerset, Wiltshire and Gloucestershire accounted for 56 per cent of the total, with the remainder coming from more distant parts of England, from Wales, Scotland and Ireland, or from overseas. There is further evidence of long-distance migration from Ireland in the records of the Catholic community in the city. By 1785 there were over 400 adult Catholics in Bath, more than a quarter of whom were Irish. The social and occupational structure of the Bath Catholic-Irish community is, however, likely to have been as diverse as that of the small Jewish community. Jewish settlers in Bath came from various parts of Britain, and from continental Europe. They included professional men and tradesmen, as well as men like Joseph Moses, who earned his living as a street trader in 1764.[6]

There were also African, Afro-Caribbean and Asian people living in Bath in 1700–1820, although little is known of their numbers or experience. There are scattered references to 'black' paupers and casual labourers, but it seems likely that personal service was their most probable occupation. The first definite evidence of the presence of Asian servants occurs in 1812, by which time Bath was established as a favourite place for retirement of military officers and former employees of the Indian civil service and East India Company merchants. The economy of Bath was linked with the slave trade, which may explain the presence of some ethnic minorities in the city. Investment in Bath from Bristol, which owed much of its prosperity to the trade, was one aspect of this involvement. Moreover, the Duke of Chandos was implicated by his role in the Royal Africa Company, while the Pulteneys owned large American plantations, and, in addition, many of Bath's wealthy residents and visitors derived their income from overseas estates. It was fashionable in the eighteenth century to have a black boy among the household servants: in 1759, for example, the *Bath Journal* offered a thirteen-year old for sale, advertised as 'quite black, well-built, intelligent, musical, trained as a footboy and skilled in waiting at table'. Humanitarian sentiments co-existed with complacency about slavery, however, and Bath was caught up in the national anti-slavery campaign of the late 1780s and early 1790s. Two of the local papers supported abolition, but the political élite was unsympathetic to the cause. The corporation held aloof, and a petition against slavery (signed by over one thousand people in Bath) was presented to Parliament by Somerset MPs, because the city's representatives declined to do so.[7]

Information about the occupations of Bath's inhabitants during the eighteenth century is extremely sparse. The sources of evidence are few, and they relate chiefly to the skilled trades and the professions. For the period 1706–69 the enrolments of apprentices to freemen provide some indication of the most popular trades, while by 1773 the *Bath Guides* list members of certain professions. Directories of trade and commerce, newspapers, and visitors' accounts of the city also yield some evidence, but there is insufficient data to support anything more than generalizations.[8]

Accommodating the visitors and meeting their needs employed a substantial proportion of the labour force, but, at the same time, Bath was not without trade and industry. Two fairs a year were still held, albeit of dwindling importance and partly superseded by a larger fair at Lansdown during the month of August. The regular food market grew in size and economic importance as Bath developed. Guides to Bath and other watering places usually contained comments about the availability, quality and price of provisions, which made the markets a particular concern of the corporation. The shambles area was improved around 1745, and in the 1760s stalls for market gardeners selling produce were laid out. In the following decade, associated with the building of a new Guildhall, a permanent marketplace was built. Markets were held on two or three days each week, and were regulated by the corporation through a system of inspection and the licensing of traders. The Bath market became something of a feature, and was said to surpass anything in London in 'its excellent order and abundance'.[9]

Although there was no large-scale industry, crafts and retail trades flourished in Bath. Manufacturing on a small scale in craft workshops was characteristic of the city in the eighteenth century, and continued to be so in the nineteenth century. What relatively large-scale industry there

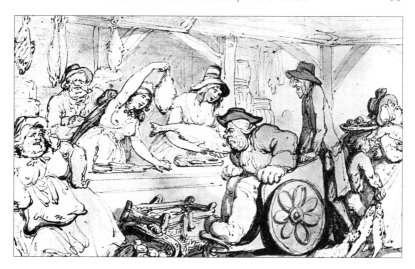

8. 'The Fish Market', by Thomas Rowlandson, *The Comforts of Bath*, 1798. (Victoria Art Gallery, Bath)

was often went unnoticed by visitors, and was conveniently ignored by many contemporary commentators on Bath, because it was located in peripheral areas beyond the old centre or the newly-built parts of the city. There were two cloth mills at work in the parish of Walcot in 1730, and industrial villages grew up beyond the city limits. The manufacture of wool cloth continued in the parish of Lyncombe and Widcombe, and at Twerton, long after it had ceased in the city itself. By the end of the century other industries were established in Bath, but their presence was not intrusive. Brewing, glass manufacture, soap-making, and iron-making were of increasing significance in the local economy. However, these were relatively small enterprises and they were located in the unfashionable area of Bath along the riverside. Consequently, they did not impinge on the dominant image of Bath as a resort of frivolity and fashion.

Despite its specialization, Bath, clearly had a variegated economic base in the eighteenth century. Its occupational structure (as far as it can be reconstructed) is set out in Tables 2 and 3, but this quantifiable evidence tells us little of the occupations of the unskilled or the semi-skilled. These workers are subsumed within the unhelpful categories of 'other' or 'miscellaneous'. Yet Bath obviously did offer opportunities to the unskilled rural immigrant. The building trades prospered as the town expanded, and this was a labour-intensive industry, especially in Bath, where steep, uneven sites had to be levelled, and much of the work entailed in building the squares and crescents required little more than muscular force. Strength was also the prime requisite for those who worked as 'chairmen', carrying the wealthy visitors about the town. The

Table 2   Occupations of Bath inhabitants in the eighteenth century

A   Enrolment of apprentices: occupations of masters

	Numbers of apprentices enrolled		
Occupations of masters	1706–27	1728–49	1750–69
Clothiers and weavers	1	3	—
Tailors	73	55	61
Cordwainers	96	70	47
Drapers, milliners, mercers and haberdashers	17	13	22
Other textiles/dress	13	22	21
Building	81	91	129
Other crafts	47	39	67
Victualling	97	67	71
Medical	33	27	34
Other professional services	1	—	—
Transport and entertainment	46	49	62
Miscellaneous	3	—	—
Total number of apprentices enrolled	508	436	514

B   Percentage of apprentices enrolled in occupational groups

	1706–27	1728–49	1750–69
Clothing and shoemaking	39.4	37.4	29.4
Building	15.7	20.9	25.1
Crafts	9.3	8.9	13.0
Victualling	19.1	13.1	13.8
Professional	6.7	6.2	6.6
Services	9.1	11.2	12.1
Miscellaneous	0.6	—	—

Source: Adapted from Table 18(A), p. 215, Sylvia McIntyre, 'Bath: The Rise of a Resort Town, 1660–1800' in Peter Clark (ed.), *Country Towns in Pre-Industrial England* (Leicester: 1981).

Table 3   Occupations of Bath inhabitants in each parish, 1801 census

	Agriculture (A)	Trade, manufacturers and handicraft (B)	(A) and (B) as % of parish population	Other
Bath City				
St James	2	372	9.4	3,588
St Michael	1	933	25.2	2,766
SS Peter and Paul	1	2,305	93.6	159
Walcot	253	1,935	11.0	15,371
Bathwick	34	104	3.8	2,582
Lyncombe and				
Widcombe	93	575	20.6	2,122

Source: Table 18(E), p. 217, Sylvia McIntyre, 'Bath: The Rise of a Resort Town, 1600–1800', in Peter Clark (ed.), *Country Towns in Pre-Industrial England* (Leicester: 1981).

numbers of chairmen (licensed by the corporation, which published a tariff or list of charges according to distance and steepness of the road) rose in the period 1744–99 from 120 to 340.[10] Some men would have found work in delivering coal from door to door, or in loading and unloading cargo at the riverside. Others may have worked in the capacity of mere 'hands' in the inns, lodging houses, coffee rooms, workshops and small factories of the city. Men and women (though comparatively few) worked as 'bath guides' – supervising the clientele at the spa, providing the bathing costumes, and generally being at the beck and call of the visiting company as they took the waters. Both men and women survived by working as costermongers or street sellers, offering a range of goods from fruit and vegetables, to haberdashery, ballads and pamphlets. A willingness to carry provisions about the town for retailers, or to act as porters or basket-carriers to overburdened visitors laden down with purchases from Bath's tempting shops, made it quite easy for those immigrants without skills to earn money – but the proliferation of poor strangers seeking such a livelihood provoked the corporation into establishing a licensing system in 1767, which curtailed these activities. Domestic service was an important sector of employment, particularly for women. Indeed, Bath seems to have offered more labour opportunities for women than for men and this is one reason for the greater

9. ' A Town Cryer on the Parades', John Nixon, 1795. (Victoria Art Gallery, Bath)

10. 'A Street Sweeper, New King Street', John Nixon, undated. (Victoria Art Gallery, Bath)

number of females recorded in the 1801 census returns. Servants were needed by Bath's permanent residents as well as by its temporary inhabitants, not only as footmen, ladies' maids, or general domestics, but also as gardeners and laundresses. Those who worked for the visitors were sometimes employed directly, but they could be supplied by the lodging house or inn-keeper. When Louis Simond stayed at the White Hart in 1810, for instance, he noted that 'the servants have no wages – but, depending on the generosity of travellers they find it their interest to please them', and he went on to say that the servants cost him about 5s. (25p) a day.[11]

Skilled immigrant workers to Bath faced the power of the citizens or freemen who, under the control of the corporation, determined who had the right to practise trades within the city. The corporation increasingly encouraged the purchase of freedom, as a means of raising revenue, although whether they were legally entitled to do so is uncertain; by 1810 the purchase price was over £250. The most powerful company was that of the Merchant Taylors, reflecting the role in the local economy of the wool and cloth industry. Membership of a company and freedom of the city gave a man considerable influence and scope for ambition, even if he did not practise a trade. The Quaker Richard Marchant served an apprenticeship to his father and became a Merchant Taylor, but his career was that of a land speculator, building developer, and agent for men engaged in urban development, such as the Duke of Chandos.

Freeman heads of families in Bath apprenticed their sons, and the sons of near relatives, to a wide range of occupations, numbering 68, for much of the eighteenth century. Between 1724 and 1769 the most numerous apprenticeships were as shoemaker (137), carpenter (122), tailor (81), barber and wig-maker (77), apothecary (65), mason (51) and baker (50). These occupations were all related to the demands of the visitors, but the general growth of population in Bath inevitably increased the demand for services of tradesmen, such as bakers, grocers and chandlers. Moreover, a growing diversification of employment as the city expanded is suggested by the fact that the proportion of apprentices entering the manufacturing sector (other than building) rose in this period from 11 per cent to 25 per cent. However, citizen control of trades in Bath was eroded as the result of a dispute between the Company of Merchant Taylors and William Glazeby, who traded in the city as a tailor from 1756, but whose right to do so was challenged by the company in 1759. Legal wrangles dragged on until 1765. The final decision went against the Merchant Taylors, and laid down that the power of regulating and fining non-freemen lay with the corporation. This effectively destroyed the power of the companies, who thereafter never paraded their privileges through the streets of Bath. Only one apprentice tailor was enrolled in the following three years and by 1774 the total number of enrolled apprentices in any trade in Bath had fallen to two. The skilled sector of the labour market was thus opened up to those who had the money to purchase freedom, which became the only means of attaining citizenship. The increased competition from incomers led to violence and intimidation by tailors trying to protect their interests – several of them were involved in attempts to compel cut-price journeymen to leave the city in 1784.

The immigrant and Bath-born labouring classes lived somewhat apart from the upper classes, unless they were resident servants, but class segregation in the social organization of space was less marked in Bath before 1820 than it became later, when the process of suburbanization speeded up. Overcrowding was a common experience, as pressure on the housing stock arose from the influx of workers who were required to build the Georgian city, or who were attracted to it as a general labour market. Consequently, once-fashionable lodgings became tenement buildings, let out by the room. Gardens and stable yards in the Avon Street area, developed for lodgings in the early eighteenth century, became filled in with courts and workshops. Also, new artisan housing for skilled workers was built throughout the eighteenth and early nineteenth centuries, in Morford Street, Ballance Street, and Lampards Buildings. All of these were in close proximity to the King's Circus and the Royal Crescent. To sustain the comfortable life styles of wealthy residents and visitors it was necessary to have laundresses and dressmakers, chimney sweeps and gardeners living nearby.

Little is known of the living standards of the labouring classes in Bath during this period, or of levels of unemployment at any time, although seasonal unemployment was probably commonplace. The building industry (which would have employed substantial numbers of unskilled workers, who were likely to be laid off in the winter months) remained depressed for ten years or so after the crash of 1793. Neale has suggested that living standards fell for most of Bath's workers in the late eighteenth century, by at least a third, and perhaps by a half, between 1780 and 1801. He estimates that the average weekly earnings of unskilled labourers rose by 20 per cent between 1779 and 1800, but that purchasing power – the 'real' wage – fell sharply. A penny loaf purchased in 1800 weighed only half what it had in 1780.

Poverty and protest

Throughout the eighteenth century poverty and hardship fostered the recurrent threat of social upheaval. Sporadic outbreaks of violence and class hatred reflected a smouldering popular resentment of wealth and privilege. Across the country, the old order sought to protect its power and influence at times of turbulence at home and revolution abroad, by resisting all reforms, retaining control of the political sphere, and maintaining the status quo. The aristocracy and gentry developed charitable activities in towns where they were influential, such as Bath, as an extension of their rural tradition of creating dependency among the tenantry on landed estates. The lower orders were expected to render due deference, loyalty and gratitude in return for largess from the élite.

Applications for relief inevitably went up during economic depressions, but the numbers of poor relieved, and the timing of the foundation of charities, were related less directly to economic circumstances than to the level of anxiety among the wealthy classes about the threat to sociopolitical stability from the labouring poor. Charitable activity increased at times of political unrest and decreased when the relationship between rich and poor became more harmonious. The ideology that inspired much 'do-gooding' is exemplified by the evangelical pamphleteer Hannah More, who was based at Bath in the 1790s, conducting her mission to quarry workers and miners on Mendip from Great Pulteney Street. More's numerous *Cheap Repository Tracts* were published by Samuel Hazard of Cheap Street, and were widely circulated in the city. Nearly every bookshop in Bath stocked them, and street hawkers queued at Hazards to buy discounted bundles. The dominant theme of these moralistic tracts was that the social hierarchy was ordained by the Almighty, and that any challenge to the prevailing order invited divine retribution.[12]

Despite the attempts by the upper classes to impose social control on the lower orders, popular protest erupted in mob violence and riot in Bath during the late eighteenth and early nineteenth centuries. The writer Philip Thicknesse was hung in effigy by a mob from Batheaston in 1780, ostensibly for having offended local patriots by intervening on behalf of a man taken by a press gang for naval service. Thicknesse himself believed the incident was provoked by 'the Gambling and trading part of the town', who had been offended by his mockery of the pretensions of Bath in his recently published *Valetudinarian's Bath Guide*. In June 1780 Bath saw its share of violence during the nationwide Gordon Riots, which demonstrated anti-Catholic feeling in support of 'Church and King'. A Catholic priest was attacked, the city's Catholic chapel was burned to the ground and nearby Catholic-owned property was looted. The Bath Volunteers failed to control events on the Friday and withdrew after one rioter was shot. Violence continued overnight, until troops from Wells and Devizes reached the city on Saturday. The leader, a footman named John Butler, was executed for his part in the riot. The loyalism of the mob was no consolation to the traders and authorities in Bath, for damage to the city's economy and image was immediate. Many wealthy visitors departed hurriedly, and the linen-draper and magistrate Francis Bennett urged the corporation to do all it could to restore the 'former lustre' of Bath's name as a peaceful place of safety.

Between 1792 and 1804 the élite in Bath responded to the rhetoric of revolutionary France, and to the growing radicalism among the labouring classes, by campaigning so vigorously against 'sedition' that the period was dubbed Bath's 'Reign of Terror'.[13] The campaign was coordinated by the Bath Association for Preserving Liberty, Property and the Constitution of Great Britain against Republicans and Levellers. The city's branch of this national organization was chaired by the mayor, its committee drawn from magistrates, members of the corporation and principal property owners. Its activities created a tense, repressive, atmosphere. French visitors were regarded with suspicion, allegedly seditious meetings were banned, and informers were encouraged to betray radical sympathizers. Several tradesmen were boycotted as suspected Jacobins. The association took part in the national public bonfire ceremonies in the winter of 1792–3, to burn effigies of Tom Paine, whose egalitarian tract *The Rights of Man* had been declared seditious and its author tried *in absentia* for treason. It was a criminal offence to publish, circulate or possess a copy of this polemic. A journeyman tailor, Benjamin Bull, was arrested in August 1794 on the orders of the mayor after an informer reported him to the authorities. At his family lodgings in Wine Street, thirty-eight copies of the pamphlet were found. Bull was imprisoned, but his destitute family was supported by public subscription, on the condition that he publicly renounced his sedition. Here again charity was used as a means of coercion. The tailor duly declared himself 'truly penitent' in the *Bath Herald*, a month before his release.

Radical organizations included a Bath branch of the London Corresponding Society, according to an informer, and the United Britons (a secret association which sought to promote cooperation with the United Irishmen) may have had contacts in the city. The Bath Irish came under suspicion in May 1798 when rumours circulated that, after the failed republican rising in Ireland that year, they were harbouring and arming United Irishmen, although the *Bath Chronicle* dismissed the rumours as unlikely. Numerous individual radicals were prosecuted for 'sedition', chiefly tailors and shoemakers who, in the authorities' opinion, were 'much addicted to inflame and promote sedition'.[14] Only a minority of prosecutions was successful, but nonetheless the threat of the force of law was a weapon of intimidation. Coercion in the workplace also occurred. Benjamin Bull had been sacked for his political opinions a week before his arrest, and the Bath and West Society (a powerful employers organization) actively sought declarations of loyalty from employees. In these circumstances it is hardly surprising that several thousand workers signed the Bath Association's membership book at the Guildhall.

Although political radicalism was effectively suppressed by the turn of the century, when popular protest in Bath was prompted by food shortages some protestors adopted political slogans. Leaflets circulating in the city included one headed: 'Peace and a large Bread, or a King without a Head.' In March 1800 anonymous letters to the mayor and several employers threatened attacks on their property if prices were not lowered. An attempt to fire Stotherts' Ironworks followed, and a brewery on the quay was burned down. Garden robberies, poaching, violent robberies from millers and butter-sellers became increasingly commonplace. The 'moral economy', or sense of natural justice, that inspired many food riots prompted 200 women to mob dealers in the market in May 1800, forcing them to sell their produce cheaply. The angry women then rampaged out to Larkhall, where they set upon a gardener and carried off supplies of potatoes. They were eventually dispersed by the yeomanry.

In response to social disorder the wealthy residents of Bath followed the example of other cities and set up a Provision Committee in December 1799. Over the following year it raised £3,000 by donations, which was used to buy food and coal for resale at low prices, to avoid the stigma of charity. The corporation took action in February 1801 by offering free stalls in the market to bakers from the rural areas around the city. Poor-relief rates rose, but high prices absorbed much of the increase, and ratepayers, themselves adversely affected by inflation, became vociferous in their complaints about the standard of relief, which was lowered in some poorhouses after investigations of accounts and expenditure. In the years 1800 and 1801, £14,000 was distributed in charitable relief, but not all those in need were allowed to make purchases from the Provision Committee. This privilege was reserved for applicants with a written recommendation to the fund from a subscriber, who provided details of the applicant's name, address and family size. During 1801 a third of the city's population, some 10,000 people, were subsisting on a weekly distribution of rice. Local newspapers offered recipes for making rice bread and other dishes, but they lost no opportunity to remind the poor that they owed the rich 'respect, gratitude and obedience', and emphasized that 'idleness, discontent and riot, will make things worse'.

With its extremes of wealth and poverty, and a substantial labouring class, Bath was clearly a complex city in its heyday as the resort of fashion. It retained its dominant image in the opening decades of the nineteenth century, but that singular picture did not reflect the occupational diversity of the city or the changes that had resulted from its expansion.

Bath was becoming a favoured place for the permanent residence of the wealthy upper and middle classes, who chose to settle there in growing numbers rather than merely visit for a season's entertainment. This foreshadowed the altered image of Bath that emerged later in the Victorian period. Whereas the spa had been widely perceived as a temple of frivolity and fashion in its Georgian heyday, its dominant image in the nineteenth century was that of a sedate, unfashionable and conservative backwater, inhabited largely by maiden aunts and retired colonels. Bath then became the butt of satirists as a place where:

It sounds rather strange, but I tell you no lie,
There's many good people that come here to die
... These folk, like Sir Lucius, find comfort in dying,
Because in the Abbey there's very snug lying.[15]

This image, like the earlier one, emphasized only one aspect of the diverse realities of Bath's history. In the turbulent decades from 1820 and on into the early twentieth century, Bath was much more than a haven for old age and not all of its inhabitants were 'genteel residents'.

Chapter 4

The City of Genteel
Residence, 1820–1914

The need for Bath to develop a new image was created by the economic consequences of its decline as the resort of fashion. Whereas in the eighteenth century Bath had courted 'the quality' for the season, in the nineteenth century it increasingly sought to tempt 'the gentility' to take up permanent residence in the city. The genteel image it developed, in a bid to replace the loss of upper-class visitors with middle-class incomers, was also influenced by the general change over time in social values and attitudes.

The corporation's decision not to rebuild the Lower Assembly Rooms when they were destroyed by fire in 1820, but to erect a Scientific and Literary Institution on the site, reflected a move away from the frivolity of the eighteenth century to the more high-minded interests characteristic of the nineteenth century. The mood of the moment was caught in 1834 by Captain Roland Mainwaring, who proclaimed that by this decision 'Bath stands redeemed from the imputation of being a city devoted to pleasure and dissipation'.[1] Another change from the decadence of the Georgian age was reflected in the religiosity of Bath in the early Victorian period. The spate of church and chapel building and the growth of charitable societies expressed a new moral earnestness that dominated what in 1864 was claimed to be 'probably one of the most religious cities in the kingdom, at least externally'.[2] Indeed, religious enthusiasm threatened to destroy the public amusements of the city:

> The clergy of this town by their preaching and exhortations have endeavoured to suppress the various amusements of the place, and indeed so comprehensive have been their denunciations, that scarcely an entertainment of a publick character has escaped; concerts, balls, races, theatrical exhibitions, and even horticultural shows, have each of them been the subjects of clerical vengeance.[3]

The city was therefore undergoing another transformation. From being primarily the mecca of the rich in search of seasonal amusement, it was to become much more a permanent retreat for pensioners and annuitants.

This process had begun before 1820 but it gathered pace thereafter. What remained constant between 1820 and 1914, embodied in the language of the *Bath Guides* and in the utterances of local dignitaries, was a sense of the city's unique quality, informed by the legacy of history. The ancient legend of Bladud, the link with classical antiquity through the Roman baths, and the architectural heritage of the Georgian master-pieces were repeatedly publicized as enduring reminders of past glories. The past was also drawn upon to advertise the city's cultural traditions, by frequent references in the official guides to the famous artistic and literary figures associated with Bath in the eighteenth century.

A new image for Bath

In 'selling' Bath as a place primarily of genteel residence, its more imme-diate attractions were emphasized; the other, industrial and commercial character of the city was ignored or camouflaged. Naturally, Bath con-tinued to advertise the qualities of its hot springs in curing rheumatic disorders. It also drew attention to its mild winters and (after 1841) good railway communications with all parts of the kingdom. Particular prominence was given to the agreeable combination of high quality shops and the availability of cheap food, coal and lodgings. Another virtue that Bath proclaimed unfailingly in its attempt to attract new residents was the very low level of its municipal, poor and water rates. The city could offer fine buildings and parks, an increasing range of private schools, and amenities such as municipal supplies of water, gas and – by the 1890s – electricity. Diversions and amusements were still plentiful, at the Assembly Rooms, the theatre and concert halls. Parti-cular prominence was invariably given to the city's growing reputation as a desirable place of residence, since living among the 'right sort of people' was perhaps the most compelling reason of all for deciding to settle in Bath.

The refined and respectable image projected in the official guides was reinforced by commentators and journalists, who largely accepted it without question and echoed it in their own writings. The author of a magazine article in 1844, for example, informed his readers that:

> The visitant is well aware that Bath is not a city of trade. No manu-facture worthy of note is carried on within its limits, nor is it the resort of commerce ... Of all places in the Kingdom, Bath is best fitted for the retirement of individuals with independent incomes, whether small or large. For those past the meridian in life, its quiet-ness, beautiful neighbourhood, and warmth of climate particularly recommend it ... Trade in Bath consists principally in the sale of arti-cles connected with the refinements rather than the necessities of life.[4]

Marketing Bath's new image proved so successful that the city became identified with its social élite. By the end of the nineteenth century its name was virtually synonymous with staid maiden aunts and retired military men:

> It is indeed a wonderful place of resort for very old people, of whom you see scores creeping placidly in the sunshine, or doddering about in corners sheltered from the wind ... Of these veterans, the large majority are composed of the retired military, among whom still linger the black stock with its satin 'fall', the pipe clayed buckskin gloves, the bamboo cane.[5]

The proclaimed old-world air of the place, the courtesy of its suitably deferential shopkeepers and 'the uncommon civility of attendants at the Baths'[6] were especially appealing to a class of people anxious to preserve the traditions of a paternalistic society at a time of rapid socio-economic and political change. All the attractions and advantages of the city as a place of genteel and economical living were summarized in a letter quoted in the *Guide Through and Round Bath* of 1900. Signing himself 'A Contented Man', the writer declared that the city provided him with:

> refined society, where elegance and taste are the rule, vulgar show the exception, public amusement, delightful scenery within 10 minutes walk, house rent lower than anywhere else in a place offering the advantages of Bath, my table is *cheaply* supplied, and of the best, traders uniformly civil, obliging and fair ...[7]

Partly as a result of this marketing exercise, Bath continued to grow and develop as it adjusted to its changing role as a residential city. The physical expansion of the city incorporated middle-class suburbs that extended the spectacular developments of the eighteenth century. Bath remained one of the great cities of England until 1851, with a population of over 50,000. Thereafter its rate of growth lagged behind the general level of urban expansion. Yet, even when the aggregate population in Bath remained static during the second half of the century, suburban numbers grew apace.

It is from within such a framework of physical growth and the social transformation of Bath into a residential city that we now turn to other developments, starting with communications. Communications in and around the city were improved by the activities of the Bath Turnpike Trust in the 1820s and 1830s, and by the later advent of the railway age. The corporation undertook some municipal improvements during the 1820s, and in the following decade laid out the Victoria Park, but new building projects in Bath from 1820 to the 1860s were almost entirely ecclesiastical, industrial or commercial. At this time only a few suburban villa residences stretched up Bathwick Hill, Lansdown Hill and on the southern slopes of Lyncombe and Widcombe. However, the city expanded in size in the late nineteenth and early twentieth centuries as a consequence of major housing development and of changes to its administrative boundaries. During the thirty years before the First World War, Bath acquired a great suburban skirt that incorporated neighbouring rural parishes.

The appointment of John Loudon McAdam as surveyor to the Bath Turnpike Trust in 1826 marked the beginning of ten years or so of changes to the city's infrastructure, notably an increase in the number of vehicular bridges over the River Avon. Cleveland Bridge, between Bathwick and Walcot, was constructed in 1827, and housing development in Cleveland Place soon followed. New Bridge, on the Bristol Road, was widened and refashioned during the 1830s, and North Parade ceased to be a cul-de-sac in 1835 when work began on North Parade Bridge. Further down the Avon, in the increasingly industrial part of the city, the Victoria Suspension Bridge was erected in 1836.[8] The Great Western Railway line from Bristol to London opened along its entire length when the Box tunnel (a major feat of engineering for its time) was completed in 1841, but the twelve-mile section between Bristol and Bath came into operation a year earlier. The Midland Railway Company constructed a spur to Bath from its Birmingham–Bristol line in the late 1860s, and in 1874 this was linked to the Somerset and Dorset line serving the south coast.

Numerous churches, chapels and cemetery chapels were built between the 1840s and 1890s, including the Swedenborgian church (1844) off Manvers Street, a Moravian chapel (1845) in Charlotte Street, and St Mary's Roman Catholic church (1880s) in Julian Road. Domestic building was more varied in both style and materials than it had been in the Georgian period. Housing along the Upper Bristol Road was constructed mainly of Bristol pennant rather than Bath stone or, in some instances of pennant stone at the front and cheaper red brick at the back.[9] In the late nineteenth century there was another building boom in Bath. The council was then involved in improving civic amenities, and private investment in speculative building financed extensive suburban housing developments. Desirable detached and semi-detached villa residences on the outskirts of the city were widely advertised in the 1880s and 1890s, and in the Oldfield Park area there was a large development of terraced artisan dwellings. This was a popular location for meeting the housing needs of Bath's railway and post office clerks.

Officially, Bath's population increased at a modest rate, to reach 54,240 by 1851. It then remained virtually static until the last decade of the century, falling by 8 per cent to 49,839 between 1851 and 1901, but over the next ten years it increased by almost 2 per cent, to reach 50,721 in 1911. What these figures conceal is the redistribution of the city's population away from the inner city districts and towards the suburban areas. Furthermore, the administrative boundaries of Bath became progressively outdated in the later nineteenth century. As a consequence of suburban growth, the two satellite parishes of Twerton and Weston functioned increasingly as part of the city. They were officially incorporated within its boundaries in the early twentieth century, but this was a long-overdue recognition of their function. The aggregate population of Twerton and Weston grew from 6,046 in 1851 to 17,025 by 1901. If these numbers are added to Bath's population, as part of the operative area of the city, then the decline in population between 1851 and 1901 of 8 per cent becomes an increase of the order of 10.9 per cent in the same period.

The expansion of the suburban parishes was a long-term trend in Bath, discernible from the early nineteenth century, but the effects of the process were not fully understood by some of its leading citizens. The Revd George Tugwell (rector of Bath from 1870) confidently declared in a speech at the mayor's banquet of 1890 that: 'The city grows in all directions.' He went on to suggest that the population of the suburban parish of Bathwick, a mere 250 in 1791, would probably be returned as between 5,000 and 6,000 in 1891.[10] His optimism, at a time when the city's population was officially in decline, reflects a local tendency to identify Bath with its suburban inhabitants, while ignoring the state of the inner-city parishes. It is true that the migration of wealthy citizens to suburban areas initially increased the population density of inner-city parishes, as the poorer classes crowded into the premises left vacant in the centre. This, however, was a short-lived phase. Employment opportunities in the city itself were, in all probability, reduced with the decline of the Bath season, but alternative work was available in the textile trade in the suburban parish of Lyncombe and Widcombe, and just outside the boundary at Twerton. Even so, from 1801 to 1851, the trend was for the aggregate population growth of the inner-city parishes to be substantially smaller than the increase for the city as a whole. Moreover, by the 1830s some of the poor, in their turn, removed themselves to tenements on the outskirts of Bath.

Underlying the overall decline of 8 per cent in the city's population between 1851 and 1901 there was a marked differential in the fall and rise of populations in inner-city and suburban parishes. This was not simply a reflection of the flight from the city of the prosperous commercial and professional classes, retreating to their gothic villas – artisans and labourers were also moving to the suburbs. In the last quarter of the nineteenth century the process of suburbanization was greatly accelerated. Only 18 per cent (20 out of 111) of the new houses built in Bath during the twelve months from October 1899 to October 1900 were located in the three central parishes of the city. Those who were left behind in the inner city areas generally comprised the poorest sector of the population, compelled to live near their place of work. On the other hand, needlewomen, charwomen and laundresses may well have lost valuable contacts and custom, as gentry families and the middle classes drifted to the suburbs.

Suburban growth tended to increase the geographical segregation of different social classes. Speculative housing developments were aimed at specific classes, so the suburbs quickly became identified with the social status of their inhabitants. The shopkeepers and humble tradesmen who moved out to new villas found themselves among neighbours of a similar socio-economic background. Moreover, as the process of suburbanization accelerated, so the physical distance from the poor became a barrier to understanding the condition of inner-city slums. The reputation of the urban poor assumed alarming proportions to those who rarely came into contact with them, but who, in the comfort of a drawing-room behind shuttered windows, read lurid newspaper accounts of the 'animal' behaviour of the under class. As the drift to the suburbs began to encompass the lower-middle classes and the socially aspiring working classes, it also increased the gulf between the 'respectable' and the 'rough' among the lower ranks of Bath society.

The social structure of the city was always more complex than many contemporaries and some historians, influenced by the image of Bath, have assumed. The opinion of the Revd Warner, that 'the higher classes of people and their dependants constitute the chief part of the population, and the number of lower classes is small',[11] was representative of the erroneous views of people of his class and time. Yet this paternalistic analysis of the social structure, based essentially on two classes, persisted long after Warner wrote in 1801. A modern analysis would separate the groups identified by Warner as 'dependants' into occupations, according to their economic function. The large numbers of shop assistants, craftsmen and domestic servants working in Bath in the nineteenth and early twentieth century were, nonetheless, widely regarded as 'dependants' rather than 'workers'. It fitted the projected image of Bath, as a city of 'little trade and no manufacture', to minimize the working-class presence by camouflaging all those sectors that earned their livings by providing goods and services for the upper classes, or being directly employed by them.

In reality, the working classes formed the great majority of the population in Bath, and the broad trend over time was for the size of this group to increase. The male labour force grew by 35.3 per cent (from 9,409 to 12,734) between 1851 and 1901, while in the same period the female labour force expanded by 23 per cent (from 8,712 to 10,713). The combined numbers of males and females living on independent means also rose, from 2,875 to 3,155, but this was a slight increase compared with the growth in the commercial and industrial labour force.

Throughout the years between 1820 and 1914 Bath's population was subject to a process of gentle ageing. It consistently had a larger proportion of elderly people than most other cities of comparable size. Nevertheless, it would be a mistake to accept the view that Bath was a geriatric community, the 'cradle of old age', as one contemporary described it in 1900.[12] The attraction of Bath as a place of retirement raised the proportion of its population over the age of 60, but there was also a continuous migration of young women into the city in search of work. The comparative lack of male employment opportunities was responsible for an out-migration of young men, which created a large disparity between females and males of marriageable age.

The variation in population growth between different parishes and wards in the city was echoed by important differences in the age structure and gender ratios of the populations of inner-city and suburban parishes. A comparison between Bath as a whole and the suburban parish of Bathwick in 1841 reveals that there was little difference between the two in the age distribution of the male population, but the ratio of females to males in Bathwick in 1841 was 229:100. Women outnumbered men in the total population of the United Kingdom throughout the period 1820 to 1914, but Bath shared with Cheltenham a severe imbalance between the sexes, which reflected the popularity of spa towns as places of genteel residence for wealthy unmarried and widowed women, and also the demand for female domestic servants. The disparity between females and males in Bath remained in the region of 140 to 150 women per 100 men from 1841 to 1901, a demographic feature that varied between parishes and changed over time. The highest ratio of females to males in 1891 among the inner-city parishes was 148:100, in St Michael's parish. The ratio in the suburban parish of Bathwick in the same year was almost two to one at 196:100. In the poorest areas of the city, in the wards of Lyncombe and Widcombe and St James's, the respective ratios in 1901 were 121:100 and 138:100. The superabundance of females was particularly marked in the two most socially exclusive wards of the city. The ratio of women to men was 210:100 in Bathwick and 251:100 in Lansdown.

The persistent imbalance in the gender ratios of Bath's population is of particular significance in the context of the city's reputation as a marriage market. This had been one of its traditional functions for visitors since the height of its fashionable appeal in the Georgian age. Yet in terms of its demographic structure Bath was the least likely location for the arrangement of marriages. Even with the annual influx of visitors for the season, there was a universal lament about the shortage of men at public functions. It was reported in *London Society* in August 1870 that 'It is the misfortune of Bath society that at most parties there is a scarcity of gentlemen', and this complaint reverberated down the decades to 1914. In the marriageable age groups of 21–40 year olds, men were greatly outnumbered and most particularly so in the parishes that would be represented in a 'respectable' marriage market.

Yet ambitious mothers still held to the belief that Bath society was the ideal setting for displaying a daughter to attract a suitable marriage partner. The numbers of foreign language teachers, music tutors, and drawing masters listed in city directories from 1820 to 1914 suggest that many hopeful young ladies were busily engaged in acquiring the superficial accomplishments deemed necessary for making a 'good match'.

As Bath adjusted to its changing fortunes in becoming a residential city, the corporation faced a dilemma over the need to provide attractive features for the visitors, without losing potential new residents by putting additional burdens on the rates. Opinion was evidently divided as to the best option for the local economy. Vested interests relying primarily on the tourist trade were supported in their desire to promote Bath as a health resort by those members of the political élite who looked back nostalgically to the city's past role and function. They were opposed by those who did well economically from the influx of new wealthy residents, and by new residents themselves – who were encouraged to settle in the city because of its low rates and generally cheap living costs. The debate over spending ratepayers' money on amenities for visitors is illustrated by events in August 1882, when the council considered a proposal for general repairs to the baths and the construction of a 'cooling room' for bathers at the New Royal Baths, at a total estimated cost of some £1,000. The spa was actually enjoying a revival of popularity in the 1880s, but, nonetheless, Alderman Gibbs commented that he had never known trade in the city to be worse than it was at that time. He went on to move the following amendment: 'Considering the present depression of trade and agriculture which affects all classes, and the large amount of expenditure, actual and prospective in other civic departments to which the rates are already subjected, it is *not* desirable to undertake further outlay than is required for the necessary repairs at the Baths.'[13] Alderman Gibb's amendment was rejected, but the ambivalence of some of the political élite and the need to attract visitors form a continuous thread in municipal politics from the eighteenth century to the present day.

Promoting the image of Bath was, in general, good for business. Indeed, the civic leaders' efforts to guard jealously the reputation of the city could have a profound influence on policy decisions affecting the lives of all the residents of Bath. The city, like many others, was a victim of the first major epidemic of Asiatic cholera in Britain during 1832. The first incidence of the disease in Bath appeared in July of that year. Energetic measures to restrict its spread were undertaken, but the recently established local board of health was faced with an awkward dilemma. If it were to release the daily total of cholera victims to the central board in London, as it was duty bound to do, there was a substantial risk of very damaging publicity appearing in the London press just at the start of the Bath winter season, when visitors would normally arrive. A majority of the city's board of health decided against the release of the figures. No information on the epidemic was given to local newspapers and a prayerful silence was maintained in the hope that the cholera outbreak would soon die out. It did not.

To finance the necessary measures against the epidemic, money had to be raised from each of the city's six parishes, according to the size of their populations. Most of them bluntly refused to provide the required sums from the rates, because the cholera was largely confined to the poorest area of the city in the Avon Street district. The board of health was therefore forced to apply to London for the authority to compel the parishes to pay up. The reply was frankly mystified. Why should Bath need to raise so much money to combat the cholera, when there was no evidence of disease in the city? In order for the board of health in Bath to be empowered to implement its preventative measures, evidence had to be submitted to the central board. It was provided only after assurances were received that the returns of cholera victims would remain confidential and out of the press. The need to protect the city's reputation as a health resort, and to avoid frightening off prospective visitors for the season, very nearly prevented the authorities from protecting the bulk of the city's residents from disease in 1832.[14]

Another example of the conflict of interest between residents and visitors occurred in the late nineteenth century, when the city council was involved in developing civic amenities. Extensions to the Guildhall, plans for the Empire Hotel, and a new art gallery were all part of the improvements. The clash of interests was sharply brought out in a piece of satirical verse provoked by proposals for the art gallery:

> The latest fad that folly can devise
> To squander money, falling from the skies;
> 'A Gallery of Art', the biggest boon,
> For still the parrot cry is, 'Room, more Room'.
> Not for the labourer, or the artisan;
> Let such men herd in slums as best they can.[15]

In this instance the needs of the poor were felt to have less claim on the civic purse than those of other, more powerful interests. Yet the writer's attack on the council's wasteful expenditure was, in reality, in defence of the interests of the wealthier ratepayers rather than the largely unenfranchised poor. Slum clearance and subsidized municipal housing, as an alternative to the art gallery, would have required the council to borrow money from the local government board, and to have levied substantially more from the rates.

Nonetheless, although there were conflicts of interest over spending from the rates, the general perception persisted from 1820 to 1914 that Bath's economic prosperity depended on its ability to attract outsiders.

Wealthy new residents were welcome, but the need to attract visitors was also widely held to be crucial to the city's success.

Taking the waters: visitors and the Bath season

While Bath was becoming more of a residential city, it still retained an interest in attracting visitors, not least because of a reluctance to abandon its former glory, but also because there were many vested interests dependent upon passing trade. Bath was no longer the premier resort of fashion by the 1820s, but it still had a unique feature in the hot springs. Marketing its appeal as a spa treatment centre continued to be a matter of importance to the authorities and others. More visitors meant improved business for doctors and shopkeepers, better custom for hoteliers and lodging-house keepers, and more employment for dressmakers, laundresses, chairmen and, later, cab drivers. There were, indeed, many vested interests concerned to promote the image of Bath as a health resort for visitors between 1820 and 1914. However, the gradual realization that the city's principal role was changing brought about a crisis of confidence, which was reflected in the ambivalent attitudes of the council to the spa facilities, and in the perennial debate over whether or not to raise the rates paid by residents in order to provide amenities for visitors. The response to Bath's social decline as a resort encompassed both a determined optimism and a sense of loss at the city's fading reputation. The 1830 *Bath Guide* listed numerous diversions for the visitors, and proclaimed: 'From a perusal of the foregoing scenes of amusement and recreation, it will be readily conceived that in a full season, no place in England affords a more brilliant circle of polite company than Bath.'[16]

An enduring attraction for visitors and residents consisted of the city's shopping facilities, which were regularly advertised in contemporary accounts. The following example, dating from 1887, serves for others of similar description in the period 1820–1914:

> The shops of Bath are a revelation to the stranger, and give token of the fact that Bath is still the centre of fashion and luxury not only to the fashionable visitors, but to the whole of the West of England. Kings of Milsom Street would do credit to the Rue de Rivoli or Regent Street, for sustained splendour and gorgeous raiment.[17]

Yet by 1832 it was widely recognized, if not officially acknowledged, that 'Bath was deserted by fashion, after having served as its Temple', and in the same year the *Bath Chronicle* gave expression to the prevailing ambivalence. In January 1832 it reported that 'we have every reason to believe that the present season will be one of the gayest which Bath has

11. Milsom Street looking south from George Street in the 1840s. Originally built as fashionable lodgings, Milsom Street became the most important shopping street in Bath. (Bath Library)

witnessed for some time'. However, later in the same month it informed its readers that the master of ceremonies was striving unsuccessfully to encourage more patrons to 'this once-favoured city'. The fall in numbers of visitors made an impact on local events, leading, for instance, to the curtailment of the Bath races from three to two days in 1833. Similarly, a Sydney Gardens gala in 1838 seems to have lost money for its organizer. It was reported that 'the attendance was not commensurate with the exertions of the proprietor'.[18]

Visitors who came to Bath for the season, which lasted from November to around Easter, were in general less wealthy and more solidly middle class than their counterparts during the city's Georgian heyday. Improved communications, first by road and then by rail, were vital in making Bath more accessible to visitors from all over the country, but they were accompanied by unexpected hazards and disappointments. At the beginning of this period, travelling to Bath still entailed arduous journeys by coach. Road improvements made such journeys somewhat more comfortable than in the past, but local newspapers' accounts of many incidents of petty highway robbery on roads leading into the city throughout the 1830s suggest that they could still be dangerous expeditions. The advent of the railway age raised hopes of an influx of visitors. Yet it was Bristol-based entrepreneurs rather than Bathonians who dominated the group

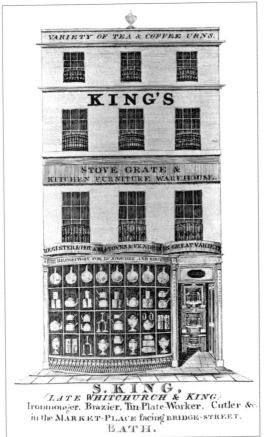

VARIETY OF TEA & COFFEE URNS.

KING'S

STOVE GRATE &
KITCHEN FURNITURE WAREHOUSE.

REGISTER & HOT AIR STOVES & FENDERS IN GREAT VARIETY
REPOSITORY FOR IRONWORK AND SIEVES

S. KING,
(LATE WHITCHURCH & KING)
Ironmonger, Brazier, Tin-Plate-Worker, Cutler &c.
in the MARKET-PLACE facing BRIDGE-STREET,
BATH.

12. S. King, Market Place, 1837. An example of the integration of craft and retail establishments characteristic of small businesses in Victorian Bath. (Bath Library)

which promoted the Great Western Railway (GWR), and there was some local resistance to railway development. The company's plans were approved by Parliament in 1835, but were opposed by the Kennet and Avon Canal Company and by the Bath Turnpike Trust, which administered and maintained fifty-one miles of road, collected the tolls from fifty-one gates and operated five weighbridges in the city. Loudon McAdam, surveyor to the Turnpike Trust, spoke out publicly against the 'Calamity of Railways', but it was not only those who were directly threatened by competition who doubted whether the railway would benefit Bath in its attempts to attract visitors. A correspondent to the *Bath Chronicle* in May 1835 put forward the view that Isambard Kingdom Brunel's scheme was 'a plan to reduce the population of your fair City', by luring potential visitors to London.[19]

The corporation, nonetheless, assisted the GWR company over the purchase of land for the line, the station and goods yards, in the expectation of a boost to the number of visitors, although it also imposed certain restrictions. These chiefly concerned bridges and tunnels, and

13. J. Abraham, Bartlett Street, 1837. The advertisement of royal and noble patronage was characteristic of Bath's genteel image. (Bath Library)

the protection of the water supply in the parishes of Lyncombe and Widcombe and Bathwick. The area around the GWR station (later known as Bath Spa) was intended to make an impressive entrance to the city. Two new roads were laid out. Dorchester Street (running westward to join Southgate Street at the city bridge) and Manvers Street (running northward to join Pierrepoint Street) were planned as terraces of substantial houses, with the Royal Hotel and the Manvers Arms (renamed the Argyll Hotel) standing on the corners facing the station. The GWR line from Bristol to London opened along the entire route in 1841, but when the twelve-mile section from Bristol to Bath went into service (August 1840) huge crowds attended the inaugural ceremony, and such was the interest in the new form of travel that twenty trips each way were made between Bath and Bristol on the opening day. The regular service thereafter was ten trains each way on Mondays to Saturdays, with four on Sundays, at a single fare of 2s. 6d. (12½ p) first class and 1s. 6d. (7½p) second class.[20]

However, the main impact of the railway was not on the tourist trade, but on speeding up the process whereby the industrial area of the city became concentrated in the southern part of Bath along the Lower Bristol Road, where transport networks converged. The two new hotels facing the railway station (built in Georgian style) were symbols of the commercial hopes that were invested in the coming of the railway and the expected revival in the numbers of visitors, but the Royal Hotel and the Manvers Arms stood in isolation for some time. The economic climate did not encourage speculative building. Manvers Street and Dorchester Street remained undeveloped until later in the century.[21]

Despondency about the city's prospects as a health resort deepened with the realization that the GWR had not boosted visitor numbers. Official interest in the spa diminished to such an extent that the corporation let the baths to a private individual in the early 1860s. After a trial period the lessee terminated the agreement in 1864, and no other entrepreneur could be persuaded to take up a new lease. In the same year, the post of master of ceremonies became redundant. The lack of visitors was beginning to affect seriously the city's hotel trade. York House had already been turned into a post office, and numerous smaller hotels had gone out of business. The famous White Hart, opposite the Pump Room, closed down permanently in 1864. The severity of the situation prompted renewed activity, heralded in an address by the mayor to the corporation: 'Having thought much lately of the change that Bath has undergone, I have come to the conclusion that we ought to make a vigorous effort to revive its prosperity and that we cannot do better than follow the old lines.'[22] In response, a committee was set up. It proposed replacing the White Hart with a prestigious new hotel, equipped at basement level with the most modern bathing facilities, and fitted with lifts to take patients from their suites to the baths. The baths were re-opened in 1867, and the Grand Pump Room Hotel was itself completed two years later in 1869, the year which is traditionally seen as marking a revival in Bath's prosperity. The new baths, built entirely with corporation money, were widely approved:

> Everyone who sees the beautiful suite of baths adjoining the hotel ... sees also what the city has gained in this respect. Conveyed by a lift from bedroom floors, the patient is not subject to hazardous and comfortless exposure, while the variety of baths, suited to various forms of complaint, is a great advantage.[23]

The Grand Pump Room Hotel was not, however, an instant success. It only slowly began to attract an increasing number of visitors, although some recovery in the local economy was apparent form the late 1860s. Another large hotel of good repute opened shortly afterwards, and it was reported that private family hotels had multiplied and that houses and lodgings had been better let than for many years.

At the same time, more railway developments improved national communications with Bath and brought renewed hope of visitors from the Midlands, the North and, via Liverpool, from even further afield. During 1869–70 Queen's Square station (more recently known as Green Park station) was built as the terminus of a spur from the Midland Railway's Birmingham to Bristol line. When, a few years later (1874), the station was linked with the Somerset and Dorset line, access to Bath from neighbouring counties and the south coast was improved. More visitors may have journeyed to Bath on day trips, but the line raised the worrying possibility of more competition from seaside resorts.

In the year 1881–2, 60,000 bathers passed through the four city baths; the revival of the spa was well under way. Moreover, the council agreed at its March meeting in 1882 to further promotion by spending £300 annually, 'in advertising the advantages of the hot mineral springs. W. H. Smith and Son, advertising contractors, have undertaken to provide large show boards and display at 100 principal stations for five years at £200 per year.'[24] These advertisements featured Minerva leaning on a shield in the upper part, with details of the yield and temperature of the springs and with a selection of photographs of the city. The virtues of the springs were extolled and compared advantageously to continental spas. A version of the poster, in the form of a circular, was sent to every medical practitioner in the United Kingdom. Expenditure on advertising was strongly supported by Alderman Wilkinson, Chairman of the Baths and Pump Room Committee, who reckoned that 'for every pound spent on … advertising there would be a £10 return to the citizens of Bath'. The number of visitors certainly rose once the spa was being vigorously promoted. The number of bathers using the city baths more than doubled in the decade after 1876, to reach 86,223 in 1886. During 1888 this figure rose to 94,835. The renewed interest in the Bath waters benefited the corporation, the medical profession, the hoteliers and tradesmen, such as the enterprising Mr Cater, who secured the monopoly of bottling the spring water. It was claimed to be therapeutic to the gouty and the rheumatic and it proved highly profitable to Mr Cater, who devised a process for aerating it to preserve the carbonate of iron content.

The authorities, now firmly committed to the spa and the need to encourage visitors, were determined not to be left behind by advances in medical science. During the 1880s the city surveyor, Major Davis, and Dr Henry Freeman, surgeon to the Royal United Hospital and later a mayor of Bath, were sent on an extended tour of European spas to study new treatments. On the basis of their report, the council built a complete new suite of douche and massage baths at the corner of York Street and Stall Street. When they were opened in 1889 they were an immediate success. 'Continental' treatments were very much in vogue and it was claimed that visitor revenue doubled 'almost overnight'.[25]

The mineral water hospital itself played an integral part in the image and function of the city as a health resort. Lists of patients discharged were printed every month in local newspapers. Some patients were sent out because of misconduct, others discharged themselves before treatment was completed, some were classified as 'improper', meaning that they were unsuitable for treatment. For the remainder, medical staff employed a simple classification in the published lists, as 'cured', 'much better', 'better', 'no better' or 'dead'.[26] Because the outcome of all cases was published, it was obviously in the interests of the hospital to demonstrate a high rate of cures or substantial improvements. This added to its prestige and encouraged donors and subscribers to give generously to its funds. It is likely that at least some of those 'cured' by the waters had, in reality, spontaneously recovered from their ailments.

Meanwhile, the redevelopment of the spa from the 1860s had led to the excavation of the Roman Baths.[27] These were to become one of the city's enduring tourist attractions. Part of the pediment of the temple of Sulis-Minerva had been discovered when the Pump Room was built in 1790, but there were no attempts to uncover more remains until after the White Hart Hotel closed down in 1864. An enthusiastic antiquarian, James Irvine, was employed at that time as clerk to the works by the architect Sir Gilbert Scott, who was carrying out restoration work on the abbey. Irvine knew of the discoveries of 1790 and, deducing that most of the Sulis-Minerva temple lay under the White Hart opposite the Pump Room, he began exploratory excavations as soon as the hotel closed. When demolition and rebuilding on the site was underway (1867–9) he carefully recorded all the findings unearthed. The authorities took no official interest in the Roman remains at this stage, but over the next decade Irvine successfully engaged the interest of Major Davis, the city surveyor, in his discoveries. Davis instigated excavations which revealed the Roman reservoir built around the original spring beneath the King's Bath. Once this project was completed (1878–9), he went on to carry out further excavations in the following year, which led to the uncovering of the Great Bath. This provoked considerable local excitement and the council, somewhat belatedly, recognized the potential of the site as a visitor attraction. An Antiquities Committee was soon set up, and funds were raised to complete the excavation.

The project was bedevilled by conflicts of interest and personality clashes. Some local tradesmen, concerned about the effect on their businesses of the disruption around the site, took the council to court for causing a nuisance. Extra funds had to be raised to purchase the Poor Law Offices, which stood on part of the Roman site. Major Davis became involved in an acrimonious public debate about who had actually discovered the baths. As an antiquarian himself, but also city surveyor, Davis found himself facing a dilemma in 1886, when the douche and massage baths were being built: he was naturally in sympathy with those who wanted to preserve the archaeological remains discovered on site but, as an employee of the city council, it was his duty to build the baths as quickly and cheaply as possible. Such was the antipathy towards Davis, who was the focus of considerable hostility in the late 1880s and 1890s, that his conduct as city surveyor was the subject of a committee of enquiry. He was exonerated, albeit guardedly, from accusations of misconduct, but he remained a controversial figure in Bath.

By 1889 visitors could view the Roman antiquities, although no immediate attempt was made to tidy up the site, and the Great Bath was left uncovered. For some nine years it remained exposed to the elements, and it suffered considerable erosion from the weathering process. It was not until 1892 that a scheme was proposed to extend the Pump Room and thereby incorporate the Roman antiquities into the complex. The project included a new concert hall to relieve the overcrowding in the existing Pump Room, which was a cause of complaint now that visitor numbers had increased. Plans were put out to competition, which was won by the London architect J. M. Brydon who had planned the Guildhall enlargement of 1891. Major Davis was effectively excluded from this competition by the manoeuverings of a faction on the council which managed to get the brief rewritten at a late stage, ostensibly on the grounds of cutting costs. This however, was not the end of Davis's career. The discovery of the Roman baths and the general upturn in Bath's appeal as a spa in the closing decades of the nineteenth century gave a boost to civic pride. The Pump Room extension, completed in 1897, was followed by the commissioning of Major Davis in 1899 to design a new purpose-built hotel as another prestigious amenity for visitors. The building of the Empire Hotel (completed in 1901) and of the parade in front of it reflected the optimism generated by Bath's late Victorian prosperity but, in reality, this had petered out before the Empire opened its doors.

The social tone and character of Bath changed over time, as it developed its genteel image after 1820. It became more solidly middle class, and its visitors also changed. Conferences began to be of increasing importance by 1900. The Society of Architects, among many other similar bodies, held their annual conference in the city between 1906 and 1910, as did the British Medical Association and the Institute of Mechanical Engineers. In January 1913 the city entertained 400 doctors from London, who were taken on a motor tour of the area before being received by the mayor and the chairman of the Baths' Committee for tea at the Pump Room. Other items on the itinerary were demonstrations of methods of treatment, a description of the Roman antiquities, and an address on the radioactive waters of Bath.[28]

Meanwhile the social scene during the Bath season remained outwardly vibrant, but patterns of leisure were altering throughout the country during this period. The entertainments and amusements offered to visitors changed with national trends, but also in response to the increased number of middle-class permanent residents. Newspaper accounts of theatrical performances, concerts, balls and gala celebrations give a somewhat misleading impression of the gaiety of social life in Bath. These traditional attractions were still on offer, but the city could make no claim to high culture in the period 1820–1914, and private entertainments by and for residents increasingly replaced the public social life of earlier times. The Theatre Royal sank to a level of provincial mediocrity early in the nineteenth century, no longer the nursery for the London stage, as formerly it had been in the career, for example, of Sarah Siddons. Theatrical decline reflected the structural shift from a high-class resort to a middle-class residential city. It was not regularly well patronized, and even Amateur Night, one of the most popular features of the later nineteenth century, was not always well supported. Similarly, musical concerts were less frequent than they had been in the late eighteenth century, although the private *soirée* became an important event in the social calendar. People's Concerts twice a week at the Guildhall often lost money for the promoters. The ball remained the supreme social event, attended by the élite and the socially aspiring, in order to see and be seen in the 'right' company. Yet even these events changed over time. Public subscription balls, a unique feature of Bath's entertainment in the 1700s, became much less significant. Increasingly, between 1820 and 1914 balls were annual events organized by clubs or societies for their members (predominantly residents); or they were celebration or inaugural balls held to mark national and local events. The Bath races, reinstated as a biennial event in spring and summer after mid-century, were always the excuse for a week of carnivals, fêtes and balls. Card-playing assemblies flourished in the season, and the Assembly Rooms also provided billiard tables by the later nineteenth century.

Exclusiveness was practised in public entertainment, to preserve the right social tone. In the 1860s a guinea (£1.05) paid for a season of subscription balls, with 5*s*. (25p) extra for the card assembly, while 6*d*. (2½p) was the charge for tea. These were indeed 'moderate prices for admittance to one of the most polite assemblies in the kingdom', but it was not only the cost that excluded those of low social status from these gatherings: 'Certain rules are drawn up, by which all retail traders, articled clerks of the city, theatrical and other public performers are excluded from its saloons.'[29] Similarly, uniformed attendants were employed in the Victoria Park and other pleasure gardens to chase away the rough and 'undesirable'.

The growing numbers of wealthy permanent residents offset to some extent the depression which Bath, in common with other English spas, experienced in the early part of the period from 1820. Throughout the year from October 1835 to October 1836 the Assembly Rooms attracted sufficient patronage to remain open between Easter and November, i.e. out of season. Similarly, the customary practice of shops selling high-quality goods closing down during the summer months became eroded in the 1830s and 1840s, by which time all-year-round demand made this unnecessary. The growth of clubs and societies listed in the city directories from the 1820s onward also reflects the increase in the permanently resident population, as well as the general development of leisure activities. Some organizations, such as the Athenaeum and the Bath and County Club, had a membership beyond the city limits and provided a meeting point for visitors and residents. Others, like the Floral and Horticultural Society (formed in 1834), were likely to have a distinctly local membership. The national interest in sport, in new forms of activities, and in 'rational recreation' was shared by the residents of Bath, who in the later nineteenth century formed boating and rowing clubs, athletics societies, football and bicycling clubs. Organizations for the serious-minded also flourished. Old established ones, the Natural History and Antiquarian Society for example, were joined by new ones, including the Bath Ladies' Microscopical Society, which was formed around 1887–8 and was still in existence in 1910–11.

Many of the occasional entertainments in Bath would have attracted both visitors and residents, according to taste and class. Madame Tussaud's travelling exhibition, which visited Bath in November 1831, is one example, while Wombwell's Menagerie (which came to the city regularly over a period from the late nineteenth century) is another. Hanoverian bands, which enjoyed great popularity in Britain around the turn of the century, could be heard frequently in Bath at promenade concerts held in Sydney Gardens and elsewhere. These concerts were held in the summer months, organized by the Band and Fête Committee. No doubt the promenade concerts were enjoyed by people living in the city, although their addition to the attractions of Bath also reflected efforts made in the 1890s and early twentieth century to expand visitor numbers outside the traditional 'season'. Drinking the waters in the open air had always been recognized as one of the enjoyable features of many continental spas, but English health resorts were slow to adopt the idea. The authorities in Bath did so in 1910 when, as 'a great movement forward in the direction of the city's future as a summer resort', the Hot Water Mineral Fountain was opened under the Colonnade in the Institution gardens. By the time of the First World War the corporation's success at turning 'the routine of water-sipping into an alluring out-of-door amusement' had made the gardens at the Colonnade one of the most popular rendezvous of visitors during the spring and summer.[30]

As the city became predominantly a place of genteel residence, long-established bodies such as the Literary and Scientific Institution were supplemented by numerous clubs and societies catering for a variety of tastes. Temporary membership was offered to visitors by some of these organizations in the early 1900s, including the Chess Society and the Bath Lawn Tennis Club. The city's respectable image was firmly based on the social status and values of its new middle-class inhabitants, but visitors to Bath were also likely to be 'the right sort of people' who could be admitted to one's club, albeit only on 'certain conditions', as some organizations stipulated. Those who settled permanently in the city shared on a long-term basis the short-term experience of the visitors, who were integrated only to varying degrees into the life of polite society in Bath.

Residents and residential life

The new residents who moved to Bath in this period were predominantly middle class, but they were not a homogeneous group. The social status of some families and individuals was undoubtedly less secure than that of others. Furthermore, differences in age, gender, occupation and financial circumstances would have shaped the aspirations and perhaps limited the degree of their integration into the social and political life of Bath. Personal tastes and preferences would also, to some extent, have determined the level of participation of the newcomers.

The growth of Bath, and particularly the process of suburbanization, contributed to the erosion of the cohesiveness that had typified social life in the city when it was dominated by a small, wealthy élite. Cliques or 'sets' emerged as the city grew, and all-embracing public entertainments declined in significance. These different social groups overlapped or merged at times and within some organizations, but they always retained a clear distinctiveness. This fragmentation of the social élite was commented upon by a writer in *The World* of 1876, who noted that society at Bath 'ramifies into four distinct classes – with great assiduity and skill a native may continue to belong to three of them; but even this would require some amount of ingenuity. There is a High Church set, a Low Church set, a literary set and a fashionable set.'[31]

There is some evidence to suggest that the outsiders who were attracted to the city's suburbs were increasingly drawn from the less wealthy sections of the respectable classes, many of them living on fixed incomes and limited means. It is revealing that the increase in the number of these genteel residents, which accounted for most of the suburban growth in the later nineteenth and early twentieth centuries, did not create a corresponding demand for domestic servants. Between 1871 and 1901, a period of rapid suburban housing development and of an apparent increase in middle-class settlers, the numbers of resident domestic servants employed actually declined, while the aggregate number of charwomen and washerwomen rose steadily to reach 1,061 by 1901.[32] These women could be employed on a daily basis or have work put out to them, thereby saving the cost of maintaining them in the household. The 'paraphernalia of gentility' was perhaps increasingly beyond the means of some of Bath's new residents, who could not afford the level of servant-keeping that obtained in the mid-Victorian period, and who were forced to make economies in their household management. Dinner parties, *soirées* or musical evenings, 'at homes' and other private entertainments became more fashionable throughout the nineteenth century, encouraged partly by the Victorian enthusiasm for the family as the focal point of life, but the decline in support for the theatre and other public amusements in Bath may also reflect the financial circumstances of some incomers to the city.

14. The Victoria Art Gallery, Bridge Street. (Authors' collection)

Women, even those of the right social status and sufficient wealth to participate fully in the social life of Bath, would have been further constrained by the conventions of the times. For many of them it seems that the church and charitable activities formed the hub of their social life, and were deemed as especially suitable for unmarried or widowed women of the middle and upper classes. Mrs Arabella Roxburgh, granddaughter of a baronet from Yorkshire, is representative of many wealthy widows who retired to Bath in the later nineteenth century. She lived unostentatiously, devoting much of her time and income to works of piety and charity. During her lifetime she presented a number of pictures to the city, in the hope that they might form the nucleus of an art gallery. Many local charities benefited from her will after her death in November 1897: she left £12,000 as a fund for providing annuities for unmarried women or widows, and a quarter of the residue of her estate was designated for the provision of scholarships to the Bath Technical School and other educational establishments. The remainder of her fortune, some £8,000, was left to the city for the purpose of founding the art gallery.[33]

It was over the question of improving amenities for the city, financed wholly or in part from the rates, that the new residents of Bath were most likely to form a distinct interest group. In such instances, however, they often found themselves in alliance with other ratepayers, and it was as such that they acted in concerted opposition. Low rates were one of Bath's persistently advertised features and every suggestion for improvements that might lead to their increase was resisted. The strength of feeling that existed was demonstrated at an uproarious meeting in the Guildhall on 8 November 1869, when the question of a free public library in Bath was raised in the context of general improvements, including the extension and development of the water supply.[34] Other factors, as well as the likely impact on rates, influenced the vote against the motion in support of the library. The venture was particularly strongly opposed by working-class ratepayers, who believed it would be used mainly by the middle classes.

The wealthy incomers to Bath seem to have been more favourably disposed to contributing to civic amenities voluntarily rather than through the rates. Plans for an art gallery in the city had been mooted for many years before it was eventually built at the turn of the century. Sir Jerom Murch (many times mayor of Bath – see below, Chapter 5) had constantly advocated such an institution and he left a legacy for that purpose when he died in 1895. Mrs Roxburgh, as described above, had followed his example in 1896, but had taken the precaution of attaching a time limit of five years to her bequest. Unless the art gallery was built within that period, the city would lose her legacy of £8,000. Subscriptions were invited for the double purpose of an art gallery and a free library, but determined opposition to the inclusion of a library led to a compromise, whereby the gallery was built in conjunction with a reference library to house the Guildhall collection of books of local interest. The provision of a public library was again deferred, but subscriptions, many from prominent citizens, were sufficient for the gallery and Guildhall library to be commissioned as a memorial to Queen Victoria's Diamond Jubilee in 1897, although it was not completed until several years later.

For a glimpse at the social calendar in Bath during the closing years of the nineteenth century there is no better guide than the regular column – 'Penelope's Diary' – in the *Bath and County Graphic*. It covered a wide range of activities, from the sporting fixtures of Bath High School for girls to religious lectures and the private parties given by the social élite. In reporting such events as a garden party given by Mrs Yorke-Fausset in the grounds of Bath College, in aid of the Royal Victorian

Home for Women, 'Penelope's Diary' illustrates the Victorian practice of making a social event out of a moral obligation:

> The weather was perfect, and tea under the spreading branches of a huge old cedar was very refreshing. Tables were dotted about the grounds bearing basket work made by the inmates of the Home, which is for the reception of inebriates and other cases. It is actively supported by the Duke and Duchess of Beaufort, the Duchess of Bedford, the Countess of Dudley, Lady Battersea, and many other ladies.[35]

The roll-call of illustrious patrons or guests was an integral part of the 'Diary' and Penelope also took a keen interest in the decorations at social events, which were invariably described as 'charming'. She also lovingly recorded details of the glamorous dresses on display, as in the following extract from an account of an evening reception and ball held by the 'Prince of Mayors', George Woodiwiss, in 1897:

> Miss E Marshall was gowned in white moiré, with silk trimmings … Miss Spender wore a soft blue silk with very long train and long sleeves, a style which suited her slight figure; then the Misses Cary looked exceedingly well in a rich white satin, relieved by very little trimming, well-adapted to their height and figures.[36]

No doubt those singled out for a mention of their appearance enjoyed a warm glow of satisfaction, but the intimate tone of this and other pieces, and the full descriptions given of décor and dresses, suggest that Penelope was writing for a wider audience than the social élite. Bath, with its cheap living and 'right sort of people', provided a sanctuary for many middle-class women who were never invited to the glittering occasions that they took pleasure in reading about. Keeping up to date with 'Penelope's Diary' was perhaps some compensation for their own reduced circumstances, making them feel that they too participated in the social scene, if only vicariously.

The new image of Bath was so firmly established by the turn of the century that accounts of the city often focused almost exclusively on its role as a place of genteel residence. In the *Shilling Guide Book* series, brought out by the Ward Lock publishing company of London during the First World War, the volume on Bath informed its readers that life there had 'become more vigorous and prosperous than of old' because:

> while thousands still flock to Bath for the sake of the healing waters, the city has become the permanent abode of a dignified and well-to-do community, attracted thither by interesting associations and a beautiful neighbourhood, by stately streets and crescents and enchanting parks and gardens, that have won for the place the proud and well deserved title of 'Queen of the West'.[37]

By 1914 Bath was so closely identified with its social élite and its firmly established genteel image that the complexities of its functions were largely overlooked. In reality, although it was characterized by extremes of social structure, Bath was predominantly a small-scale industrial city during the period 1820–1914. It was home to a substantial labouring population as well as to its new middle-class residents. In the next chapter, we examine the growth of industry and changing occupational distribution, as well as exploring some aspects of working-class society in Bath.

Chapter 5

The City at Work,
1820–1914

The city of Bath has traditionally been seen as outside the main trends of industrial and commercial development in the eighteenth and nineteenth centuries. Contemporary understanding of its economy was somewhat distorted by the belief that the prosperity of Bath was dependent on the wealth it could attract from outsiders. Moreover, historians have arguably been too ready to accept the dominant, genteel image of Bath and to ignore much of the evidence that challenges that image.

The entrepreneurial activity, and considerable investment, associated with the construction of Georgian Bath stimulated not only the building industry itself, but also the development of extensive stone quarries, the growth of industrial villages, the formation of the Turnpike Trust, the construction of tramways and the canalization of the River Avon, all before the mid-eighteenth century. Thereafter, continued building and rebuilding and high levels of expenditure on quality consumer goods attracted numerous tradesmen, general labourers, and craftsmen to the city.[1] The development of the surrounding complex of industrial villages owed more to national trends in economic development than to the city's function as a spa resort or place of genteel residence. Incipient industrialization was underway between 1800 and 1830, with the establishment of steam-powered manufactories in brewing, soap-making and glass-making. Stotherts' ironmongery developed into a foundry, while woollen mills were erected on the River Avon at Twerton, and coalmining was attempted at Batheaston.[2] Further substantial changes were to alter the character of the city over the rest of the century.

The growth of industry and occupational change

Trade and small-scale industry (which was frequently represented in the same business) formed the major sector of male employment in the city and by occupational definition approximately three-quarters of the population enumerated in nineteenth-century census returns were of the

Table 4   Occupational distribution of males in Bath, 1831

Occupation	Number of males over 20 years of age
Capitalists, bankers and other educated men	1,196
Building trades	1,074
Labouring (non-agricultural)	1,480
Retail (including some craftsmen)	2,797
Domestic service	670
Shoemaking	529
Furniture and coachmaking	351
Tailoring	349
Labouring	110
Total	8,556

Sources: Census of population, 1831. R. S. Neale, 'The Standard of Living 1780–1844: a regional and class study', *Economic History Review* 19 (1966), p. 593.

working classes (see Table 4). Between 1841 and 1891 Bath's occupational structure differed from the national average only between various categories of employment, but not substantially in terms of social class structure. Lower than average proportions engaged in manufacturing (1841: Bath, 25.78 per cent; England and Wales, 30.77 per cent. 1891: Bath 22.26 per cent; England and Wales, 32.72 per cent) were balanced out by higher than average male employment in building, transport and dealing. The size of the working population increased throughout the period 1851–1901, even though the aggregate numbers remained fairly static. Over those fifty years, the male labour force increased by 35 per cent and the female labour force rose by 23 per cent.

These structural realities have received too little recognition. Although the prevailing character of economic activity was relatively small-scale compared with factories in the great industrial towns, Bath should, nevertheless, be recognized as a city with a strong industrial sector. It ranked with many medium-sized industrial towns, and its nineteenth-century population was too large to be sustained simply by seasonal trade associated with its role as a place of entertainment. Evidence of the complexities of the city's industrial and commercial past lingers on in street names, such as Midland Wharf and Brassmill Lane, and in the remnants of industrial buildings along the river. Far from being a place without trade, industry, or commerce, it was essentially – and increasingly so, from at least 1851 – a working city, whose prosperity depended primarily on mass demand from all of its residents and on its success in meeting needs in a market much wider than Bath itself. By the turn of the century, as a local historian reminds us, Bath:

> generated its own electricity, produced its own gas, possessed two busy railway yards and was served by three railway companies, exported giant dockland cranes and shorthand primers to every corner of the world, brewed its own beer, milled its own flour and wove its own cloth, modelled the world in 'Plasticine', fitted out the Queen Mary with furniture and panelled rooms, produced its own building materials and even its own cars.[3]

Throughout the nineteenth century, the city was experiencing significant economic changes, reflected in the changing structure of industrial and commercial occupations. Despite the difficulties of occupational definitions varying in the decennial census, the broad trends that can be identified show an increasing proportion of all occupied males employed in the building industry, rising to over 16 per cent by 1901, when this sector was particularly buoyant because of the suburban building boom of the last decades of the nineteenth century. Cabinet-making and coachmaking (both representative of the traditional small-scale enterprises characteristic of Bath's industry) expanded, and new industries – such as printing and bookbinding, and engineering – were established. Retailing and commerce were both subject to major expansion. Allied to industrial growth, there was an increase of employment in various forms of transport, which occupied 1,134 male workers (including 247 railway workers) in 1901. By 1900–10, bus companies, the trams, and several taxi firms were also an integral part of the transport sector. Local industries in relative decline from around the mid-nineteenth century included brewing, soap-boiling, and steam-dyeing, and Bath shared the national experience of falling numbers in certain trades where new technology reduced the demand for labour. Industrial production for a mass market increasingly replaced handwork in tailoring and shoemaking, for example, both of which sectors had employed substantial numbers in Bath. The 453 tailors of 1841 fell to 308 by 1901, and their numbers were further reduced over the next decade to 261 in 1911. In the same period the fall in the numbers of shoemakers was even greater, from 605 to 202 between 1841 and 1901, and down again to 167 by 1911.

However, the numbers of males employed as cabinet-makers, French polishers and upholsterers rose from 228 in 1841 to 342 in 1901. Those engaged in coachmaking increased from 111 to 204 over the same period. Many of Bath's small-scale enterprises were featured at the Great Exhibition in 1851, and achieved national and even international recognition.[4] The quality products of Knight and Son, upholsterers to the Prince of Wales, were shipped all over Europe, while there was a

15. James Heath, Broad Street, 1880–1. Bath was a centre for furniture- and carriage-making. Royal patronage ensured that the products were sold throughout the country and overseas. (Bath Library)

large demand from London for the 'Victoria carriages' built by the Bath coachmaking firm of Fullers. Moreover, new industries grew up alongside the traditional crafts. Between 1841 and 1901 the number of men employed in printing more than trebled, rising from 58 to 199. By 1911, 212 male workers in Bath were printers or lithographers. Sir Isaac Pitman's printing business, founded at Nelson Place in 1845, was a part of the general expansion of printing and publishing in Bath. Pitman (born at Trowbridge, Wiltshire, in 1813) wrote several books on spelling reform, commercial practice and educational matters, and published his own *Phonetic Journal*; he is remembered chiefly as the pioneer of shorthand. In 1859 he had new premises built on the Lower Bristol Road and these were enlarged in 1913. Pitman's served markets far beyond Bath, as a major printing and publishing company and one that was internationally known for its shorthand primers and instruction books.[5]

Engineering and machine-making was another expanding sector. This category accounted for only 37 males in 1841, but those numbers rose to 410 by 1901. The engineering firm of Stothert and Pitt, a particularly successful business, originated as an ironmongery and developed into a foundry at its Newark Street works before moving to a larger factory on the Lower Bristol Road.[6] In 1851 metals and engineering industries generally employed 540 'hands'.[7] The name of Stothert and Pitt became virtually synonymous with dockside cranes from around the 1860s, but, before this specialization, the company manufactured a diverse range of items such as treadmills, pumping engines, garden rollers, leather-tanning machines and apparatus for heating, cooking, and washing in hospitals or other large institutions. The company exhibited, and won prizes, at the Great Exhibition of 1851, the Paris Universal Exhibition (1867) and the London International Inventors' Exhibition (1889). Its products could be found in towns and cities throughout the United Kingdom, the Channel Islands, continental Europe, Canada, Australia, South America, and the subcontinent of India.[8] In 1911 the metal and associated industries (which included the manufacture of electrical appliances, cars and motor cycles, as well as engineering and machine-making) employed 961 of Bath's male workers.

One new industry, located at Bathampton, but almost certainly drawing some labour from the city itself, was the manufacture of 'Plasticine'. This modelling material was invented by William Harbutt, who came to Bath in 1874 as head of the Art School but later ran his own Paragon Art Studio in Bladud Buildings. Plasticine was developed in 1897 for use in his art classes but Harbutt also sold it in small quantities to local shops. Advertising soon led to a growth in demand, and in 1900 production on a commercial scale began in an old steam flour mill on the Kennet and Avon canal at Bathampton, where a gas engine was installed to power the mixing and blending machines. Plasticine also had industrial uses, and it remained one of the chief products of the company for most of its 83 years' existence, although Harbutts diversified over time into a broader range of artists' materials and related items.[9]

Female industrial workers in Bath, as in the country generally, were concentrated in particular trades. Clothing was the outstanding one and, overall, it was a growth area for the employment of women and girls in the city. In 1831 some 10 per cent of the female labour force was engaged in the manufacture of cloth or clothing, but this rose to 16.8 per cent by 1901. Staymakers increased their numbers substantially between 1841 and 1901, from 75 to 233, rising to 255 in 1911. Production became mechanized from the 1870s with the establishment of Bayers' corset factory in the south of the city, beside the river, and the founding of Drew, Son and Company as a corset manufacturer and wholesaler, with premises at Gascoyne Place and in Trim Street. The fact that the change to mechanized, factory production did not displace staymakers, but actually increased their numbers, suggests that the Bath corset-makers were serving the needs of an extensive and growing market. Indeed, Drew, Son and Company advertised its speciality corset as obtainable from all drapers and ladies outfitters 'throughout the Kingdom and Colonies'. Moreover, the company claimed that its product had larger worldwide sales than any comparable undergarment.

Within the commercial sector of employment, wider opportunities existed for both men and women by 1900. Commercial occupations accounted for just under 12 per cent of male employment in 1871, rising to over 19 per cent by 1901. The numbers of clerks, merchants, agents and accountants, porters and messengers, all rose substantially over a thirty-year period. No female clerks were recorded in Bath before 1871. It seems likely that the primary cause of the growth of their existence, from 8 in 1871 to 111 by 1901, lay in the rapid expansion of the commercial sector, rather than the introduction of the typewriter. Later in the twentieth century the female typist became the archetypal woman at work, who largely replaced male clerks and office workers. These new opportunities for women in the commercial sector in Bath were accompanied by an increase in male employment in commerce in the late nineteenth century.

The relationships between Bath's occupational structure and its functions as a leisure and health resort, and as a place of genteel residence, are complex, but it seems clear that the most important economic developments from the 1820s to the early twentieth century were not directly related to the visitors or to the influx of new middle-class residents. In 1841, Bath had twelve hotels. Together with the lodging houses in the city they employed 130 female workers. The number of hotels increased, over a fifty-year period, to 24. Female employment also increased, as the numbers working in this sector rose to 438 by 1871, and to 542 by 1901. Yet the fastest growth in this sector (over 200 per cent in 30 years) occurred between 1841 and 1871 (rising from 130 to 438) when, by all accounts, the numbers of visitors coming to take the waters were relatively few. The moderate expansion over the following thirty years (just under 24 per cent) reflects Bath's resurgence as a health resort from the 1870s to 1900, but the occupational distribution of females, aged ten years and over, in Bath in 1901 suggests that the spa function of the city was not a leading sector of its economy. Between 1901 and 1911, the total number of women employed in hotels and lodging houses actually fell by almost 50, to 494.

Moreover, although indoor domestic service (excluding hotels) was (at just over 17 per cent) the largest single category of employment for women in 1901, the numbers had not risen significantly since 1871, despite the influx of new middle-class residents to the growing suburbs. No full-scale study of servant-keeping in Bath has yet been undertaken by any historian, but an analysis of households in Northampton Street and Rivers Street over the period 1851–81 revealed that the lower-middle-class and professional middle-class households in those streets employed on average only one resident female servant.[10] These findings support the view that the 'paraphernalia of gentility' was beyond the means of many of Bath's genteel residents, who seem to have made economies by reducing the numbers of servants they employed. Furthermore, the numbers of male servants declined substantially from 860 in 1841 to 340 in 1901 and thereafter fell dramatically to a mere 79 by 1911. This also suggests that the servant-keeping classes in Bath were, in general, less well off by the beginning of the twentieth century. Keeping a man servant was the first sign of affluence (their wages were persistently higher than those of women), but even in the mid-nineteenth century Mrs Beeton, in her definitive *Book of Household Management* (1861), concluded that the expense could not be justified on an annual income of less than £1,000.[11]

The trends within professional occupations, for both men and women, seem related more directly to wider changes in society than to the growing popularity of Bath as a place of genteel residence. Male professional occupations fell from 13.4 per cent of all male occupations in 1851 to 10.9 per cent by 1901. Within this broad category, clergymen and teachers increased, but both occupations were having to expand their services to meet the needs of a mass society. The numbers of clergy rose most rapidly before 1871, in line with the pace of church building. The growth in numbers of teachers was more evenly spread, reflecting the expansion of educational provision in Bath before the Act of 1870, which established state education. This was clearly related to middle-class demand, although charity schools and private establishments catered for some children of lower social classes before the 1870s. The city directory of 1902 listed 17 boys' schools, 34 girls' schools, 7 language teachers, 81 music teachers, and 1 military and naval tutor. Male teachers rose from 59 in 1841 to 155 in 1901, while over the same period the number of female teachers increased from 182 to 397. Women in Bath, as throughout the country, gained entry in significant numbers only in the lower-paid professional jobs, such as teaching and nursing. Nurses and midwives numbered 106 in 1841 and 325 in 1901, but in that year there was only one female doctor in Bath and there were no female lawyers in the city. By 1911 the numbers of nurses and midwives had risen to 387, but women had made no inroads to the higher professions in Bath.

The male professions that mainly served the needs of the better off experienced a reduction in their numbers. There were 52 lawyers (including barristers and solicitors) in Bath in 1841; these had increased to 87 by 1871, but fell back to 61 by 1901 and thereafter rose to 70 in 1911. A sharper reduction took place in the number of physicians, falling from 105 in 1841 to only 81 in 1901. There appears to be little connection between Bath's resurgence as a health resort in the late nineteenth century and the demand for medical practitioners, although by the early twentieth century it is possible that some of these professional classes were living outside the city and 'commuting' in to places of work.

The city directories, however, give some indication of a growth in demand for services and trades associated with permanent residence in Bath. From the 1880s into the early twentieth century new entries or increased numbers can be found of house agents, furniture removers, domestic agencies, painters and decorators, specialist paper-hangers and sellers, tuners, and repairers of pianofortes. There is also some indication

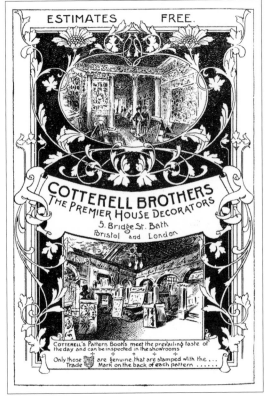

16. Cotterell Bothers, Bridge Street, 1903. This was one of the many trades catering for the new residential middle class who settled in Victorian Bath. (Bath Library)

that companies diversified to meet new demands. The City Metalworks, for example, directed its advertisement in the 1909 directory to the market for its products and services for heating private houses, greenhouses and conservatories.

Nonetheless, dependence on local consumers and visitors to Bath lessened as the base of the city's economy broadened. Population growth certainly expanded local demand for a wide range of goods and services, but throughout the nineteenth century Bath became more of an industrial and commercial city, dependent for its economic success on meeting national demands. The expansion of some traditional craft industries and the birth of new enterprises were responses to the increasing wealth of the nation, but developments in transport and communication were also crucial to the growth of national markets.

At the beginning of the nineteenth century the Avon Navigation was of particular economic significance. Local products, such as Bath stone and beer, were shipped by barge to Bristol docks for distribution to other parts of the United Kingdom. (The beer went chiefly to Swansea and Cardiff, to supply the South Wales coalfields.[12]) Then, in 1810, after fifteen years of construction work at the cost of around £900,000, the Kennet and Avon canal opened.[13] Thereafter, it was possible to

MILSOM & SON'S Piano-Forte Saloon, 2, Argyle Street, Bath.

Piano-Fortes Let on Hire at Ten Shillings per Month.

17. Milsom & Sons, Argyle Street, 1866–7. Milsom's was supported by a host of private music tutors who fostered the development of female accomplishments in Bath. (Bath Library)

transport goods from Bristol to London in four days, despite extensive locking systems on the canal at Widcombe in Bath, and at Devizes in Wiltshire. In the months of March and April 1830, 9,415 tons of goods were carried on the canal from Bath to destinations in the southern counties or London, whereas in the same period the comparable tonnage on the Avon Navigation from Bath to Bristol docks was only 1,655.[14] The canal, in its turn, was superseded by the railway. The Kennet and Avon Canal Company was one of the main opponents of the Great Western Railway Bills of 1834 and 1835, and once the second Bill was passed the company attempted to cut costs and increase revenue by various means. From 1837 traffic was allowed to operate by night as well as by day, and in 1841 fly-boats of up to fifteen tons (giving a larger capacity than before) were permitted on the Bath to Reading section of the canal, and economies were made in manpower and wages. The company could not, however, withstand the competition from the railways. Once the GWR line from Bristol to London was operating, goods could be transported in hours over distances that took days by canal. Canal company receipts fell from over £51,000 in 1840–1 to less than £40,000 in the following year,[15] and in 1852 the Kennet and Avon was taken over by the GWR.[16] The railway network expanded further when the Midland Railway spur-line to Bath (1869) linked the city with the manufacturing areas of the Midlands and the North. This stimulated the growth and specialization of some local industries, but it also increased competition by bringing in products from outside the locality. In this respect, it made a particular impact not on the economy of Bath, but on the long-term decline of the nearby Somerset coalfield, as cheaper coal raised in the

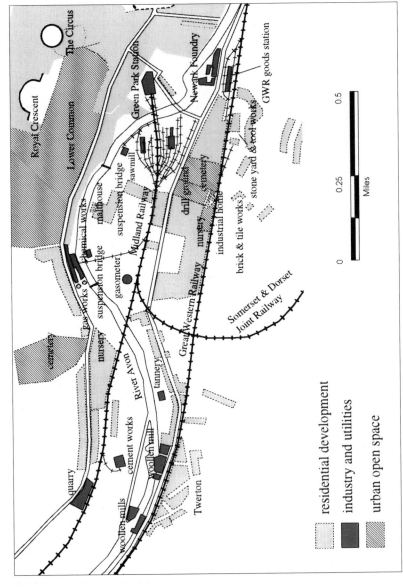

Map 5 Industrial Bath in the railway age. The location of industry in the nineteenth century continued the pattern established in Georgian Bath. The railway network extended the growth of industry first situated alongside the River Avon. Note the presence of the Newark Foundry of Stothert & Pitt, the sawmill, malthouse (for the brewing industry), chemical, gas and cement works and the woollen mills of Twerton.

The Circus

Royal Crescent

Lower Common

Green Park Station

Newark Foundry

GWR goods station

sawmill

suspension bridge

malthouse

chemical works

Midland Railway

suspension bridge

gas works

gasometer

cemetery

nursery

River Avon

tannery

Twerton

woollen-mills

cement works

woollen mill

quarry

drill ground

cemetery

nursery

industrial homes

brick & tile works

stone yard & tool works

Great Western Railway

Somerset & Dorset Joint Railway

residential development

industry and utilities

urban open space

0   0.25   0.5

Miles

18. Bath & West of England Steam Power Dye Works, Broad Quay, 1880–1. In the early 1800s, Broad Quay had been the site of major breweries and it remained at the heart of industrial Bath alongside the River Avon and the Great Western Railway (see Map 5). (Bath Library)

developing Midlands coalfield eroded the traditional markets for Somerset coal. The location of industry in Bath remained much the same while these developments in transport progressed, but from the 1840s onwards the focus of activity was on the railway lines and associated goods yards, rather than the quays and wharfs along the waterways.

As its economy diversified, Bath continued to attract labour from far beyond the city limits, particularly female labour. Domestic service continued to be an important sector of employment for women. Although we have shown that the level of servant-keeping declined over time, there is evidence to suggest that domestic work was readily available for those who did not share the growing working-class antipathy to service, as alternative opportunities grew. Moreover, as late as 1911 the largest single occupational group of women in Bath was the category of domestic service. There were 3,824 women employed as 'domestic indoor servants', a further 424 worked as 'washers, ironers, manglers, etc.' and another 301 earned their wages as 'charwomen'. Out of a total 10,446 females aged ten and upwards engaged in occupations, the number employed in 'domestic offices and services' of all kinds was 5,388 – over half of all Bath's female working population. Domestic agencies advertising in Bath frequently aimed their publicity at prospective employees as much as employers: 'Good servants of every description wanted immediately' recurs in advertisements from the 1870s onward. Similarly, the expanding industrial and commercial sectors also attracted female labour into

Bath, some for work and training in the clothing trades. Much of the high-quality women's clothing sold by Jolly's of Milsom Street (as with other similar companies) was made up in the firm's workrooms. Jolly's employed 17 women in 1861, including draper's assistants, milliners and mantle-makers, as well as domestic servants. Of these, 7 were born in distant counties beyond the west country region.[17] In 1911 the textiles and dress trade employed over 2,000 women in Bath. In addition to the 255 corset-makers, there were 859 dressmakers, 232 milliners, 223 tailoresses and 117 shirt-makers or seamstresses. Over 100 women were occupied as dealers in articles of dress, and another 264 were miscellaneous 'other workers'.

By the 1890s several strictly run church hostels and other similar organizations existed for the purpose of helping young workers who migrated to the city. Most of them were concerned with women, although there was a branch of the Young Men's Christian Association (YMCA) which had premises in Broad Street. Without reference to class or occupation, the YMCA promoted itself as a body concerned for 'the spiritual, intellectual, social and physical welfare of young men', to which ends it offered Bible classes and evangelical lectures, a library of 'selected works', newspapers and periodicals, draughts, chess, bagatelle, and a gymnasium. The Young Women's Christian Association (YWCA), in contrast, had more specific interests and provided fewer general facilities. Its aim was 'to promote the welfare of young women in the various workrooms and houses of business in the city'. Bible and other classes, and religious lectures, were organized, but the only other diversions on offer were a reading room (supplied with 'suitable periodicals' and one weekly newspaper) and a library stocked with 'a selection of religious and instructive works'. The YWCA also provided accommodation, in Stall Street, for 30 young women 'coming to Bath as strangers'. It ran a separate servants' home and registry, offering shelter for servants 'of a respectable character' when out of work. Such subtleties of discrimination, between women engaged in trade or commerce and those who worked as domestic servants, was further refined by the Young Women's Friendly Society (YWFS) (affiliated to the national Girls' Friendly Society), which operated from premises in Russell Street. The YWFS dealt with a 'better class' of client than did the YWCA, aiming to provide 'pleasant and domestic evenings for young women engaged in business or tuition'. It, too, provided some accommodation and, despite its title, seems to have imposed no upper age limit: the organization's entry in the city directory for 1893 stated that 'Ladies are also boarded at a moderate rate.'[18]

The typical resident of Bath in the period 1820–1914, if such a mythical creature existed, was neither a destitute beggar nor an upper-class pensioner. The typical resident was female, in that women outnumbered men, and she was more likely to be a domestic servant or a dressmaker than either a street hawker, a prostitute, or a woman (whether widowed or single) of independent means. Among the adult male population of the city, engineers and cabinet-makers were more representative than either upper-class pensioners or unskilled labourers. This large section of the population, encompassing a wide range of occupations and social status, was often overlooked by contemporary commentators and has been somewhat neglected by historians, other than R. S. Neale, who has been credited with 'discovering' Bath's working classes. Even Neale was rather more interested in the skilled artisans than in the standard of living of the unskilled and common labourers, who were dismissed as 'the lumpen proletariat', lacking a 'true' Marxist class-consciousness.

As we have seen, Bath changed significantly over the period from 1820 to 1914, and it did so in more complex ways than its dominant image suggests. It was not merely that its role as the resort of fashion was eroded and replaced over time, by its becoming a favoured place of genteel residence. Simultaneously, it was becoming more industrial and commercial, and supporting a larger working class. Some old craft industries experienced a revival; new industries became firmly established; retailing and commerce were both subject to major expansion. The labour force in Bath increased, primarily as a result of developments that were nationwide, rather than in response to the influx of new middle-class residents or to the brief resurgence of the spa after the 1870s. Changes in the occupational structure of the city, from the earlier decades of the nineteenth century to 1911, owed much more to new forms of transport, technological advances in industry, structural changes in retailing, and the general growth of government and commercial activity. The city continued to attract migrants from the rural hinterland and beyond, as an expanding labour market, and in the late nineteenth century its numerous charities still drew vagrants and tramps to Bath: numbers conveyed by the police to the casual ward of the workhouse in the period 1885–94 indicate a rising trend. Over that period, with some fluctuation in 1891–2, numbers rose from 4,675 to 6,577.[19] The genteel image had nonetheless been firmly established by 1900. It reflected the realities of Bath's admittedly declining appeal as a fashionable resort and of the process of suburbanization which was attracting many new, middle-class residents to the city. What the dominant image obscured was the significant change underway in the occupational structure of the city, which reflected another, but equally valid reality: from at least the mid-nineteenth century, Bath was a predominantly working-class, small-scale industrial city.

Working-class society, social control and living standards

The splendour of Bath's Georgian architecture and the comfortable solidity of its large Victorian and Edwardian villas often evoke images of gracious living and a degree of affluence that are quite at odds with the realities experienced by the majority of the city's residents. Only a fortunate minority lived at such desirable addresses as the Royal Crescent or Newbridge Hill. Moreover, the process of suburbanization increased residential segregation of the social classes in Bath throughout the nineteenth century, and particularly so from the 1880s into the earlier twentieth century.

In the early nineteenth century the inner-city parishes were the main centres of manufacturing, and housed most of the working classes. For example, skilled craftsmen predominated in the parish of St James in 1831, when it was home to 12 per cent of the male population of Bath, but accounted for a much higher proportion of the city's artisans. The proportion of adult males in St James's employed in building, furniture-making, coachmaking, shoemaking and tailoring was twice that of Bath as a whole.[20] On the other hand, Lyncombe and Widcombe, lying outside the city boundaries until the mid-1830s, was a suburban industrial parish and one of the poorer ones up to 1840. The textile industry was located there, as was much of Bath's growing industrial sector of the later nineteenth century. Small shopkeepers predominated among the inhabitants of the inner-city parish of SS Peter and Paul, while larger shopkeepers were particularly numerous in the central parish of St Michael (which included the fashionable shops of Milsom Street). Walcot was a very large parish, housing over half of Bath's total population in the mid-nineteenth century, and many of the poorest parts of the north and west of the city lay within its boundaries, although the Lansdown district of Walcot was a comparatively wealthy residential area.[21]

By the 1830s, urban decay in the southern parts of the city had created Bath's most notorious slum, in what was known as the Avon Street district. Natural and physical barriers defined this area, rather than administrative ones. Most of it was in St James's parish but some parts extended into the parishes of Walcot, of St Michael's, and of SS Peter and Paul. The commercial thoroughfares of Southgate Street, Lower Borough Walls, and Westgate Buildings marked its eastern limits. The open spaces of Saw Close and Kingsmead Square lay to the north, with wasteland to the east, and the River Avon was its southern boundary. Some 10,000 people, or about one-fifth of the population of Bath, lived within the Avon Street district in the mid-nineteenth century. This was by no means a constant figure, but one that changed over time and fluctuated with the seasons, as migrant workers and other itinerants moved in and out of the city. Avon Street itself was described in the 1820s as the home of 'at least 300 people who obtain a living by begging, thieving, or on the miserable wages of prostitution'.[22] Shops were open on Sundays, public houses for almost the whole of every day, and street-corner gambling and obscene language were frequently complained of by Bath's respectable residents. Newspaper reports often highlighted the

19. 'The Buff Club at the Pig & Whistle, Avon Street', Richard Cruickshank, 1825. Among the assembled company are several gentlemen, a farmer, a soldier, a chimney sweep and girls of ill-repute. Avon Street was the red-light district of Bath. (Victoria Art Gallery, Bath)

association of Avon Street with criminal activity, as in July 1820 when six inhabitants of the street were imprisoned for brothel-keeping, and in September of the following year, when seven juveniles aged 17 to 19 were sentenced to death at the Somerset assize for various offences of assault, robbery, and highway robbery.[23] From the 1830s, the Avon Street district succeeded Holloway as the main area for the reception of travellers; by the end of the nineteenth century the 'nymphs of Avon Street' were no longer in evidence, although prostitution still flourished in other parts of this southern district. From the late 1840s, an increasing presence of poor Irish living in over-crowded lodgings attracted negative reporting which gave Avon Street an enhanced reputation for violence and disorder:

MON – AN AVON STREET RIOT –

Richard Barret, an Irishman, was charged with being drunk and disorderly in Avon St., on Saturday night.

It appeared that a crowd of people were assembled before the door of the Fountain public-house, in consequence of some outrage committed by the prisoner, while he was at a window upstairs, threatening the mob outside. Presently afterwards some woman connected with him, hurled a lump of coal upon their heads. Some of the crowd, in retaliation, smashed the window, when the prisoner rushed out of the house, furiously wielding a poker, and followed the people down the street, attempting to strike indiscriminately, as he proceeded.[24]

20. Avon Street, c.1910. Originally built as fashionable lodgings in the 1730s, Avon Street became a working-class district within a generation, and by the early 1800s had acquired a reputation as a notorious slum district. (Guildhall Archives, Bath)

The notoriety of Avon Street persisted into the early twentieth century, even though conditions improved in terms of population density, overcrowded and insanitary housing, inadequate water supply, and the incidence of epidemic disease. Within the southern slum district as a whole, however, the changing character of Avon Street was perceived more clearly than it was by outsiders. The 'locals' who lived there around 1900 regarded Little Corn Street, the haunt of itinerant tinkers, as the roughest of the streets, dubbing it 'Little 'Ell' because of the frequent outbursts of violence among its inhabitants. Avon Street, in contrast, had risen in comparative social status to become recognized as a relatively wealthy street, inhabited by respectable tradesmen and lodging-house keepers, many of whom owned their own property. Even the travellers who lodged there were 'well off', for they could afford to pay 3*d*. (1.25p) for a bed while their poorer counterparts went to cheaper, unregistered lodgings elsewhere, or resorted to the casual ward of the workhouse.

Similarly, Holloway became a somewhat more respectable working-class district, as the southern slums across the river became the chief lodging-house area of the city, and new artisan cottages were built at Calton Road and in other parts of Holloway. The changing status of

21. Little Corn Street in the 1930s. A poor working-class street, known as
'Little 'Ell' because of the character of its inhabitants. Note the presence of
the handcart with which a family might avoid rent arrears by doing a
'moonlight flit'. (Guildhall Archives, Bath)

streets or districts within particular parishes has not been studied extensively, but a further example of the process can be found in Northampton
Street, in the parish of Walcot. Northampton Street (together with
Morford Street, Ballance Street and Lampards Buildings) was one of
the sites developed as artisan dwellings in the late eighteenth and early
nineteenth centuries, despite its close proximity to King's Circus and the
Royal Crescent, which housed the professional and the upper-middle
classes. By 1851, however, Northampton Street's 39 houses were occupied
by 82 chiefly lower-middle-class households (defined by rateable value
of the houses, and the occupation of head of household). 'Gentrifica-
tion' was clearly underway in nineteenth-century Bath. Between 1851
and 1881 the number of houses in this street remained constant, but the
number of households fell to 65. Tradesmen predominated among male
heads of household in Northampton Street in 1851, but thirty years later
residents included more annuitants and fundholders, as well as representatives of the lower professional classes, such as schoolteachers.[25]
    Differing levels of income, occupations and social values all contri-
buted to the formation of subtle hierarchies, even within outwardly
homogeneous residential districts. The gulf between the 'rough' and the

'respectable' among the labouring classes was particularly marked, although it was perhaps never as great as the contemporary middle classes perceived it to be. There is evidence to suggest that working people gave their own meanings to such key words as 'respectability' and, moreover, that some elements of 'rough' behaviour (notably heavy drinking) were quite commonplace among working men as a whole until the later nineteenth century.[26] Nonetheless, an extreme example of the violent disorder that could be caused by Bath's slum dwellers was recalled by the travelling showman 'Lord' George Sanger, in his description of an incident at the Lansdown Fair in the 1820s. A mob of savage roughs from the city's slums arrived at the fair towards evening, bent on destruction. They were led by a gigantic, red-haired virago called 'Carotty Kate', a notorious figure 'as strong as a navvy' and much feared in Bath, where she lived at a place called Bull Paunch Alley:

> Half-stripped, with her red hair flying wildly behind her, she incited the gang of ruffians with her to wreck the fair. The drinking booths were the first to suffer. The mob took possession of them, half killed some of the unfortunate owners, and set to work to drink themselves into a state of frenzy more acute than before. The scenes that followed are almost indescribable. Not content with drinking all they could, the ruffians turned on the taps, stoved in barrels, smashed up bottles, and let the liquor run to waste. Then they started to wreck the booths. Canvas was torn to shreds, platforms were smashed and made bonfires of, waggons were battered to fragments. Everywhere was riot, ruin and destruction.[27]

Carotty Kate and company were eventually rounded up by the stall-holders, who took revenge for the damage to their property by resorting to physical violence themselves. The men were dragged on a rope through a deep pool at the bottom of Lansdown Hill. Then, after being allowed to recover and 'drain' on dry ground, they were dragged uphill to the wagons where they were tied, two at a time, to wheels and thrashed with whalebone whips. Kate herself was spared a ducking, but was fastened to a cart-wheel to witness the flogging of the men. Then she was seized by six stout women and caned by two more until their fury was spent. The police, equipped with heavy staves, intercepted the returning mob and a bloody battle ensued. Many arrests were made, after numerous injuries had been inflicted, and one officer was crippled for life.

This is a particularly vivid example of the 'roughs' of Bath on the rampage, but street disorder and violence were commonplace in the poorer districts and the provision of extra police on occasions such as the annual fair, the races, or at election times, was not always sufficient to ensure the maintenance of public order in the supposedly quiet and civilized city of Bath.[28] In the early nineteenth century, the city's streets were plagued by juvenile gangs, as well as the notorious beggars, and hawkers and street traders of every description. Bath was reputedly one of the major centres of crime outside London, and it was said in 1828 to have a distinct criminal class, comprising some 60 per cent of the 'boys of the town', who survived by crime alone, chiefly stealing from shops and picking pockets.[29] The general level of street noise and disorder was quite out of keeping with Bath's reputation as a quiet resort for the invalid and the elderly. Even among the 'respectable' working classes, resorting to violence was a means of enforcing community values, which persisted into the early twentieth century.

Respectability included a powerful moral stigma against illegitimacy, as Louie Stride (born in 1907), the bastard child of a prostitute, recalled in her memoirs. After numerous 'moonlight flits' from one slum district of Bath to another, mother and child made another move, around 1910, from a tenement in Walcot to a small, hovel type of cottage at the back of a sweetshop in Holloway. The next morning, all the women in the neighbouring cottages 'attacked my mother verbally and in person called her a "Scarlet Woman", and they threw her goods out in the yard, "coming to live amongst a lot of decent people with a Bastard", they weren't going to tolerate that and they didn't'.[30] For Louie and her mother, this meant another 'handcart ride', to a part of the lower town, where prostitutes and their bastards were less of an affront to respectable inhabitants. Yet Holloway, viewed from without and from the perspective of the dominant middle-class culture, was seen as an homogeneous district in terms of socio-economic structure and cultural values. Together with other areas of working-class residence, such as Snow Hill, the Dolemeads, and all of the Avon Street district, it was perceived as 'poor' and 'rough'.

What outsiders overlooked, or found difficult to comprehend, was the degree of social stratification that existed within working-class communities. Not even at the height of its notoriety as Bath's worst slum was Avon Street inhabited only by the very poor. It was a 'poor' area in comparison with more select parts of Bath: four out of five of the 182 houses in the streets, courts and alleys connected with Avon Street and Milk Street had a rateable value of less than £15 per annum in 1839, compared with the King's Circus where three out of every five houses were worth over £150 per annum and none was rated at under £110.[31] In Avon Street itself, the majority (69 per cent) of the 90 houses were within a rateable value of £5–6 in 1862. Just over 12 per cent were rated at less than £5 per annum, but almost a fifth (18.5 per cent) were valued at over £10 per annum.[32] Moreover, 35 houses, or 38.9 per cent of the total, appear to have been owner-occupied, and the pattern of ownership of property in Avon Street indicates that some of its residents were petty capitalists. Fifteen people owned two properties in the street in 1862, and a further eight people owned between three and six houses.

22. The steps leading down from the Paragon to Walcot Street. In Victorian times the steps were dimly lit by gas light. (Authors' collection)

The publicans, shopkeepers, lodging-house keepers and master craftsmen who lived in Avon Street and the surrounding district formed the upper socio-economic strata of the area's working classes. From 1832 onward (when the Reform Act introduced the £10 property qualification for the franchise), some of them also provided political leadership to a populous working-class part of the city.

Because inadequate recognition was given to the hierarchy of status within the working classes (and to differing, class-based perceptions of 'respectable' or acceptable behaviour), the process of suburbanization, which increasingly took the better off away from the inner-city parishes, reinforced the fears of the authorities and the middle classes that social segregation had left the urban poor bereft of moral leadership. What then followed was legislation to reform or improve aspects of urban working-class living, but this was invariably framed within the parameters of middle-class culture, and often infringed on traditional freedoms. Throughout the nineteenth century and beyond, the working classes were subjected to increasing interference and regulation in the work-place, in the public streets, in their leisure pursuits, and even within the

23. Northgate Lane, off Northgate Street. A rare glimpse of conditions in the courts and alleys of Victorian Bath.
(Authors' collection)

family. Differing sets of values between legislators and those most affected by new regulations made some degree of conflict inevitable.

Both the rough and the respectable among Bath's poorer residents were affected by the reorganization and extension of the forces of law and order. Until 1836 Bath had three autonomous police forces, each with different powers, and police authority did not extend to the Holloway district south of the river, in the parish of Lyncombe and Widcombe. A new borough police force was established in 1836, under the central direction of the Watch Committee and the Chief Constable. Thereafter the whole city was policed by a single authority, and the instigation of regular day and night patrolling of the streets led to more acceptable standards of public order. Closer regulation of street activity was an important function of the borough police, and no doubt the relative success of the force made the streets of Bath safer and more pleasant for all of its residents, particularly in the last quarter of the century. However, the 'move on' policy of police in the central commercial streets threatened the livelihood of the urban poor who made their living as hawkers and costermongers. Emma Rose, for example, was charged in

1863 with causing an obstruction in Southgate Street, by placing a basket of fish near the footway. She was fined 1s. (5p) and costs, or three days' imprisonment. In passing sentence, the mayor observed that 'the Bench were determined to repress the use of obscene language that now prevailed in some parts of the city'.[33] Conflict between the police and the street traders continued, and the strict supervision by a full-time professional police force (supported by wide powers under local by-laws) created new areas of conflict. The uniformed authority focused its attention on working-class districts, where closer regulation of lodging-houses, pubs and popular forms of recreation (such as gambling) was met with widespread suspicion. Hostility showed itself in sullen resentment, verbal abuse of the police, and occasionally in physical assault. Following the arrests of people discharging fireworks in London Street on 6 November 1876, it was recorded in the Watch Committee Minutes that 'the mob consisting of 4 or 5 hundred persons resisted the Police with such effect that the prisoners had to be conveyed to the Police Station by way of Cleveland Bridge when bottles, stones and other missiles were freely thrown at the police whose helmets and clothing were damaged'.[34]

The respectable classes of Bath evidently shared with the police force a concern about the proliferation of pubs in the poorest parts of the city. A memorial presented to the annual licensing meeting in 1867 pointed out that there were 74 bakers' shops and 51 butchers' shops in the city and borough of Bath, but that within the same area there were '300 places for the sale of intoxicating drinks'. Experience showed, the memorialists claimed, 'that poverty, immorality, and crime are in proportion to the facilities afforded for the sale of spirituous liquors'.[35] Heavy drinking – 'the curse of the working classes' to many respectable Victorians – undoubtedly caused poverty in many families, and some public houses and beer shops were closely associated with criminal activity: a police return sent to the Watch Committee in 1869 referred to fifteen that were known to the force as the resorts of thieves and prostitutes. Nonetheless, most public houses had a wider function that was rarely recognized, as meeting places and venues for various clubs, and as an informal source of news about jobs or lodgings. Their landlords were summoned most frequently for serving drinks after hours, or allowing gaming on their premises – 'offences' in the eyes of the law, but such prosecutions were often perceived by landlords and their customers as an infringement of traditional personal freedoms.

From the 1870s, legislation created new categories of offences, which brought some parents into conflict with the law. Compulsory vaccination of children against smallpox and enforced attendance at school for all between the ages of five and thirteen were two improving measures which, incidently, led to some previously blameless characters appearing before the Bath magistrates. Vaccination was neglected by many parents, who did not understand its implications, but it was also resisted on principle by some who either resented what they saw as undue interference in family life by the authorities, or who had genuine fears about the process. It was, however, only a minority of parents who did not comply with the law, and preventative measures were increasingly successful in reducing the incidence of smallpox epidemics. This success, it seems, led to some degree of complacency among parents and the authorities themselves. Of all children born in Bath in 1905, 1906, and from January to June 1907, the percentage vaccinated was 82.6 per cent, 72.1 per cent, and 67.9 per cent respectively. Prosecutions declined as the level of vaccinations declined.[36]

Non-compliance with the law on this issue was, perhaps, more likely to be due to negligence or to ignorance than to principle or to rational fears, but parental resistance in the poorer parts of the city to compulsory schooling was inextricably bound up with working-class culture, the family economy, and the survival strategies with which the urban poor coped with daily life. Compulsory schooling struck a severe financial blow to the household economy of many poor families, who not only lost the often crucial earnings of children, but found an extra expense imposed on their limited budgets by the fees required for schooling. Yet, both before and after compulsory attendance at school was introduced, it was only a small minority of parents in the poorer working-class districts of Bath who did not avail themselves of the opportunities for their children to gain some education. Charges brought against parents by the school board reveal a predictable pattern of summonses to addresses in the Avon Street district, the Dolemeads, Holloway, Snow Hill and Larkhall – all those areas of the city which were distinctively working class and which housed the poorest of Bath's residents. The abolition of school fees in the late nineteenth century no doubt contributed to the rise in average school attendance in Bath, which reached 86.8 per cent between 1899 and 1901.[37] But as late as 1901, the census report estimated that 209 boys and 80 girls aged ten and under fourteen (or 11.5 per cent and 4.4 per cent respectively) were engaged in occupations.[38] A local government inspector of schools commented in 1902 that 'ambition to improve themselves either mentally or financially seems to be dormant among the class that form the bulk of the population'.[39] For those who made up the small but severely deprived under class, who lived their lives in the culture of poverty, education beyond that of the streets had no value. A contribution to the family economy was of more immediate concern than a formal education, and it is not surprising that only about half of the total of 55 child workers identified in Bath in 1910 were registered as pupils of St Paul's School in Avon Street.[40]

Little can be said with confidence about the standard of living of 'ordinary' residents of Bath, because of the lack of evidence on wage-rates, earnings and prices. Neale has drawn some broad conclusions, for the period 1780–1850, from his analysis of wage-accounts kept by the overseer of highways in Walcot parish, in relation to the weekly publication in local papers of a selection of retail prices in Bath market, but it should be borne in mind that his sources were very few, and that the data on earnings was confined to labourers working on the highways. However, Neale considered it 'probable' that the movement of wages for this particular group indicated the direction and magnitude of wage levels for the whole group of non-agricultural labourers who, in 1831, numbered 1,480 and constituted approximately 20 per cent of the adult male workforce in the city. His general conclusion was that living standards fell in the early nineteenth century, but that by 1832 'real wages' (that is, the purchasing power of earnings in relation to prices) were at a level comparable to those of 1780. In 1835 they reached a level 22 per cent higher than the base year of 1780, but declined thereafter, and it was not until 1841 that real wages showed a definite and sustained improvement. Neale estimates that during the mid-1840s the standard of living of labourers, if fully employed, was about 50 per cent higher than it had been in the late eighteenth century.[41]

No detailed study exists on wage levels in Bath in the period between 1850 and 1914, but there are two indicators that suggest that a gradual improvement took place in the standard of living for at least some sections of the working classes. Firstly, the changes in the occupational structure of the city – including the growth of employment in regular, if not always better-paid jobs in commerce and new industries such as printing and engineering and a decline in traditional, often low-paid and casual labouring jobs and in the craft industries of tailoring and shoe-making – must have had a beneficial effect on the overall standard of living of the working classes in Bath. Also, the wages of domestic servants increased at an above-average rate, which affected many female workers in Bath, even at the expense of fewer jobs being available. Secondly, it is generally agreed that real wages (taking into account the level of prices) at a national level improved by 60 per cent or more for the average urban worker between 1850 and 1900.[42] This improvement was effected more by a fall in prices than by a rise in actual wage levels, but the purchasing power of the working classes increased as a result. It is most likely that on the whole the working people of Bath shared in the nation's experience of growing prosperity, although the poorest among them, the labourers, hawkers and casual workers, were the least likely to have benefited.

Class differences in public health remained a constant, even after important gains were made by 1914. The life chances of the working classes were bleak compared to those of the higher social orders. In 1842 the average age of death among gentlemen and professional persons living in Bath was 55 years; among the families of labourers and artisans in general it was 24 and 25 years respectively, but the families of shoe-makers died at the average age of only 14 years.[43] This startling figure has not been satisfactorily accounted for, but, nonetheless, it illustrates the marked variations in life expectancy among Bath's residents. This was influenced by place of residence as well as by income and occupation, for the incidence of disease was naturally greatest in the poorest areas of the city. In the cholera epidemic of 1832, a quarter of the 74 cases in Bath occurred in Avon Street. Seven years later, it was also the chief centre of a smallpox epidemic which affected a total of 300 people. When cholera broke out again, in 1848, the Avon Street district as a whole (which housed one in five of the total population) was once more among the areas of the city where the disease was particularly prevalent, although other locations of low-quality housing (such as Snow Hill and the Dolemeads) were equally conspicuous.[44]

In general Bath shared in the reduction of mortality rates that took place throughout England and Wales. Between 1841 and 1880, the annual average general mortality rate for Bath fluctuated between 22 and 24 per 1,000, which was close to the national average for England and Wales for the same period. From 1881 to 1900, both rates declined in tandem. The figure in Bath went down from 18.5 (1881–90) to 17.1 (1891–1900) compared with 18.6 and 17.5 nationally. Incorporated within a decline in the city's mortality rate was a less marked disparity in those of different districts. In the 1840s Lyncombe and Widcombe recorded the highest rate, at 30.5 per 1,000 population, whilst the lowest figure came from Bathwick, at 19.8 per 1,000 population. Even within a single district, as in Lansdown in 1843, the rate was roughly twice as high in the poor districts such as Avon and Milk Street compared with the wealthy areas like the Royal Crescent and Marlborough Buildings. By the last two decades of the century there was a narrowing of the gap between the highest and lowest district mortality rates. While the annual rate for Bath was 15.1 per 1,000 for the period 1897–9, Walcot had the highest district rate (16.5), followed by Lyncombe and Widcombe (12.1), and Bathwick recorded the lowest figure (11.2). Clearly assisting the downward trend of mortality in all districts was the movement of population away from the unhealthy central and low-lying districts to the less crowded and better-housed suburbs.

Overcrowding in the central parishes had been reduced during the second half of the century by the gradual migration of the population to the suburbs. In 1851 a total of 11,647 persons lived in 1,349 houses in the inner-city parishes, whereas in 1901, in the same parishes, 7,577 individuals were living in 1,342 houses.[45] This represented a significant improvement in living space: fewer one-roomed households and more people living in two and three rooms. Nonetheless, poor housing was one of the social problems common to all urban centres in the nineteenth and early twentieth century, which Bath's working classes as a whole shared. The Dolemeads, developed as a working-class district in the mid-nineteenth century, quickly degenerated into a slum. A few

24. The Dolemeads, c.1910. An example of early municipal housing built in red brick. (Guildhall Archives, Bath)

decades later a large part of this district was an 'insanitary area', as defined by the Housing of the Working Classes Act (1890). The houses, on a low-lying site, were damp, and the whole area (known to its inhabitants as 'Mud Island') was frequently flooded. Particularly severe flooding in 1882 and again in 1894 eventually prompted the council to undertake improvements involving, unusually in Britain at this time, council-house building. A scheme for building small houses was approved in September 1898, but final sanction from the local government board (to raise a loan of £10,500) was not given until December 1899. Redevelopment entailed raising the site above its pre-existing level, by as much as thirteen feet in some places, and it was not until the summer of 1901 that the first seven houses (in Archway Street) were declared 'fit for human habitation', in a public ceremony. By the end of 1902, Excelsior Street had been completed. A total of 42 new houses were erected in the Dolemeads by 1907. The majority were let at rents of 5s. (25p) a week, compared to a rent of about 3s.6d. (17½p) for the substandard housing they replaced. Dolemeads' tenants had once been notorious for not paying their rent, but the Medical Officer of Health (MOH) was gratified to report, at the end of six years of improvements, that there was neither a bad debt nor any arrears among the council's tenants in the new houses. The MOH accepted the opinion of 'a gentleman who knows the locality', who explained this exemplary behaviour by suggesting that: 'Whereas a man used to spend 3/6 a week in "drink" and 3/6 a week for rent, he now spends 5/- a week for rent and 2/- for "drink". Formerly the wretched houses drove the men and women to public houses, now they live at home.'[46]

Nonetheless, the MOH did not fully accept the argument of those housing reformers who believed that 'in order to elevate the slum dweller, we must first do away with the slum'. On the contrary, he shared the views of the civic representatives of Birmingham (with whom he had visited several European cities, under the auspices of the National Housing Reform Association) who asserted that 'the Housing Problem can only partially be solved by attending to the neglect of the house owners; the poorer classes of this country primarily need educating to the value of cleanliness, neatness and general house pride, to enable the advantages of the English system of housing to be enjoyed to the full'.[47]

The council itself carried out redevelopment schemes in several parts of the city in the late nineteenth and early twentieth centuries, not only in the Dolemeads but also in the James Street, Avon Street and Milk Street areas, and at Lampards Buildings. It also experimented in housing reform by adopting a scheme first used in Nottingham, whereby subsidies were offered to property owners as an inducement to improve substandard housing. A small district in Bath known as the Amebury, bounded on the north by Corn Street and on the south by Somerset Street and Back Street, was redeveloped in 1909–10 by the owner, who accepted £150 from the authorities in return for demolishing several houses and erecting in their place wash houses and sanitary accommodation to serve the needs of tenants in the remaining houses.[48]

Bath's housing problem was not on the same scale as that of the large industrial cities, but the need for adequate housing at affordable rents was proportionally much the same. In spite of the council's efforts, not all of Bath's residents were adequately housed on the eve of the First World War. The total number of houses in the city found unfit for human habitation (under various Housing Acts and regulations) was 39 in 1911, 22 in 1912, and 22 in 1913. These numbers are not large but, during the same period, a further 162 houses were found to be 'seriously defective from the point of view of danger to health or structural faults'. Moreover, the MOH acknowledged that an unspecified number of small houses were 'unsuited for family life', even though they could not be represented as unfit for habitation. Such houses were a constant source of trouble to the authorities. Let at low rentals, they tended to become overcrowded and the subject of 'notices', requiring clearance or improvements under the Public Health Acts. By 1914, the council had built 98 new houses and improved many more. Of the new properties, 7 were 'double tenements' (divided into two one-bedroomed flats), and the remainder were self-contained houses. These dwellings were let at rents from 3s. to 3s.6d. (15p to 17½p) for tenements, and from 4s. to

6s.6d. (20p to 32½p) for houses. The MOH was confident that there was sufficient accommodation for the better-paid artisan class in Bath, but in his report for the year 1914 he emphasized that there remained a need for two- and three-bedroom houses at rentals of from 3s. to 5s. (15p to 25p) weekly. The poorest section of the working class, especially those with large families, were still disadvantaged in the housing market.

Overall, the material conditions of life had improved for every social class in the city by the end of the nineteenth century as a result of better systems of sanitation and of water supply. But suburbanization and housing reform benefited chiefly the better off among the working classes, who could afford the artisan dwellings built in Oldfield Park and elsewhere, or the relatively high rents of the new council houses and of properties improved by private landlords. Nonetheless, even the very poor lived in less overcrowded conditions, as more of the population moved out to the suburbs, and public health regulations gradually improved many aspects of life. Standards of living rose for most people, partly as a result of cheaper food (much of it imported), and as the nationwide social reforms of the Liberal government of 1905–14 introduced old age pensions, school medical inspections, health and unemployment insurance and the provision of school meals. Yet in terms of relative deprivation, little had changed. Extremes of wealth and considerable variations in life-chances, according to social class, persisted. It is probable that in Bath, as elsewhere at the turn of the century, about 30 per cent of the population lived in poverty. This level of deprivation was indicated by the pioneering social investigations of Booth in London (1880s) and B. S. Rowntree in York (1899). Furthermore, on the eve of the First World War, a 'respectable' working-class family with a head of household in full-time employment, at an average wage of 'round about a pound a week', found it a constant struggle to make ends meet.

Chapter 6

The Voice of the People, 1820–1914

The contrast between image and reality which has informed much of this book so far is extended in this chapter to the political behaviour of the Bath electorate, to social class relations in the city, and the class-consciousness of its working people. The history of modern Britain reveals that in the radical politics of the early decades of the nineteenth century some sections of the middle and working classes campaigned in alliance for parliamentary reform, but that the 1830s also witnessed the emergence of distinctly working-class politics. Disappointment over the limitations of the 1832 Reform Act weakened the class alliance and contributed to the development of Chartism, the first working-class mass movement in British history. The challenge of Chartism, defeated by a combination of force, paternal welfarism, and internal dissensions, had petered out by 1850, but some of the ideas that informed the movement were carried forward to later decades. In the third quarter of the century, however, there was a fundamental change of political atmosphere, as the working classes became essentially reformist. Rather than challenging the system, they sought to make progress through incorporation within the existing framework. This was further extended with the revival of socialism during the last two decades of the century, which was integral to the development of independent working-class politics and the formation of the modern Labour Party – as a social-democratic rather than a revolutionary body – in 1906.

In Bath, social harmony was an integral part of the city's genteel image during the period 1820–1914 and, indeed, there were several factors that made it an unlikely setting for violent class conflict and independent working-class movements. The dominant contemporary view of the city as a place without trade or industry, inhabited by substantial numbers of wealthy upper-class and professional middle-class residents, embodied the assumption that its social structure made class relationships more harmonious here than in the manufacturing centres. A wide variety of benevolent charities, administered and supported by wealthy citizens in Bath, reinforced dependency and social subordination. Moreover, social historians have found that class conflict was, in general, less marked in places like Bath, with a mixed economy, than it was in single industry towns. The scale of production also had some influence on class tensions. These were lessened where there were greater opportunities for upward mobility, as in the small units of production typical of Bath's craft and industrial sector.

The dominant image of Bath has influenced many historical studies of the city during the Georgian period and has been largely repeated by those which have focused on selected aspects of life in the city during the nineteenth century. R. S. Neale challenged that view in his comprehensive social history of the city from 1680 to 1850. He identified a class-consciousness among some of Bath's tradesmen and artisans in the 1830s, but concluded that by 1850 middle-class interests and upper-class hegemony had combined to block the aspirations of an emerging working-class politics. Thereafter, Neale argues, Bath became a conservative backwater, epitomized by its genteel image, bereft of radical politics and characterized by social class harmony which was sustained by paternal benevolence from above and due deference from the working class. This image is echoed in some studies of Bath during the nineteenth century. The local historian John Wroughton, in contrast to Neale, has identified stability as the key word in understanding the city during the tumultuous 1830s, the Age of Reform.[1] Roy Hope, writing on education in the city from 1830 to 1902, found 'attitudes of acceptance, resignation and social conformity tended to prevail among its comparatively contented working population'.[2]

Yet the political behaviour of Bath's population did not always reflect its genteel image, particularly in the earlier nineteenth century. Moreover, in spite of its high social classification as a spa and a place of middle-class residence, far from being a wholly conservative city it was, rather, a centre of liberal strength. The Conservatives always remained a political force, but mostly from a minority position from 1850 to the First World War. Beneath the much-vaunted social harmony of the mid-nineteenth century, politics continued to be permeated by conflicts of class interest. In this chapter we explore the contrast between the image of Bath and the realities of its people's politics, between outward social harmony and the persistence of class conflicts. Firstly, the participation of the working class in some popular movements of the nineteenth century is considered. Aspects of the electoral behaviour of the population in relation to parliamentary politics up to 1914 are discussed, before we move on to comment on organized labour at the turn of the century. Thereafter, the focus shifts to municipal politics, and other local agencies in which the conflict of class interests was most apparent to the people of Bath.

Popular movements and parliamentary politics

Bath shared in the revival of radicalism from around 1812 on into the 1840s, which reflected the national mood for parliamentary reform.[3] Radical opinion demanded an end to rotten boroughs and extensions to the franchise. Until the Reform Bill was passed in 1832, political activists in Bath were preoccupied largely with the national campaign for reform. They also organized local meetings and petitions, and became increasingly active in parish vestries, which they used as public platforms from which to protest over issues such as tithes and assessed taxes. The basis of the campaign was an alliance of the unenfranchised. It involved numerous tradesmen and artisans, some labourers, and middle-class radicals and Whigs sympathetic to reform. The leadership was middle class, but in the 1830s several working-class initiatives threatened to destroy the existing cooperation. Independent working-class politics posed a challenge to middle-class supporters, who tended to withdraw when it seemed that they might lose control of the aspiring lower classes.

Bath returned two MPs to Parliament, but before the Reform Act of 1832 only the thirty members of the corporation had the right to vote. Nonetheless, many of the unenfranchised took a lively interest in elections, particularly as the campaign for radical reform gained in popularity. In 1820 the city was represented by Lord John Thynne, the Tory brother of the Marquis of Bath, who was himself the recorder of the city, and the Whig General Palmer who had been first elected at Bath in 1808, as a nominee of the Marquis of Camden, the Lord Lieutenant of Somerset.

Palmer, no radical, but sympathetic to reform, had fallen out with the Marquis of Camden by 1820, and there were rumours of a plot to oust him from his seat by getting the lawyer Sir William Scott elected in his place. Scott, it seems, was then expected to step down when the Marquis of Camden's son, Lord Brecknock, became of age to stand for Parliament. This was widely regarded as an attempt at Tory gerrymandering, aimed at strengthening the grip of aristocracy and thus blocking reform. Local radical opinion was outraged at the prospect 'that Bath will have the honour of being represented by two relatives of two Marquises, and thus draw closer the bonds of union betwixt our Body Corporate, our Noble Recorder, and our Noble Lord Lieutenant'.[4] Palmer declared he would contest such an election as illegal, on the grounds of interference by a peer in an election to the Commons. In the face of public opinion the plan was abandoned, and both Palmer and Lord Thynne were re-elected in 1820.

However, once Lord Brecknock was of age he stood for election, in 1826, at which point Bath did indeed become represented by Lords Brecknock and Thynne. Elections in 1828 and 1829 produced the same result, provoking the radical *Bath Journal* to comment in 1829 that 'Never were the citizens of Bath made more sensible of their degraded condition, for never were members returned more completely in opposition to the well known wish and judgement of the people in county, city or borough.'[5] Palmer lost to Lord Brecknock by only one vote on that occasion, and thereafter he became the hero of local radicals as the representative of liberty and freedom.

He became even more the focus of enthusiasm when, at the election of 1830, the corporation proved more responsive to public opinion and Palmer regained his seat with a majority of two votes. Large and jubilant crowds were on the streets to greet the result, and Palmer and Lord Thynne were 'chaired' in procession through central Bath. Both MPs sought the goodwill of the unenfranchised, by distributing, as they passed, silver coins and 'tickets' for some 600 gallons of beer. The rejection of the Whig's first Reform Bill forced another election in May 1831, by which time the public mood was even stronger for reform. Lord Thynne and Palmer were again elected. Palmer's victory was greeted with much enthusiasm and with cries of 'The Bill, The Whole Bill, Nothing But the Bill.' He was duly chaired through the crowded streets, but Lord John Thynne, the Tory, suffered the indignity of being pelted with so much rotten fruit that he was driven to take refuge in the White Hart.[6]

There was widespread indignation in Bath when the Lords rejected a second Reform Bill, after it had been passed by the Commons in early October 1831. The immediate response was a display of mourning. Many shops closed and a muffled peal was rung from the parish church of St James. Some days later a large but peaceful demonstration of protest took place, attended by an estimated 20,000 people. The main assembly was in Queen Square, but the contingent from the radical working-class parish of St James set out independently to meet up with the main body in front of Sydney Gardens Hotel, at the end of Great Pulteney Street. The enfranchised and unenfranchised, the respectable classes and the organized workers of Bath, all came together in this grand procession, which was accompanied by numerous bands. The crowd carried many banners, inscribed with such slogans as 'The United Trades', 'We Are All Agreed' and 'The Bill or Nothing Else'. Speaking from the hustings, the middle-class leadership enthused over the strength of support for reform and urged the necessity of avoiding violence. There was much rhetoric spoken about 'the wonderful and unparalleled unanimity' that existed between 'the lowest classes and those immediately above them', but the voice of the working people was heard only faintly. One representative of the journeyman hatters of nearby Oldland Common addressed the crowd, to speak in praise of the king and his ministers, 'in their endeavours to obtain for us a just and equal representation'.[7]

In nearby Bristol, news of the Lord's rejection of the bill sparked off mass riots. The Bath troop of the North Somerset Yeomanry was called out to assist the authorities in Bristol, but the commander was prevented from mustering his troops. An organized crowd of about 1,000 people set upon Captain Wilkins, forcing him to take refuge in the White Hart, which they then attacked. Wilkins escaped, but a section of the crowd then set off to occupy the Guildhall, in an attempt to prevent police interference. Order was restored by the early hours of the morning, after 300 constables had been called out and 6 arrests made. The event suggests the existence of an organization with knowledge of the authorities' intentions, and the ability to raise a strong force to thwart their objectives.

Another working-class initiative was taken the following month, when some 3,000 people attended a meeting at the tennis court, Morford Street, to form a political union. The meeting was chaired by Mr Keene, editor of the *Bath Journal*, but no other leading middle-class radicals attended. They had declined the invitation to do so with a variety of trivial excuses, although J. Hawksey Ackersley wrote expressing his qualified support, on condition that the proposed union should follow the pattern of the Birmingham Political Union (1830), which was an organization firmly under middle-class control. In the absence of middle-class reformers, the main influence on the artisans and petty tradesmen who met at the tennis court were delegates from the militant, working-class Bristol Political Union (1831). One of them spoke regretfully of the absence of middle-class leaders, but in terms which implied a continuing commitment to the notion of class cooperation: 'They leave us to do as well as we can without them. The time may come when they will want us, and our presence will be valuable to them; should that time arrive, we will not leave them as they now leave us, to do as well as they can, we will not retaliate.'[8]

The Bath Political Union was formed with a majority of artisans on its council. James Crisp, a Baptist master hatter and long-time radical, was elected as its president. Within six months the Bath Political Union claimed a membership of 1,500.

The formation of the Bath Political Union was an outward sign of the tensions emerging in the class alliance on which the reform campaign was originally based. Such strains became even more apparent after the Reform Act became law in June 1832. The provisions of the Act brought into the franchise adult males who occupied houses of an annual rateable value of £10 or over. The effect was to increase the Bath electorate from 30 to 3,000, many of the new voters being artisans and petty tradesmen who had been pressing for change. The event was celebrated in Bath with a Grand Reform Gala in Sydney Gardens,[9] but the Act fell far short of meeting the aspirations of working-class radicals. It had, nonetheless, created a substantial working-class electorate in Bath. Their votes, about a quarter of the total, were proportionally rather more significant than those of their counterparts in many medium-sized industrial towns like Rochdale and Oldham. Poll-book evidence suggests that the newly enfranchised tradesmen and artisans formed the bedrock of support for the radical MP, J. A. Roebuck, in his electioneering in Bath between 1832 and 1847.[10]

At the first election under the new franchise, in December 1832, there was no Tory candidate. Both the Earl of Brecknock and Lord Thynne had withdrawn, and such was the strength of anti-aristocratic and anti-Tory feeling that no other nominee was put forward, although R. B. Foster of Lansdown had offered to stand so that 'the rank, wealth and worth of Bath should not be totally unrepresented'.[11] Palmer stood again, with a second Whig or Liberal, H. W. Hobhouse. Radicals apparently regarded Hobhouse as a Tory in Liberal disguise, and concern about his lukewarm attitude to further reform prompted a search for a third candidate. Roebuck, a young man of 25 who had been recommended by radicals in London, was put forward as a candidate, albeit an unlikely one: he was a political democrat, probably a republican and certainly an atheist.[12]

Roebuck offered the electorate a radical programme, including support for shortened parliamentary terms, further extensions to the franchise and the secret ballot, the abolition of slavery, religious liberty and the abolition of tithes, repeal of assessed taxes and a general reduction in government expenditure. He appealed to a broad constituency of the new electorate, and was popular with many of those still excluded from the political system. A crowd of 7,000 assembled at the Orange Grove to observe the official nomination of candidates, and a similar crowd turned out for the declaration of the poll. Palmer and Roebuck were elected, to the delight of the crowd.

Even at this triumphant moment, the class alliance was under strain. Many working-class radicals regarded the Reform Act as the beginning of a wider process of change, whereas some middle-class supporters were content to regard it as an end in itself and had no wish to support demands for a full democracy. By 1837 disunity was a feature of radicalism in Bath. Roebuck was losing some voters partly because of his belief in religious toleration, exemplified in his support for a government grant to the Roman Catholic seminary at Maynooth in Ireland. His working-class supporters were also dismayed at his advocacy of 'inhumane' treatment of the poor under the Poor Law Amendment Act of 1834, discussed more fully below. At the same time, the local economy was depressed, which enabled the Tories to argue that five years of radicalism had been bad for business. In the general election of 1837 both Palmer and Roebuck lost their seats to Tory candidates. Roebuck claimed that his defeat was due to 'Tory gold, Tory intimidation and Whig duplicity', in what was known locally as 'The Drunken Election'. Large-scale 'treating' and the possibilities of coercive influence with an open voting system certainly influenced electoral choices in the late 1830s, but the newly enfranchised electorate was a volatile mass, not tied to any party by traditional allegiances. The people were likely to vote on the particular issues at specific times, and it seems that the result reflected a rejection of some parts of Roebuck's politics.

Meanwhile, in the autumn of 1837 a Bath Working Men's Association (BWMA) was formed. The BWMA held its first public meeting in October 1837, presided over by a shoemaker, Thomas Bolwell, and chaired by the president of the Bath Political Union, James Crisp. The guest of honour was Henry Vincent from the East London Democratic Association, a 24-year old compositor who became a prominent Chartist leader. The meeting adopted a programme demanding universal suffrage, no property qualification for MPs, annual parliaments, and the secret ballot. What was significant about this event was that it was a meeting of working-class people, organized and addressed by working men. The class divide was growing between middle- and working-class radicals, reflected in the priority that each class gave respectively to the secret ballot and to universal suffrage. Middle-class radicals who were also tradesmen in Whig- or Tory-dominated wards were particularly concerned about the conflict of interest set up by open voting: 'Get the Ballot. If possible with an extension of the Suffrage, but if we can obtain no more, by all means let us get the Ballot', said Mr Jolly, the up-and-coming radical Liberal draper of Milsom Street.

Disappointment over the limits of the Reform Act turned politically aspiring labouring men away from cooperation and attracted many to Chartism. Chartism was a nationwide umbrella movement centred on demands for political reform, set out in the Charter published in London on 8 May 1838, but gathering together local grievances which were given expression through nationwide agitation.[13] The Charter was introduced to an enthusiastic Bath audience in June 1838 by Thomas Bolwell (by then chairman of the BWMA), with Henry Vincent and several local working men as speakers. One of these, George Bartlett, a shoemaker and supporter of the physical-force Chartist leader Feargus O'Connor, said of the middle class that they 'left us to fight our own battle. Thus they acted as they ever do act ... they obtained power for themselves.'[14] Here was evidence of the suspicion and distrust, following the limited achievement of the extension of the franchise in 1832, that caused a rift between radical middle-class leaders and resentful working-class allies. Bartlett was later arrested and found guilty of sedition, and imprisoned for nine months. Whilst advocating the violent overthrow of a corrupt political system, at his trial, he nevertheless forgave the magistrates as equal victims of circumstance.[15]

The experience of Chartism in Bath was similar to that in many regional capitals and in cities where political radicalism had established itself long before the drafting of the Charter. The city had substantial numbers of Chartists, but was less militant than nearby industrial centres, such as Trowbridge and Bradford-on-Avon (Wiltshire) or Frome

(Somerset), and there were attempts in Bath to reach a political accommodation between Chartists and other reforming groups. The Bath Chartists, numbering some 1,800–2,200, held regular meetings in the city. They were involved in activities in Wiltshire and Somerset, supported the national petition to Parliament, sent a representative to the National Convention of 1839 and also agreed to support the idea of a 'Sacred Month' or general strike, if the petition was rejected. A demonstration planned for Whit Monday 1839 was banned from the city, where 130 police, 600 special constables, 80 parish constables, a troop of Hussars, and 6 troops of yeomanry were mustered by the authorities. The Chartists held their meeting nonetheless, but in a field at Midford (three miles south of the city), and barely a tenth of the anticipated crowd of 15–20,000 turned up. Local leaders, Henry Vincent and W. P. Roberts, had been arrested and the show of force was an effective deterrent. The largest contingents at Midford came from Trowbridge and Bradford-on-Avon, with 250 from Bristol and only about 100 from Bath, with smaller groups from Frome, Westbury and elsewhere. The meeting was a set-back for local Chartists. The county magistrates, declaring it to have been a total failure, predicted that no similar gathering would recur. Nonetheless, further repressive measures were taken against Bath Chartists in the ensuing autumn, when spies infiltrated private meetings, and arrests were made on charges of sedition.[16]

Despite all this, the movement retained a considerable following. By 1841 there were weekly Chartist meetings in the city. A poster for one of them appealed to the poor of Bath and alerted the working classes against being bought off by charitable handouts from wealthy citizens. It exhibited the language of class antagonism. The poor were heavily taxed to keep members of the royal family living in luxury, the rights of the people could only be restored by an extension of the franchise:

SUFFERERS – You are oppressed, but have no power to rid yourselves of oppression. The power has been wrested and withheld from you – you have been robbed of your rights, which is THE CAUSE of your destitution ... It is time, however, THE SYSTEM SHOULD be changed and Honest Popular Government be established, which alone can permanently benefit the Working Classes ... IF JUSTICE WERE DONE YOU, THERE WOULD BE NO NECESSITY FOR CHARITY.[17]

At the same time, by emphasizing moderation and good order, the leadership was attempting to rebuild links in support for Chartism, with middle-class radicals from the Anti-Corn Law League.[18] This body had been founded in 1839 to fight for repeal of the Corn Laws (1815), which restricted the entry of foreign grain to this country. The league attracted support from middle-class Liberals in Bath, who blamed the Corn Laws for urban distress caused by food shortages and the rising price of bread. This argument was rejected by the Bath Tories in a series of posters and through the editorial columns of the *Bath Chronicle*, where the opinion was put forward that repeal would lead to unemployment on the land and a general lowering of wages. The Anti-Corn Law League tried to prove that all classes stood to gain from repeal but, in the country as a whole, attempts at an accommodation between the league and the Chartists were not successful, because of the latters' suspicions that the economic interests of employers and workers were hostile to each other. In places like Bath, where political radicalism based on class alliance had been the norm for some twenty years, attempts at cooperation were more appealing to the working-class Chartists and more likely to succeed. Moreover, the demands for a repeal of the corn laws and for constitutional reform had been frequently associated in radical politics since 1815. An alliance was formed in Bath between the league and the Chartists at a meeting in the Guildhall held in December 1841, for the purpose of drawing up a petition to Parliament calling for repeal of the Corn Laws and the implementation of the Charter.[19]

By 1841 the mood in the country as a whole had turned against the reforming tendencies of the Whig government. Moreover, although with hindsight it is apparent that militant Chartism had failed by the early 1840s, the threat that the movement posed to the established order evoked a conservative response. There was a strong swing to the Tories nationwide in the election of 1841, which brought Peel's ministry into power. However, 'genteel' Bath went against the national trend and J. A. Roebuck regained his seat. He and the radical Lord Duncan decisively beat the Tories. It is significant that it was in this same year that the Bath Chartists made an accommodation with the Anti-Corn Law League. The realization that independent, extra-parliamentary politics as represented by Chartism was unlikely to succeed disposed Bath's working-class radicals to renew class cooperation at local level, and persuaded those with a vote to support the parliamentary party whose policies accorded most closely, albeit imperfectly, with their aspirations.

Not all of the people of Bath rejoiced at the 1841 demonstration of renewed radicalism. The *Bath Chronicle* declared:

> Bath is a dark blot on the present general election. At a time when other places are, to their high honour, throwing off the trammels of modern Liberalism, Bath has put them on in their worst shape. It has returned not merely radicals or ultra-radicals, but persons who are 'something else'. We are taunted throughout the country with having sent to Parliament two disciples of revolution … 'Hotbed of all that is wild, reckless, and revolutionary in politics' is the phrase which is abundantly used in speaking or writing of Bath.[20]

Bath as a hotbed of revolutionary politics in the early nineteenth century was not easily accommodated within the image of a genteel city. Its radical politics of the 1820s and 1830s subsided, however, after the 1841 election. Chartist activities continued, but on a diminishing scale, culminating in the last recorded meeting in Bath, in March 1848, the year of European revolutions and the Communist Manifesto. Thomas Bolwell presided, and this final meeting of potential revolutionaries was addressed by a long-standing radical, the master hatter Cox, the 'veteran general' who had been associated with Chartism in the city since 1841.

The election of 1847, Neale argues, marked the historical moment at which radical consciousness died in Bath and paternal welfarism triumphed. The prospect of cheaper bread (the corn laws were repealed in 1846) appeared to be more attractive than universal suffrage. Moreover, the Bath Whigs and Tories cooperated in choosing Lord Ashley (later Lord Shaftesbury) to stand against Roebuck. Ashley was presented to the electorate as a social reformer dedicated to the welfare of working men, as his work in the Ten Hour Movement was said to demonstrate. (The factory reform movement led to legislation in 1847, reducing the hours of labour of textile workers.) Ashley took the seat, on a swing of about 5 per cent against Roebuck.

The election may have marked the end of Bath as a hotbed of radicalism, but did the city become thereafter, as Neale claims, a conservative backwater? Certainly, the political behaviour of its population had changed over time. Between 1820 and 1832, many working people without the vote cooperated with the middle classes in the radical campaign for parliamentary reform. The lively politics of those years was not in keeping with Bath's image. In the second stage, 1831–50, the class alliance came under strain as working people developed their own aspirations and attempted to act politically for themselves through the Bath Political Union, the Working Men's Association and the Chartist movement. The 1832 Reform Act gave the vote to the middle classes, but, although the £10 property qualification enfranchised a substantial number of manual workers, it fell far short of their demand for universal suffrage. Their middle-class allies were widely seen as having abandoned the workers. Moreover, the working classes were threatened by the 1834 Poor Law Amendment Act, which took away parish administration of poor relief and created larger Poor Law Unions, presided over by elected boards of guardians. Each union was to erect a workhouse, nicknamed 'bastilles' by anti-Poor Law campaigners, and no relief was to be given to the able-bodied poor outside the workhouse. The workhouse test, whereby an able-bodied person was deemed to be in need of relief only if he or she went into the workhouse, was particularly repellant to the labouring classes. Here again, the support of Roebuck and others of the middle class for the new Poor Law was perceived as a betrayal of the class alliance. The weakness and eventual failure of Chartism had prompted the working class, it seems, to turn back to cooperation with middle-class allies in the Anti-Corn Law League, and in returning Roebuck to Parliament again in the 1841 election. By the later 1840s, however, a less radical and more reformist working-class politics is suggested by Lord Ashley's success at the polls.

The repeal of the corn laws in 1847 and the Ten Hour Act of 1848 undoubtedly helped to renew popular confidence in the integrity of the existing system of government. The apparently new frame of mind in the third quarter of the nineteenth century also owed something to the economic background. The period 1850–75 was, in general, prosperous, and the working classes shared to some extent in the increase in national income. Working-class radicalism was expressed during these years in support for the Liberal Party. This was the party of nonconformity, espousing the cause of disestablishment of the Anglican Church and of temperance, and on these grounds it enjoyed considerable working-class support. The party was committed to social reform, opposed to coercion in Ireland, and it challenged privilege wherever it existed.

The size of Bath's electorate was more than doubled by the second Reform Act of 1867, which enfranchised all male heads of households in the city and thus gave the vote to just under 7,000 men. Both the Liberal and Conservative Parties courted the working-class vote, but in the country as a whole the majority of working men voted Liberal, particularly skilled workers. Bath tended to return one Liberal and one Tory to Parliament, with intermittent exceptions, and the Liberal vote was particularly solid in most working-class wards.

From the mid-1880s into the early twentieth century national trends were reflected in local voting, with the Conservatives gaining ground up to the election of 1906, when the Liberals were returned to power. The 1884 Reform Act (which gave the vote to many male rural workers who had not been enfranchised in 1867) brought increased competition for the working-class vote. What is noticeable about the political behaviour of the people of Bath is the continuing underlying strength of Liberalism. Analysis of parliamentary election results in the city shows that between 1830 and 1900 the Liberals retained a slight edge over their political rivals during most of the period. Between 1830 and 1850, Liberal candidates, including radicals, won 5 seats as opposed to the Conservatives' 3; in the 1850s, they won 7 seats to the 2 won by the Conservatives, and achieved the highest poll in all five contests; in the 1860s and 1870s, Liberals won 6 to the Conservatives' 5 seats and topped the poll in four out of six elections. In fact, it was only in the 1890s that the Conservative Party emerged the stronger, taking advantage of the Liberal split over Home Rule for Ireland. Between 1880 and 1900, the Liberals in Bath still won 7 seats to the Conservatives' 5, but the Conservatives topped the poll on four occasions, three of them in the period 1892–1900.[21]

The later nineteenth and early twentieth centuries were notable for a revival of independent working-class consciousness and movements. This was reflected in the growth of trade unions in the 1880s – especially the 'new unionism', which organized the unskilled and some women workers – and in the spread of socialist ideas. In 1893 the Independent Labour Party was formed, to secure the election of working-class MPs independent of the Liberal Party, and in 1900 an alliance of trade unions with various socialist bodies established the Labour Representation Committee. Arising out of these developments, the modern Labour Party came into being in 1906. Nevertheless, working men in Bath were content to be represented in Parliament by middle-class Liberal MPs. The Trades and Labour Council, established in 1891, seems to have taken few if any political initiatives beyond supporting Liberal candidates at parliamentary and local elections. The 1914 city directory does not list any socialist organizations, although there were Liberal Clubs and Associations in working-class Larkhall, in Lyncombe and Widcombe, and at Walcot, with both Liberal and Conservative Clubs in Twerton. The electorate had no opportunity to vote for a Labour candidate until after the First World War, at the general election of 1918. Yet there is evidence of some socialist activity in the city. Scattered references in the local press record occasional events, such as an 'instructive' talk on socialism given to the St James's Men's Friendly Society in January 1902.[22]

There were clearly contrasts between the image of Bath and the realities of working-class political behaviour in the period 1820–1914, especially in the first half of the nineteenth century. We now turn to the persistence of class conflict in relation to changes in the administration of the borough and some aspects of municipal politics, to the administration of the Poor Law, and to the structure and policies of the school board.

Consensus and conflict: some aspects of urban politics in Bath

Ever since the late sixteenth century, the Bath council had held responsibilities with regard to municipal property and corporation interests in the spa facilities. The charter of 1590, which formally incorporated the city, formed the basis of borough administration until the early nineteenth century. Following the reform of municipal corporations in 1835, Bath extended the size of its electorate, experienced a shift in the balance of power between the Conservatives and Liberals, and acquired new authority to establish a municipal police force. However, as we shall see, the reform rhetoric that accompanied the introduction of the 1835 Act was subverted by the commitment of the reformed council to a policy of retrenchment and to the reduction of the debt incurred by the former unelected corporation.

Pressure for municipal reform had gathered momentum as part of the radical campaign for greater democracy and the removal of corrupt

practices. It was a logical extension of the 1832 Reform Act. The Royal
Commission on Municipal Corporations was highly critical of the old
corporations in its report (1835). The men of property who governed
Bath recognized the inevitability of some concessions to democracy at
local level after 1832, but they made a small gesture in defence of the
rights of property during the summer of 1835. At a meeting in July
the corporation passed a unanimous resolution to forward to the House
of Lords, which stated its objection to the prospect of 'placing the
Corporation Estates under the Control of persons without the property
Qualification and giving such persons the power of levying Rates on the
Inhabitants'. In the same month a public meeting in support of the bill
attracted about 1,000 people.[23] This was a mere handful in comparison
to the huge crowds which had attended earlier reform meetings. Local
Tories and Whigs, who feared a radical triumph under the new system,
had formed an alliance in the Bath Liberal and Constitutional Association, to act as a united front against 'flaming Radicals', but, as described
above, many individuals who had been active in the movement for
reform before 1832 regarded the Reform Act as an end in itself, and
were unsympathetic to further change.

The changes embodied in the Municipal Reform Act (1835) created
new councils which were accountable to a greatly increased electorate.
Council debates and accounts were to be open to the public. Male
household suffrage was established for local elections, with three-year
residency and rate-paying qualifications. The Act also changed significantly the structure of municipal government in Bath; thereafter, the
council was composed of 42 councillors, 6 for each of the 7 municipal
wards: Bathwick, St James, St Michael's, Kingsmead, Lansdown, Lyncombe and Widcombe, and Walcot. These wards were created by a
redrawing of parish boundaries, which split the radical parish of SS
Peter and Paul in two. Part of it was incorporated into St James, and the
rest (with some addition from the southern part of Walcot) became
Kingsmead Ward. The remainder of Walcot parish was also divided, the
eastern, more working-class area becoming Walcot Ward, while the
wealthier part of the parish became Lansdown Ward.[24] As a result, social
class segregation and the potential for conflicts between different districts
became more evident. There were also some curious companions within
wards that encompassed diverse areas, and nowhere more so than in
Kingsmead. This contained the notorious slum of the Avon Street district, but also wealthy Queen Square, the Circus, the Royal Crescent,
and Marlborough Buildings. The electors of Avon Street and its environs
were of insufficient standing to be considered eligible for municipal office,
but their votes were crucial to the electoral success of the tradesmen
who sat on the council for Kingsmead Ward. Those electors who lived
in the Circus and its adjoining streets felt that they were not properly
represented by mere tradesmen, and preferred one of their own kind.

The 1835 Act was less radical than it might at first appear. It did not sweep away the old custom of oligarchic control in Bath. One-third of the new council was to be elected annually; a third of the elected councillors became aldermen for six years, by nomination from among themselves; and the mayor was to be elected annually as before. The fourteen aldermanic posts were used from the outset of the new system as an extension of the power obtained by the majority party. Consequently, the Bath Liberals, who did comparatively well in 1835, were able to retain overall control at times when later local elections returned a majority of Conservative councillors. Throughout most of the mid-nineteenth century the mayor and the chairmen of important committees were appointed on the basis of Liberal patronage. By such means, the dominance of the Liberal Party in Bath was preserved.

Although the reformed body was described in a series of satirical letters, published in 1836, as a 'braggart mob of saddle-makers, old clothes men, hatters, undertakers',[25] it was still men of property who governed Bath. Candidates for election had to own property worth £1,000, or occupy property of the value of £30 per annum. The first election under the new system, in December 1835, brought large Whig-Liberal gains in Bath, as throughout the country, although at least six members of the old corporation were elected to the new council. Its composition reflected the success of the challenge to the old élite posed by the new propertied middle classes, who had been excluded from the political system before the 1830s. The ironmonger John Stothert and the coach-maker Thomas Fuller were two of Bath's wealthy manufacturers elected in 1835. Only three of the new men did not own property in the city. The most significant structural change was the increase in commercial representation over time, rising to almost half (49.6 per cent) by 1861. Moreover, despite Bath's image as a place of genteel residence, it was not shopkeepers who dominated the commercial sector on the council. Men engaged in manufacturing, as opposed to retail trade, accounted for a substantial proportion of the commercial interest in the years 1836–70. Municipal reform ushered in a period of Whig-Liberal hegemony, but the Tories retained a sufficient presence on the council to remain a threat, especially as some members felt able to change party allegiance in response to public opinion. As early as 1836 complaints were being published about some councillors elected in the Liberal interest who had already 'turned their coats'. Nonetheless, in 1835 the balance of power swung from the Tories to the Whig Party, which was able to dominate the council-chamber for more than a generation, whilst the Tories always retained sufficient strength to remain in contention for power. Also, by exercising considerable influence in agencies and institutions beyond the Guildhall, the Tories were able to sustain pressure on public opinion and in the council-chamber.

In the reform era of the 1830s and 1840s, the party battles were intense.

By the 1850s and 1860s, conflicts appeared to give way to a more consensus form of politics. The Tory approach of seeing the post of mayor as above politics and investing it with due pomp and ceremony was accepted by the Liberals. Moreover, a form of civic gospel was preached in the 1860s and 1870s, outlining a spirit of unity and common purpose for all the citizens of Bath. Yet this was partly a process of image-making, and was never able to unite the disparate interest groups within the city. Beneath the rhetoric, class differences and sectional interests remained ever present in a fragmented and divided society.

The outward political consensus which was a marked feature of Bath's municipal politics from 1848 to 1851 was a part of the realignment of social classes, which was evident in relation to parliamentary politics. The electorate returned a majority of Tories to the council in 1848, the year after Ashley had defeated the radical Roebuck at the general election. The following year, the Bath Conservative and Liberal Associations agreed not to contest the local elections, an agreement that was broken only in the Kingsmead Ward, where class politics were most apparent, ranging from the poorest voters of the Avon Street district to the wealthy inhabitants of Royal Crescent and its environs. In 1850 it was agreed by the political parties that no electoral contest would take place, and in that year retiring councillors in each ward were replaced by new men of the same political allegiance.[26] The Guildhall was popularly known at this time as 'Conciliation Hall'. Yet class and sectional interests remained significant in municipal politics. As a minority, the wealthy social élite living in the upper town or the affluent suburbs, mainly Tory-voters and often Anglican in religion, had a shared interest in resisting the aspirations of the trading and labouring classes, but they were in no position to exercise power with any degree of consistent success. The strength of the Liberal group on the council was centred on the lower town, on councillors drawn mainly from the commercial middle class and supported not only by their kind, but also by working-class traders and artisans.

The men who came to greatest prominence as councillors during the nineteenth century were those who built up a network of contacts and influence through participation in local agencies outside the council. Two examples must suffice. The Conservative William Sutcliffe (1801–52) was at times a magistrate, a Poor Law Guardian, president of Bath General Hospital and honorary secretary of the Bath Ragged and Industrial School. He also founded the Sutcliffe School (a juvenile reformatory), served on the prestigious committees of the Royal Literary and Scientific Institute and of the Mineral Water Hospital. In addition, he was a member of the Bath branch of the Health of Towns Association. Sutcliffe was mayor of Bath in 1848.[27]

Jerom Murch (1807–95) was an outstanding figure in Bath's history.[28] The municipal career of this radical Liberal developed somewhat later, after he had resigned his role as a Unitarian minister and recovered from a breakdown in his health. Before becoming a councillor in 1862 he had built up support within all the key élite groups in Bath. He was descended from a Huguenot family that settled in England, in retreat from religious persecution, during the seventeenth century. Educated at University College, London, he devoted the early part of his career to the Unitarian ministry. Murch settled in Bath in 1833, where he was appointed minister of Trim Street Chapel. He later acquired a fortune of some £80,000 by marrying an heiress, Ann Meadows. A radical reformer in his outlook, Murch was politically active in Bath for over sixty years, even though he was not directly involved in municipal politics until the 1860s. He was vice-chairman of the board of guardians for nearly twenty years, and president of the Literary and Philosophical Society for over thirty years. He also served at times as president of the board of governors of the Mineral Water Hospital, chairman of the Theatre Royal Company and of the Grand Pump Room Hotel Company. He was also a member of the Bath branch of the Health of Towns Association, and took a great interest in several philanthropic organizations, in addition to being a stalwart member of the school board from the 1870s.

Murch met Conservative councillors in several supposedly politically neutral bodies. Despite his nonconformist background, he was able to penetrate the Anglican strongholds of the Bath and County Club and the Abbey Restoration Fund. His long involvement in a wide variety of bodies in Bath, before standing for election as a Liberal, enabled him to build up considerable personal support. Within a year of being elected to the council he was chosen as mayor, in 1863, and again in 1864. In fact, he held the office seven times in all, and was regarded as the mayor *par excellence*. Murch used his personal influence as mayor to attempt to build a consensus behind the civic gospel of municipal improvement. The civic gospel was founded on belief in a common moral purpose that incorporated the responsibilities of the social élites with the needs of the poorest in society, to be reconciled through the agency of municipal government. Yet in Bath, a city seen as a place where social harmony characterized class relationships, the civic gospel failed to override the fragmented and dysfunctional social structure that so often thwarted the implementation of improvement measures in the 1860s and 1870s.

One of the obstacles to achieving support for the implementation of improvement schemes such as in the city's water supply was the continuation of old powers that differed between the city parishes.[29] This state of affairs perpetuated a narrow, parochial mentality at the expense of schemes for improvement for the whole city. A fear of adding a burden to the rates limited the progress in public health provision. The city's response to the 1848 Public Health Act also promised more than was delivered in the passing of the Bath City Act in 1851. The corporation became the local board of health, establishing its own powerful subcommittee, the City Act Committee, but most of the powers such as the appointment of a Medical Officer of Health (MOH), and the registration and regulation of slaughter houses, were not acted upon immediately. It was not until 1864, under the leadership of Murch, that the city began a civic programme of improvement that was to assist not only in the revival of the city's prosperity but also provided a comprehensive corporation water supply, the appointment of a qualified MOH, extensive street improvements and the acquisition of the Royal Victoria Park. Over the next fifteen years the civic gospel was increasingly in evidence in Bath, and the corporation endeavoured to provide a unity of purpose by investing in greater amenities as a means of achieving prosperity for all its citizens. But beneath the lofty tone of moral improvement, sectional, class and parochial interests continued to set limits to what the corporation could achieve. The projected image of government by consensus and with a common purpose could not always disguise the conflicts that so often circumscribed improvement measures.

A few dry seasons highlighted the scarcity of water, and the council obtained additional powers in the passing of the 1851 Bath City Act. Theoretically, this was an important step forward in sanitary provision, as the local enactment of the powers authorized by the 1848 Public Health Act. The corporation now had the power to borrow extensively to promote a wide range of sanitary improvements, but successful implementation was another matter. Despite plans for a comprehensive scheme of waterworks envisaged for Batheaston, only a very small reservoir, containing a mere 114,000 gallons, was constructed. Instead of the estimated £30,000 loan required, the council borrowed only £6,000 and spent a total of £10,000, drawing on the difference from the surplus revenue from the corporation waterworks.

During the 1850s and 1860s, there was an increased demand for water, but, again, an inadequate response to improving the supply. In 1835, consumption had been approximately at the level of 6 gallons per head per day to 2,381 water tenants. By 1861, the number of water tenants had risen to 4,073, with an average supply of 13 gallons per head per day, although a sufficiency was reckoned to be more like 25 gallons. Total supply had increased from 94,000 gallons to 348,000 gallons, but additional sources of supply were needed to meet the ever-growing demand for water. Amidst widespread dissatisfaction at the shortage of water, compounded by the exceptionally dry summers of 1864 and 1865, the council prepared a major scheme to improve the sanitary condition of the city and to extend the municipal water supply. The issue provoked the sharpest conflicts of interest over council policy during the second half of the nineteenth century. In 1864 a new sense of urgency was given to the condition of Bath with the visit of the British Association to the city. This provided an opportunity to gain national publicity for the spa, and the authorities were clearly anxious that nothing should spoil the impressions of delegates to the conference, or impair Bath's reputation as a health resort for residents and for visitors. Their anxieties were commented upon by 'Civis', in a letter to the *Bath Chronicle*:

> It is quite delightful to see the state of trepidation into which our complacent Corporation has been thrown by the thoughts of the approaching visit of the British Association. It reminds one strongly of boys at school who have been idle, and are at last frightened at the near prospect of a sound whipping ... Let us look at the Bath Railway Station, the public flys and carriages, the pavements, the botched Market, and many other things, and ask ourselves how these will look in the eyes of travelled men – whether they are as they ought to be in 1864. Let us then no longer live upon a reputation made for us 60 or 80 years ago, and almost if not quite worn out, but let us set about in right earnest to earn one for ourselves worthy of the present day.[30]

As pressure for public health improvements grew, investigations revealed new evidence of inadequate sanitary provisions and water supply. An improvement scheme was duly prepared by the council, but this was rejected by the ratepayers at a stormy meeting in April 1866. The central objection was the estimated cost (£85,000), which alarmed a powerful lobby of wealthy residents of suburban parishes. Most of these residents took their water supply from private companies, and felt that the cost of the scheme would fall most heavily on them, while the immediate benefits would go to the poor inhabitants of the central parishes. This was a perennial conflict. It was invariably difficult to command support from all sections and interest groups for any improvement which was perceived as benefiting only one district or group, but would have to be financed by everyone. In part, this reflected the persistence of a parochial mentality into the age of municipal government, but underlying class conflict was a contributory factor. At the defeat of the 1866 Water Bill, Murch acknowledged the strength of opposition and the clash of interests involved, but still proclaimed his faith in a civic gospel of improvement:

> With all my heart, sir, I trust that future efforts may be made, and that in every respect they may succeed. For I do not abate one jot of the principle with which I started – that no greater duty devolves on those in power than that of seeing the city well supplied with water. And of this who can doubt, that, although Bath may, for reasons seeming good to her, delay the great work, she will ere long do it? She will not let heathen cities in ancient times put her to shame; she will remember what her neighbour Bristol is doing, how Glasgow has gone to Loch Katrine for water, and how London will probably go to the mountains of Wales; she will grumble a little more, and then trusting that her debts will be diminished, and her coffers

replenished, she will enable some future Mayor to boast that every house in the beautiful city over which he reigns – every house even the poorest – has its stream of pure and healthy water.[31]

The impetus to progress remained intact, despite the ratepayers' initial rejection of the scheme. A series of official reports set out the defects, which were seized upon by Samuel Sneade Brown (the self-styled scourge of the council on the sanitary question) for use in his campaign to raise public awareness about the matter. It was given added force with the appointment in 1866 of Bath's first MOH, Dr C. S. Barter, who investigated and reported on the sanitary condition of the city in 1867 and 1868. His findings were published in pamphlet form in 1869, and were a comprehensive indictment of the past neglect of public health. He naturally supported the campaign to increase the water supply, and made the telling point that every individual in Manchester had 'more than ten times the quantity of water which every individual in Bath has'.[32] By 1870, after a decade of discussions, a fairly comprehensive municipal water supply was established in Bath. At the outset, it was recognized that competing interests were involved. The parochial interest was reinforced by differential rating systems, which set district against district. The private water companies, in which some councillors and salaried officials held shares, formed another interest group. The council was sensitive to pressure over the rates from the wealthy burgesses of Lansdown, and to the needs of poorer ratepayers in Larkhall and elsewhere. One councillor urged equal justice for both parties,[33] a worthy sentiment, which did not acknowledge the political reality that with a Liberal-dominated council, the interests of Conservative Lansdown would have to take second place to those of Liberal Larkhall.

The key point about the events and debates from the 1860s to 1870 is the unpredictability of the situation. Council policy was not frustrated by the permanent opposition of a few vested interests. Instead, events were influenced by chance happenings, by individual personalities, and by the volatility of the public mood. It was the shifting alliances among the elected councillors, and the changing perception of the voters in Bath that dictated the rejection of the council water scheme in 1866 and the passing of the Bath Waterworks Act in 1870. The latter was, in effect, a compromise, resulting from the conflicts of the 1860s. The landowner Mr Gore Langton, of Newton St Loe, had employed delaying tactics in 1866 to push up the £7,000 compensation he was offered, but in 1870 he was forced to settle for only £2,500. The wealthy Lansdown lobby had successfully opposed the 1866 plans, but later found to its horror that the purity of supplies from the Charlcombe Water Company were suspect. They then campaigned, even more vociferously, in favour of a municipal water supply. However, the Act of 1870 preserved the vested interests of the private companies (albeit temporarily) and,

25. The eighteenth-century Guildhall with late Victorian extension, one of the monuments to the work of Jerom Murch, seven times mayor of Bath during the Victorian period. (Authors' collection)

ironically, suburban Lansdown was the least well-served part of the city for some time to come. Developments that took place following the 1870 Act enabled virtually all the citizens of Bath to enjoy the benefits of a good water supply. By 1878, 7,712 houses and 50,128 inhabitants were supplied with a daily average approaching 30 gallons per head.[34] The system was still only intermittent, with supplies only available at set times, but a major advance had been accomplished in both the quantity and quality of the water.

The last political achievement of Jerom Murch was to steer through council the project for extensions to the Guildhall in the late nineteenth century. At the end of his distinguished career he received a knighthood. Obituary tributes in the local press following his death in 1895 commented on his influence over the city as a whole and in council, where it was said to have been only rarely resisted, while in the *Bath Year Book* of 1896 it was observed that 'almost every local institution which could claim to exist for the public good had to place on record its grateful recognition of services which he had rendered'.[35] The characteristic language of Victorian civic eulogy should not be allowed to conceal the fact that Murch's enormous contribution to the city could only be piecemeal. It was a heroic failure that fell short of his great municipal vision – the corporation as an engine of social progress.

Murch left a legacy to the city for the purpose of building an art gallery – a venture that he had advocated for many years prior to his death.

Proposals for a gallery revived an ongoing debate over the question of a municipal lending library. The acquisition of cultural civic amenities such as libraries and art galleries gave expression to civic pride in many Victorian cities, but in Bath the matter also encompassed the wider issue of the city's general economic prosperity, with some councillors and others arguing that civic amenities would be a sound investment, adding to the attractions of the city for potential visitors and new residents, while others believed that any rise in the rates would not only antagonise existing ratepayers but also deter prospective incomers. The art gallery was eventually commissioned as a memorial to Queen Victoria's Diamond Jubilee (1897), in conjunction with a reference library to house the Guildhall collection of books of local interest. The total cost was met by the legacies of Murch and Mrs Roxburgh,[36] with additional subscriptions from residents. Many prominent citizens contributed to this form of 'municipal charity', which saved on the rates and gave the wealthy an opportunity to demonstrate their commitment to the civic good by their publicly acknowledged donations.

The spirit of civic union was popularized by leading citizens and clergymen such as the rector of Bath, who asserted in a speech of 1890: 'We are learning to set aside our differences, to throw away the scum of religious dislike, and partizan jealousy and hatred … valuing our fellow citizens only as they live together, in amity and peace, and are fellow labourers in the cause of civic good.'[37] The concept of the civic good was the 1890's successor to the aspirations for a form of political consensus in the 1850s and the civic gospel of the 1860s. The endurance of this kind of political discourse was testimony to the need to overcome the protracted wrangles in the council-chamber and to attempt to reconcile the conflicting interests of all sections of the population beyond the Guildhall.

Thus, as we have seen, beneath the veneer of social harmony in genteel Bath, class and sectional interests remained an enduring feature of municipal politics. Moreover, the contest for power was not confined solely to the hustings or the council-chamber: it was conducted over a wider arena that encompassed other agencies of government, such as boards of guardians and the school board, and to these we now turn.

In the administration of poor relief in Bath during the 1830s Tories and Whigs competed for political influence, with both parties trying to outbid the other as champions of the poor. Conservatives frequently promoted themselves as protectors of the 'deserving' poor, thus appealing to deferential working-class voters and no doubt to many independently minded others, who feared that, in reduced circumstances, their fate would be the workhouse. Liberals were more likely than their opponents to make much of the plight of the 'poor ratepayers', and so justify economies to keep their rates low, thereby maintaining the loyalty of the property-owning working-class constituency. The truly poor, without a vote determined by a property qualification, were merely the pawns in a political game.

The Bath Poor Law Union was established in 1836, with the radical utilitarian, the Revd Thomas Spencer (curate of the nearby parish of Hinton Charterhouse), as its first chairman. Given the nationwide furore over the implementation of the Poor Law Amendment Act of 1834,[38] it is not surprising that the Bath guardians were subject to some animosity, or that, as the election of a new board approached, in the spring of 1837, they sought to defend themselves against accusations of incompetence and harsh administration. Spencer particularly castigated the Tory city magistrates for their 'mischievous meddling':

> There have been perpetual messages from them to the Relieving Offi-
> cer, requesting him to relieve able-bodied men; women with illegitimate
> children; or to give orders for medical relief or for coffins, and in
> cases where the very contrary had been decided by the Board after
> careful enquiry.[39]

The magistrates responded in another pamphlet, which specifically condemned the 'inhumanity' of the guardians. The acrimonious debate continued, and attention focused on a test case for control of Poor Law administration in Bath. This concerned an old woman named Ann Perry, who was housed and fed by a Mary Price, in return for help in the house and with Mrs Price's laundry business in Avon Street. In October 1836, Mary Price applied to the guardians for out-relief on behalf of the increasingly infirm Ann Perry. The guardians offered only admission to the workhouse, but the magistrates subsequently overruled this decision and made an order for out-relief to be granted. The order remained a dead letter while the opposing groups became embroiled in a dispute that dragged on until January 1837. It involved the mayor, the magistrates, and an influential sector of Bath public opinion, in open conflict with Spencer and his supporters on the board of guardians. Eventually, the assistant commissioner was sent down from London to investigate the case. His findings supported the board, but the case culminated in the magistrates pursuing the matter in law, which found in their favour. On 13 January 1837, some three months after applying to the guardians, Ann Perry was awarded out-relief, but within three weeks she died, thus obliging the board by finding for herself an alternative permanent relief from old age, infirmity and poverty. Her case was debated as a matter of principle, clothed in rhetoric about humanity and justice, but it was fundamentally a struggle for control of the patronage and influence that could be exercised through the Poor Law.

The school board was another agency of local government that provided an arena for the contest of competing interests. In the field of elementary education it was religious divisions that superficially overlaid deeper divides. In the 1830s and 1840s religion had been an integral yet divisive factor in politics. Bath was broadly representative of the nation, in that the highest and the lowest social classes tended to be Anglican, with dissenters found chiefly among the middle classes and the upper strata of the working classes. Religious conflict often closely underlined political differences. The preservation of the Anglican Established Church was central to Conservative thinking, and nonconformists looked to the Liberal Party to remove restrictions on their civil rights. These national rivalries were reflected in Bath, where the Established Church was dominant in terms of church provision and numbers of adherents. At the religious census of 1851, the Church of England claimed over 60 per cent of sittings and total attendance in the city, compared with around 33 per cent of sittings and attendance for Protestant dissenters. Overall, religious attendance in Bath was one of the highest in the country, second only to Hastings.[40] Organized religion in Bath was essentially divisive, between Church and Dissent, in interdenominational rivalry between various Protestant sects, and between Protestants and Roman Catholics.

The Anglicans in Bath organized themselves to defend their schools, prior to the council's application to Whitehall in December 1870 for permission to form a school board following the Education Act of 1870.[41] The setting up of school boards was seen as an attack on the voluntary provision of denominational education. An appeal was launched for funds to maintain Church of England elementary schools, and a committee was appointed to meet with leading nonconformists to discuss the composition of the prospective board. It was agreed that a distribution of six Anglican and five nonconformist representatives would 'fairly represent the mind of the city'. A Protestant alliance of Anglicans and nonconformists thus attempted to prevent any Roman Catholic candidate standing for election, which would have denied direct representation to the Roman Catholic community of Bath, which comprised some 1,700 to 2,000 people in the 1870s. In the event, there were eighteen candidates for the eleven seats and an election was therefore inevitable: this took place in January 1871. All residents on the electoral roll were eligible to cast up to eleven votes, distributed in any number among the candidates, a cumulative voting system that was adopted nationally as a means of safeguarding minority interests.

The candidates consisted of three Anglican clergymen, three Protestant nonconformist ministers, one Roman Catholic priest; a barrister and a solicitor; three 'gentlemen' and two 'gentlewomen'; a self-styled professor of English literature; a silk-mercer, one engineer and iron-founder, and a provision merchant. The Working Men's Reform Association backed two radical councillors, an independent gentleman and a provision merchant, one of whom was also supported by the Bath Temperance Society. The results gave the Church of England a majority on the school board, which meant that it was essentially a Conservative body.

By January 1874, when the board's three-year term of office concluded, it had introduced through a local by-law compulsory full-time school attendance for children between the ages of five and thirteen, and made enlargements to some church schools. Its activities had cost the rate-payer little more than 5*d.* (less than 2⅕p) in the pound per annum. At the election of 1874, only two Liberal-sponsored candidates were successful, but both were nonconformists and, moreover, their election strengthened the representation of the trading and commercial classes. Thereafter, the board came increasingly under the influence of the Church Schools Managers' Union, formed at a meeting chaired by the Revd Canon Bernard (chairman of Bath school board) at the Abbey Church rooms in March 1876. The Union was a coordinating body which aimed to protect Anglican education by promoting the return of supporters of church schools to serve on the school board.[42]

Anglicans dominated the board until its demise in 1902, when it was replaced with a Local Education Authority. There was, nevertheless, sustained Liberal and nonconformist hostility to the dominance of the 'Church Party'. Liberal-sponsored candidates did not do well in the election of 1886 (only two of the six were elected), although in that year general opposition to the Established Church seems apparent in the greater social diversity of nominators, who included more tradesmen and craftsmen than previously, and in the surprising success of the independent Roman Catholic candidate, who was not only re-elected but topped the poll. By the 1890s, the organized working classes were campaigning for better educational standards, through the coordinating body of Bath Trades Council which, at the 1892 school board election, supported middle-class Liberal candidates sympathetic to its aspirations. In that year, the chairman of Bath's Liberals, W. C. Jolly, led a sustained attack on the retiring board, accusing it of complacency over truancy levels, castigating it for a negative attitude to higher-grade education for the most able working-class children, and challenging the right of the Church of England to command continually a majority on the strength of its role in elementary education. This opposition, however, was divided and lacked the coherence of the 'church party'. It had no organization comparable to the Church Schools Managers' Union.

A public elementary school place was available for every child in Bath before the end of the nineteenth century. In addition, evening classes and a technical day-school had been established, and the curriculum, although restricted by later standards, had been expanded beyond the 'three Rs' and religious instruction. The board's policies had clearly served the interests of the establishment in maintaining the religious influence of the Church, and they did not fully meet the aspirations of nonconformist parents or the needs of all children. The Roman Catholic community (too small to threaten Anglican dominance, and itself concerned to uphold denominational education) managed to maintain and extend its elementary schools but, well before 1902, the Protestant nonconformist schools of Bath had all closed down. The nonconformists found it difficult to maintain their few schools because of limited financial resources, and hoped that the board would take over their premises. It only did so in a few instances, and it was reluctant to build new schools while places were available in church schools. Many nonconformist parents found themselves forced to send their children to Anglican schools. Moreover, in 1897 only 101 of the 274 pupils at St John's Roman Catholic School, in a poor part of the lower town, were actually Catholics. Non-denominational teaching was available at Bathforum School but this establishment continued to charge fees and it educated chiefly the children of the upper-working and lower-middle classes. The board's reluctance to build schools restricted parental choice and led to a shortage of places in some districts, notably in the growing industrial parish of Lyncombe and Widcombe. The conservative attitude of the board predisposed it towards minimal standards in terms of curriculum and length of schooling, which handicapped Bath children in the labour market, according to the Roman Catholic solicitor Austen King. Chairman of the school board in 1897, King argued that 'a lot of clerks' places were taken by boys from a distance who had the advantage of a longer education than that which was given in the city'.[43] There were parents in Bath who sought non-denominational education for their children, and some who wanted higher standards at elementary level, as well as greater opportunities for secondary education. Their aspirations were not met by the school board, whose primary concerns were to uphold the interests of the Established Church and keep the rates down.

In conclusion, it may be seen that the contrast between image and reality, identified previously in relation to social and economic aspects of the nineteenth-century history of Bath, was also apparent in the broadly defined area of politics during the period 1820 to 1914. The contrast was at its sharpest from 1820 to the late 1840s, but the consensus view of Bath as a conservative backwater from mid-century onward is an over-simplification. Radical politics persisted in the electoral strength of Liberalism through to the end of the century. The notion of social harmony had some reality, but it was promoted as an ideal that served the genteel image of the city as a place apart, free from the blatant class antagonism of some industrial towns. Like the modern notion of Britain as a 'classless society', it was underlain by continuing conflicts of class interests. These were most obvious in terms of municipal politics and the clash of interest groups. Various socio-economic factors made Bath an unlikely place for the development of an aggressive class politics in the 1890s to 1914, but in this it was more representative of Britain as a whole than those few urban centres characterized by extreme radicalism.

Chapter 7

Bath in the Twentieth Century

The pace of change in Bath was slow during the first half of the twentieth century. The city grew only moderately in terms of population and physical size, and the social scene remained much as it had been around the turn of the century. The First World War made some short-term impact, but it was the Second World War that brought lasting change to the occupational structure and, moreover, was a watershed in the history of the city. Thereafter, Bath was caught up in the process of rapid socio-economic change that was at work in the country as a whole. New industries were developed and the service sector expanded considerably, while increased leisure and rising living standards combined with improvements in transport to foster the emergence of an age of mass tourism. By the 1980s Bath was recognized as a centre of international culture, and the value of its architectural heritage was acknowledged by its inclusion in the UNESCO list of world heritage sites. This inevitably sharpened the continuing debate over conservation and development, which reflects the perennial problem of reconciling the needs of the majority of the city's residents with those of wealthy incomers and visitors. Bath continues to draw upon its past to attract the tourists of today, but it remains essentially a small, provincial city of greater complexity than is suggested in the official guides or travel brochures. As in previous centuries, the reality of Bath is both more complex and interesting than its popular image.

The emergence of modern Bath, 1914–1945

The citizens of Bath shared the major experiences of the nation in the years from 1914 onward, as mass society became increasingly homogeneous. As elsewhere, the outbreak of war in 1914 brought an influx of troops to the city and an outflow of recruits to the armed forces, and, as the economy moved on to a war footing, the participation of women in the workforce increased substantially. Following the armistice in 1918 and the return to normality, many women were forced back into the home or into traditional occupations such as domestic service. During the interwar period national concern over high unemployment, poor housing and the standard of health of the mass of the people was reflected in Bath, although conditions in this provincial city were very different from those which characterized such symbols of the age as the depressed shipbuilding town of Jarrow.

The Great War of 1914–18 brought with it a level of state intervention that affected the lives of the mass of the people in unprecedented ways. The introduction of passports restricted freedom of movement, conditions of work were prescribed; the publication of news was restricted; licensing laws were tightened and the strength of beer was reduced; the quality and supply of some foodstuffs was regulated; and – from 1916 – British Summer Time was enforced.[1] In Bath the marching bands and recruiting drives of the first months of war were soon succeeded by troop trains bringing the wounded to Bath Spa station for transfer to local reception centres and hospitals. Some five million men joined the armed forces in the First World War, of which 11,213 came from Bath (out of a population of about 70,000), at least 2,969 of them as volunteers.[2] Approximately 1,000 Bathonians died in the service of their country, and an unknown number were wounded. Even as local volunteers and recruits left the city, there was an influx of troops, including some from Canada and Australia. Fights between 'British Tommies' and colonial troops were commonplace, especially after the pubs closed at night.[3] The casualties of war were nursed at Newton Park House (in Newton St Loe, some three miles from the city centre),[4] in sanatoriums, church halls or other requisitioned buildings, until May 1915, when the Bath War Hospital was opened. Ten 50-bed huts on a cricket pitch at Combe Park made up the hospital, but, as casualty figures rose, its capacity was increased until, by 1918, it could accommodate 1,300 servicemen.[5]

Production for the war effort involved eight local companies, which manufactured munitions, parts for aircraft and submarines, ammunition boxes, and an experimental 'super tank'. With the exception of Bath Aircraft Company, war production was located not in specialized establishments, but in the workshops of engineering firms such as Stothert and Pitt and the Horstmann Gear Company, and those of woodworking concerns like Bath Cabinet Makers. Stothert and Pitt was the largest employer of labour, with a workforce of 1,185 men and 225 women – the firm manufactured about 200,000 of the 205,000 high-explosive shells produced in Bath. The munitions industry as a whole employed 2,128 men and 1,044 women in the city.[6]

The need for female labour to replace men who were joining the forces gave women new opportunities for paid employment, and not only in the armament factories. Bath women also worked as tram conductors, as clerks in recruiting offices and food control centres, as ambulance drivers and nurses.[7] Many others undertook voluntary work for the war effort, in the kitchens and wards of the War Hospital, at convalescent homes, and at the Red Cross 'comforts depôt' in Wood Street. The Needlework Guild ('consisting of ladies' working parties') also made a contribution by producing some 250 articles a day, such as socks, shirts and bandages.[8]

The circumstances of war impinged to some extent on the lives of women of all social classes in Bath, as Louie Stride recalled in her memoirs. Aged seven at the time war broke out, living in squalid poverty with her prostitute mother, Louie noted that, by 1915, 'we were living a bit better ... not quite such hunger'. Her mother 'got very bold and brought men back to the attic, and I would discreetly disappear. It would be soldiers, and of course no shortage of them as Bath had a lot of big houses and schools that were taken over as billets.' One Canadian soldier became a regular caller to the attic, often bringing food from his billet at Prior Park school, and he eventually married Louie's mother. This provided reliable income in the form of 'ring money', the army allowance of 19s.6d. (97½p) for a wife and child, which enabled mother and daughter to move to somewhat better accommodation. By 1917 they were living in the Dolemeads area, where many of the inhabitants were women bringing up children alone. Some, like Mrs Stride, had husbands in the forces, others were war widows, and a few had been 'left in the lurch'. But not all the women of the Dolemeads lived without men:

> [Some] took in soldiers who deserted, usually colonials, Australians were very much in evidence ... one young woman had a very smart Australian hidden there for quite a long time, but she was rounded on, and the military police came and took him one day. She was very upset ... somewhat after she had a baby girl.[9]

Following the armistice in 1918, Bath began to readjust to peacetime conditions, although reminders of the conflict lingered on. For Louie Stride, 'things got worse again' in 1919 when her step-father was 'demobbed' and began to spend much of his weekly pension of £1 on drink. Women found the demand for their labour falling, as men came home from war, and the munitions factories closed down. Convalescent soldiers were still numerous in Bath as late as March 1920, when the Trades and Labour Council organized an entertainment for some 1,000 wounded troops. In that year Armistice Day was marked with ceremonies of commemoration for the dead, and dinners and dances to celebrate the peace. By then, however, the postwar economic boom was faltering, unemployment was rising and labour unrest was becoming widespread in Britain. Indeed, the following decades are often perceived as years of unremitting depression, of high unemployment, associated with poverty and poor standards of health and housing, but this bleak image has masked the reality of the changes from which the affluent consumer society of post-Second World War Britain emerged. The history of Bath in the interwar period is essentially that of a slowly-changing city, which shared in the general improvement in social conditions throughout the country. The city was the most populous urban area in Somerset in 1921, with a total population of 68,669, rising to 68,815 by 1931. The physical size of the city was increased by the construction of 4,242 houses between 1918 and 1938, the majority of which were built by the private sector. The lack of planning controls at the time resulted in some ribbon development on the approach roads to Bath of the type of semi-detached houses typical of 1930's Britain. The city council provided over 1,000 new homes for its working-class residents in the 1920s and 1930s.[10] During these decades many Georgian family houses were subdivided, either into flats (thereby adding to the housing stock) or into offices for doctors, solicitors and other professionals. In addition to housing developments, the city acquired three cinemas, a large cooperative store, a Woolworths, a new post-office and modern electricity offices. Several secondary schools were built in the suburbs, and a new Royal United Hospital was erected at Combe Park on the site of the temporary War Hospital.[11]

While these physical changes, benefiting the mass of Bath's residents, were underway, the city was still promoted as a health resort in the official guides of the 1920s and the 1930s, particularly as an ideal place to spend the winter. The list of treatments available at the baths ran to several pages in the guides, and some hoteliers advertised their willingness to provide special diets for guests coming to take the waters. Visitors' tickets, covering admission to the winter concerts in the Pump Room and charges for drinking the spa water, were available at 'moderate prices'. The wording of advertisements for hotels and guesthouses suggests that comfort, exclusivity and economy were regarded as prime attractions to prospective customers. Miss Gittens, for example, the proprietor of the Westbourne and Grosvenor Hotels, offered excellent cuisine served at 'separate tables', and a gas fire in every bedroom, all at a 'moderate tariff'. It seems, however, that the popularity of Bath was at a low ebb between the wars. Louie Stride, who worked as a chambermaid in Pratts Hotel in the 1930s, remembers:

Visitors for treatment usually came for three weeks and in the winter we had our 'permanents'. These were people who came back every year at a reduced rate usually. Bath was not a tourist attraction like today. The first coach loads of Americans came about 1934–5, I think, and the hotels felt it was humiliating to take such people as 'one nighters', and I remember at the posh Empire Hotel, the coaches had to go around the back at [the] Police Station where [the] Guildhall is now, as it was so demeaning. It soon got common enough, and hotels were glad to welcome them and are now.[12]

26. Pratt's Hotel in South Parade where Louie Stride worked as a maid-servant in the 1930s. (Guildhall Archives, Bath)

There was little by way of public entertainment for the visitor, other than the Pump Room concerts, which were followed by a summer season of band concerts in the city's parks and gardens. The Assembly Rooms were obsolete by 1921, when the ballroom became a cinema and the tearoom was used as a sale room, although in 1931 a Mr Cork purchased the premises and made a gift of them to the National Trust, which undertook a restoration programme, completed in 1938.[13]

Bath did not feature in the list of 148 places in which the population figures were inflated by more than 3 per cent by visitors on census night in June 1921. Nor did the other inland resorts, Cheltenham and Leamington Spa. The largest numbers of visitors recorded were in the popular seaside resorts (places such as Blackpool, Margate and Southend), but the 20 places in England and Wales in which visitors accounted for the highest percentages of resident populations in the 1921 census included such small to medium-sized resorts as Barmouth, Walton-on-the-Naze and Broadstairs.[14] These seaside resorts, specializing in quiet holidays for middle-class families, were attracting more early-season visitors than Bath or its rival spas. The 'Queen of the West' became 'a grime-encrusted … drab place of little charm'[15] by the 1930s, and city directories for the last years of that decade carry few advertisements for hotels. It seems likely that semi-permanent guests had by then become more significant than seasonal visitors to this sector of the local economy. Moreover, a shrinking market was perhaps curtailing opportunities – particularly for entrepreneurial women – to run small enterprises catering largely for visitors. The numbers of men occupied as inn- or hotel-keepers, publicans or beersellers, boarding- or lodging-house keepers, declined only slightly, from 177 in the first category and 74 in the second in 1921, to 164 and 68 respectively in 1931. But the numbers of women thus occupied fell more sharply, from 100 to 58 (inn- or hotel-keepers, publicans and beer-sellers) over the decade, and in the same period the number of female lodging- or boarding-house keepers dropped from 536 to 371. Hotels did provide employment for working-class women, and an opportunity to see how the other half lived. As Louie Stride wrote:

What a revelation it was to me, seeing well educated, and really nice, aristocratic people, and some of course, not so nice! I had some lovely rooms to look after, first floor south, one was the room (or supposed to be) which Sir Walter Scott was in when he lived in South Parade. My clients varied tremendously. Some were very difficult and cranky, so I always had to be very diplomatic, an art I soon learnt. You would soon be out of a job if you were reported for being rude, or maybe the slightest thing, some of them were very autocractic. Several long stayers I remember well. Poor old Miss Hayter, nearly blind and no relatives, or ever any visitors … when she died, the relatives were numerous, came from the ground, I think. Then, next door was Mrs Parry Jones, a very elderly lady … she suffered dreadfully from asthma, and I had to light a saucer of incense, or some such stuff for inhalation every night. Mrs Parry Jones had a glass eye, and I had to poke it out very carefully every night with a hairpin, and put it in a small glass of fluid made special. I shall never forget the feeling almost of horror to see this glass eye in my hand looking at me, [but] one soon got used to it. Also, she used a commode, and always left a 1/- [5p] on top when [she] had been obliged to use it. I must emphasise the fact that none of the rooms had toilets or bathrooms, [there

Table 5   Selected occupations of males and females in Bath, 1921 and 1931

	Males		Females	
	1921	*1931*	*1921*	*1931*
Total population	29,326	29,162	39,343	39,653
Numbers occupied*	19,292	20,125	12,141	12,280
Agriculture, mining and quarrying	1,253	1,050	27	27
Workers in metal	2,058	1,815	19	16
Textiles and dress	685	540	1,867	1,319
Food, drink and tobacco	529	427	134	59
Wood and furniture	1,403	1,221	74	45
Paper, printing, bookbinding and photography	518	622	277	342
Building and construction	906	1,225	—	2
Painters and decorators	665	774	4	20
Transport and communication	2,577	2,558	92	56
Commercial, finance and insurance	2,528	3,148	1,421	1,627
Professional	806	808	1,129	1,182
Entertainment and sport	137	172	50	51
Personal service	980	1,228	5,931	6,147
Clerks, draughtsmen and typists	966	1,226	767	985

* 1921: aged 12 years and over; 1931: aged 14 years and over.

Source: Census (England and Wales) County Reports (Somerset), 1921 and 1931.

were only] two bathrooms and loos on each floor ... All the rooms had coal fires, and jugs and basins, so coal had to be carried, and cans of hot water.[16]

However, Bath was better placed than many other cities when the interwar depression set in. It remained a largely residential city, albeit with something of a tourist trade, but it was also a local and regional shopping centre and had an industrial sector which included engineering, cabinet-making, the manufacture of cloth and articles of dress, printing and bookbinding, and other small often craft-based industries. This sector employed in the aggregate about 10 per cent of the total population.[17] There was no abrupt change in the occupational structure of Bath between the wars, but the overall trend was one of moderate decline in the primary sector (agriculture, mining and quarrying) and also in the secondary manufacturing sector, although as Table 5 shows there was a slight growth of employment in printing and associated trades.

27. Milsom Street looking north in the 1930s. King's and Jolly's offered attractions to discerning customers. (Guildhall Archives, Bath)

Within the category 'Textiles and Dress' the manufacture of cloth was insignificant in comparison to the production of clothing. Weavers and spinners, once commonplace in Bath, had dwindled to fewer than 80 by 1931. The single largest subgroups of occupations for men employed in textiles and dress were the tailoring trades and boot- and shoe-manufacturing, although neither accounted for many more than 200 at either interwar census. The majority of women textile workers were employed in tailoring, dress- and blouse-making, and as corset-makers or machinists. Their numbers fell by more than 500 over the decade. Areas of expansion, offering employment to both men and women, were chiefly in the 'white-collar' service sector. Between 1921 and 1931 the numbers of men and women occupied in commerce, finance and insurance rose by 620 and 206 respectively. Within this broad category, the growth of retailing was significant. The number of salesmen and male shop assistants rose from 830 to 1,018 between 1921 and 1931, while the number of women in this occupational group went up from 1,058 to 1,207. There was also an overall increase in the numbers occupied as clerks, draughtsmen and typists, but the figures set out in Table 5 mask some gender differences in employment. The number of male clerks rose between the census dates from 821 to 970 but the number of

28. Southgate Street in the 1930s. (Guildhall Archives, Bath)

female clerks fell from 748 to 607. Among office workers, female typists (341) were far more numerous than their male counterparts (11) in 1931.

On the whole, the unemployment rate in Britain was lower for women than it was for men (although the labour force was predominantly male), not least because lower wage rates made women more attractive as employees during the depression. Yet, as unemployment mounted, some employers preferred to give work to married men rather than to single women or, particularly, to married women. Indeed, there was a 'marriage bar' in some areas of employment for women. Such choices may explain the fall in the number of female clerks in Bath. Women were certainly excluded rapidly from those male occupations in which they had participated during the First World War, perhaps as a consequence of opposition to their presence by male trade-unionists and the prevailing notion that a woman's place was in the home. By 1921 only six female machine-tool workers and thirteen 'other workers' were employed in the metal industries, and only one woman worked as a tram or omnibus conductor. Within the professions women in Bath remained most numerous in those of lower status, such as nursing and teaching, although by 1931 there were nine women doctors in the city. However, for most of Bath's female labour force domestic service remained the chief occupation. Some part of the increase in total numbers between 1921 and 1931 can be explained by changes in occupational categories,[18] but nonetheless there was an identifiable increase in the number of female

29. Southgate Street looking towards the Old Bridge and Holloway in the 1930s. (Guildhall Archives, Bath)

indoor domestic servants, from 4,239 in 1921 to 4,587 in 1931. Over the same period the number of male indoor domestic servants rose from 195 to 235. Male labourers and unskilled workers also increased in numbers, from 1,205 in 1921 to 1,660 in 1931.

Occupational change in Bath between the wars was broadly similar to the national experience. As the primary sector and secondary manufacturing industries declined somewhat, there was a growth in white-collar occupations. The production of new consumer goods, which created

Table 6 Number of workers registered at Bath employment exchange, 1925–1933

Year	Numbers registered unemployed
1925	1,061
1928	1,143
1929	2,199
1930	2,618
1932	3,000
1933	2,350

Source: *Bath Chronicle*, in Anne Part, 'The development of the school medical service: a case study of Bath 1913–39', unpublished B.Ed. dissertation, Bath College of Higher Education (1980).

many jobs in some parts of southern England, was not a feature of the local economy, but the numbers employed in the building trade increased in the city, as they did in the country as a whole. The building industry was one with a high demand for unskilled labour, but it was subject to seasonal unemployment during the winter months. It may well be that some of Bath's working-class men were forced into this sector, as they were perhaps into domestic service, by the state of the labour market.

In the west country as a whole, unemployment was persistently lower than the national average, although it was locally high in specific occupations, such as coalmining. In Bath itself the available figures suggest that the numbers out of work followed the national trend.

At the census taken in 1931, 2,076 men and 545 women (10.3 per cent of males and 4.4 per cent of females in the total occupied population) were out of work, and the number of unemployed rose to 3,000 in the following year. No figures for the later 1930s have been located, but job opportunities were by then increasing in the area covered by the Bath and District Local Employment Committee. In the mid-1930s the Mendip quarries were taking on labour to meet the growing demand for road stone, and in 1937 some 150 unemployed men were engaged to lay a gas main from Bath to Frome.[19] Moreover, the threat of war led to the creation of new jobs at an arms factory established at Corsham (Wiltshire), and in several other 'government undertakings' set up within travelling distance of the city. From at least 1937, Bath was attracting labour from areas of high unemployment in northern England and South Wales.[20] The growth of motor traffic in the 1920s and 1930s was a contributory factor to unquantifiable but significant changes in employment patterns. The proliferation of private transport (bicycles, motorbikes and cars), and of public bus services and 'works' transport, extended the geographical labour market, and thereby fostered the trend towards commuting to a workplace often far removed from home. Bath was no 'dormitory town' but, nonetheless, as the local historian Bryan Little has suggested, between the wars an increasing number of its residents found work in the new industries, offices and factories of Bristol, some thirteen miles away.[21]

Bath was clearly not an unemployment blackspot but, with more than 10 per cent of its male labour force out of work in the early 1930s, it has a place in the ongoing debate over the links between unemployment and ill health. Moreover, as a provincial city in a period of economic transition, changes in the health standards of its population and the housing conditions of its working classes are integral to the wider debate about the quality of life in interwar Britain. For those without work, living on the dole entailed relative deprivation, if not absolute poverty, but the Medical Officer of Health (MOH) found no evidence of ill health as a direct consequence of unemployment in Bath. In his report for 1934 he stated: 'I am not aware of any definite evidence that the health and physique of the unemployed and their families differ significantly from that of the community as a whole.'[22] Nonetheless, a declining trend in the incidence of pulmonary tuberculosis among the child population of Bath in the period 1920–39 was sharply disrupted by a steep rise in the years 1930 to 1934, when the number of cases notified to the authorities amounted to 13 per cent of the total school population of 7,500.[23] This disease is closely associated with poverty and overcrowding, and it seems unlikely that it was entirely coincidental that more children were affected by it in the very years when the economic depression was at its deepest.

Yet in most respects the health and condition of schoolchildren in Bath had improved significantly by the end of the 1930s. No single factor can account for rising standards, but better housing, higher average family earnings, changes in diet, the fall in average family size and the wider role of both national and local government in caring for the nation's children all made some contribution. The development of the school meals service is one example of the increasing role of the state, although in Bath it had its origins in a voluntary scheme set up in 1904. It was introduced nationally by legislation in 1906 and thereafter expanded under various Acts of Parliament. By 1939 the school medical and dental service was also well established in the city, and in addition there were special schools for handicapped children, a child guidance clinic, and a juvenile employment committee. The average height and weight of Bath schoolchildren aged twelve, measured over a 30-year period from 1909–39, showed increases similar to those identified in York by B. S. Rowntree.[24] This evidence of improved diet was accompanied by other changes for the better. Epidemic disease was still a life-threatening risk, but the general trend was one of decline in cases of scarlet fever, measles and diphtheria. The crippling disease of rickets (caused primarily by a lack of calcium in the diet) became less common, combated in part by the provision of cheap 'school milk'. The incidence of flea-bitten bodies, lice-infested heads, of scabies, ringworm and impetigo all diminished as standards of cleanliness and children's ability to resist infection rose. Whereas the overwhelming majority of children inspected by the school medical service in 1907 were officially classified as 'dirty', in 1939 only 30 children in every 1,000 were thus designated.

The health standards of the total population of Bath also improved over time. The standard death rate per 1,000 in 1925 was 10.5 for Bath, when for England and Wales it was 12.2. This was virtually unchanged in 1939, at a rate of 10.7 for Bath and 12.1 for England and Wales. The main causes of death were heart disease and cancer, afflictions chiefly of middle life and old age. The birth rate in Bath, however, was also proportionally low, at 14.0 compared with 18.3 for England and Wales in 1925, falling to 13.8 and 15.0 respectively by 1939. The infant mortality rate in the city (i.e. the number of deaths under one year per 1,000 births) had been 126 in 1900 but by 1925 it had fallen to 51.[25] It continued to decline thereafter, although in 1939 it rose to 57, for which the MOH could offer no explanation, but he suggested that one contributory factor might have been the state of health of incomers to Bath from the distressed areas. The success of the local medical authority in reducing the death rate of children aged one to five years was recognized by the *Daily News* which, in 1925, awarded a prize of £25 to Bath. In 1928 the same newspaper gave the city £10, the second of several prizes awarded to local authorities showing the greatest reduction in infant mortality in 1927.[26] These monies were spent on maternity and infant welfare services.

In his report for 1939, the MOH commented that the standard of health of Bath's population had improved more than he would have thought possible when he first took up his appointment twenty years earlier. Writing some six years later, however, he stated that 'the most poignant of all the problems' that he had dealt with in his career were related to the housing of the working classes.[27] His belief that a shortage of suitable housing 'is by far the greatest of all the causes which tend to undermine the health of the people' was reiterated in his annual reports from 1919 to 1939. Yet, as Dr Blackett acknowledged, the local housing problem was not comparable to that of many other urban districts. Housing conditions in Bath were better than those in the country as a whole and, moreover, they improved during the interwar period.[28] The percentage of the population of England and Wales living in overcrowded conditions at the census of 1911 was 9.1 (in Leeds it was 11 per cent, in Finsbury 39.8 per cent); in Bath, in 1919, 2,846 people, or 4 per cent of the population, were housed in overcrowded dwellings.[29]

During 1920 and 1921, some 250 houses in the city were classified as unfit for human habitation and a further 979 were considered to be 'seriously defective'. Between the wars, however, as noted earlier, the local authority provided over 1,000 new homes in council houses or flats. The first interwar council estate, at Englishcombe Park, was developed in 1920. Council estates were also built at Rudmore Park, Larkhall and Southdown during the 1920s. The largest housing project was undertaken at Odd Down, where the Fosseway estate was developed in 1930 and 1931.[30] Further council initiatives were blocked by the decision of the National Government in 1933 to abolish all subsidies on housing, with the exception of slum-clearance programmes. Pockets of slum housing in the Avon Street district and in the Dolemeads were thereafter cleared and redeveloped, with workers' flats being erected at Kingsmead and some council houses being built in the Dolemeads. The provision of adequate mass housing was crucial to improving the social and living conditions of the bulk of the population in the interwar period, but in Bath, as elsewhere, the building of council houses in the 1920s and 1930s did not completely eliminate the problem. Overcrowding in parts of the inner city was still a major concern of the MOH in 1939, as it had been in 1919. Moreover, 'the difficulties of the housing situation' in the city were exacerbated by the influx of men (and their families, in many cases) attracted to nearby munitions factories from 1937 onward. In the closing months of 1939, following the outbreak of the Second World War, there was another and very rapid inflow of population to Bath, which added to the existing problems.[31] Before moving on to consider the conflict of 1939–45 in relation to the city, we turn to the labour movement and the voting behaviour of the electorate in interwar Bath. During that period the local experience was an integral part of national events, and of the process of political change that accompanied socio-economic change in the country as a whole.

The labour movement in Bath, as elsewhere, was in confident mood for a brief time when the First World War ended. There was some degree of organization in all of the city's main trades and industries, and a Trades and Labour Council representing skilled and unskilled workers was formed locally in 1893.[32] In 1918 a Labour candidate stood for a parliamentary election in Bath for the first time. By then the Labour Party had become truly national, with a new constitution that made provision for individual membership. Its electoral chances had been improved by further extensions to the franchise under the Representation of the People Act (1918), which gave the vote to all men over 21 and women over 30. (Women gained the franchise at age 21 under further legislation in 1928.) At the 1918 election, the sitting Conservative-Coalition member was returned with a majority of over 10,000 in a total poll of 20,849, but A. J. Bethell gained for Labour just over a quarter (25.2 per cent) of votes cast.

The confidence of Labour in 1918, however, was soon eroded. The early 1920s were a time when working people in general were subject to rising unemployment, falling wage rates, and determined attempts by employers and governments to reduce wages further as a means of improving the competitiveness of British industry. It was within this context that the labour unrest of the 1920s took place, culminating in the General Strike of 1926. Locally, in 1920, a wages dispute at Bath Cabinet Works quickly developed into a lockout (lasting several weeks from late July), which culminated in a return to work on the employer's terms. The Sawclose was the setting for several labour demonstrations in 1920, including a mass rally on May Day and a public meeting in August of that year in support of the miners' demand for nationalization of the coal industry. Contacts with the Somerset Miners' Association (SMA) undoubtedly heightened awareness in the city of conditions in the mining districts, and the association was supported by trade-unionists in Bath during a major industrial dispute in 1921 and again in 1926, when the conflict between coal-owners and miners engulfed the wider labour movement in the General Strike.

Between 3 and 12 May 1926, 2,300 Bath workers from nineteen unions (including two that were not affiliated to the Trades and Labour Council) participated in the national strike. It made relatively little impact on the city, however, and despite its revolutionary undertones (much exaggerated by right-wing politicians and commentators), it did not provoke blatant class hostility in Bath. Gas and electricity workers took no part in the action, and 1,000 volunteers enlisted at the Guildhall to offer their services to the authorities. Essential supplies were maintained, the *Bath Chronicle* published as usual (after bringing out an emergency one-page edition on 4 May), the railways continued to run a 'skeleton' timetable, and the press reported that the number of visitors to the city had been reduced by no more than 10 per cent of the average figure for early May. Allegations of violent intimidation against a volunteer bus driver, and two subsequent arrests, were made in a *Sunday Observer* report, but the incident was grossly exaggerated. There were no arrests during the dispute in Bath, where, as James Tarrant (secretary of the Council of Action and of the Trades and Labour Council) told the press, leaders and strikers had 'done everything to ensure that we should not cause trouble to our friends in blue'.[33] Moreover, mass meetings at the Sawclose, an open space opposite the Theatre Royal, were addressed by the Liberal alderman Cedric Chivers, mayor of Bath in 1926. The owner of a printing firm, Chivers was a major employer in the city and for many years the municipal representative of the working-class ward of Twerton. Yet conciliatory attitudes were not shared by all those involved. The Bath Electric Tramways company issued an ultimatum to its striking workers to return by noon on 8 May. The manager announced that volunteer labour would be used thereafter and that any man not reporting for work would no longer be guaranteed his job. In the aftermath of the dispute, the Tramways management insisted that employees returning to work and new recruits should sign a 'non-union' undertaking. As for the miners, they remained in dispute until the end of the year, during which time the Bath Trades Council organized numerous fund-raising events, the proceeds of which were divided 50:50 between the nationwide Miners' Distress Fund and a local relief committee set up by the SMA.[34]

In spite of the collapse of the General Strike, the labour movement in Bath retained its cohesiveness. The Cooperative Societies were first established in Bath in 1888, at Twerton, and by 1894 in the central part of the city. After the First World War they continued to expand with several additional local shops, a city-centre department store, and the formation of branches of the Cooperative Women's Guild in Widcombe, Oldfield Park and other areas. Although there was a trend towards the amalgamation of small unions into larger organizations between the wars, the Trades Council was not affected by this in terms of the number of unions affiliated to it – which was 28 in 1918 and 29 by 1930.[35] There were also attempts to organize the unemployed, which came mainly from unofficial bodies, notably the National Unemployed Workers Movement (founded in 1921 and not disbanded until after the outbreak of the Second World War). Concern over the threat of 'entryism' from the Communist Party deterred the official labour movement from actively responding to the problems of the unemployed until the early 1930s, when the General Council of the TUC decided that some leadership should be provided for those out of work, and it recommended Trades Councils as the most appropriate bodies to undertake the task. The Bath Trades Council seems to have followed up this recommendation. By the mid-1930s a Bath Unemployed Association (affiliated to the Trades Council and on occasions castigated as 'extremist' in the local press) was in existence, although there is no evidence to show the size of its membership.[36]

The Trades Council and Bath Labour Party shared premises known as the 'Labour Rooms', in the Green Park district, but it seems that the two organizations functioned as distinctly 'industrial' and 'political' parts of the labour movement. The Trades Council minute books for the interwar period indicate that it focused its attention on trade-union matters, but by 1932 Labour Party activists were concerned that 'the forces of the Labour Party and the Trades Council have not been put to the best uses'. In September of that year the party suggested a joint meeting of executive committees 'to discuss what methods may be adopted to further the interests of the Trade Unions and the Labour Party in Bath',[37] as a result of which the two groups became formally affiliated. Labour was clearly an established presence in the city, although a lack of evidence precludes a detailed analysis of its growth.

General election results show that some degree of political change was underway in Bath. Such change was a significant feature of the history of interwar Britain. The Conservatives (as such, or in the National Government after 1931) were in power for most of the period, but in the 1920s and early 1930s their strength had been seriously challenged by Labour, as the Liberal Party went into decline. Following the general election of December 1923, Labour formed its first government (a minority one, supported by Liberal MPs) early in 1924, but less than ten months later it was out of office. The election of May 1929 returned Labour to power, but mounting economic problems following the Wall Street crash led to the collapse of this second Labour administration, and the formation of a National Government with Ramsay MacDonald as Prime Minister.

In Bath the electorate favoured the Conservatives, but the Liberal vote held up and Labour attracted only minority support. It came bottom of the poll at every election it fought after the contest between Lloyd George's Coalition forces and Labour in 1918.

No Labour candidate stood for the 1923 election, perhaps as a tactic to avoid splitting the anti-Conservative vote. Given its social and occupational structure, Bath was never likely to be a stronghold for Labour, but its core support was not seriously eroded, even by the ignominious fall of the second Labour government and Ramsay MacDonald's 'betrayal' in joining the coalition National Government. The local consequence of these events was a substantial increase in electoral support for the Conservatives, but the Labour vote recovered to just under 20 per cent of the total in 1935 (see Table 7). The strength of Liberalism, however, had persisted longer in Bath than in Britain as a whole, and it was not until the post-Second World War years that Labour became the main challenger to Conservative dominance in parliamentary politics in the city. One local factor contributing to Labour's popularity in post-1935 elections may well have been the presence of men and women from South Wales and the north of England, those workers from the distressed areas who settled in Bath from 1937 onward. They arrived in sufficient numbers to 'make a significant modification in the general character of the working-class population of the city'[38] and originated from parts of the country with well-established traditions of working-class support for Labour.

The newcomers to Bath were followed by a further substantial influx of population which occurred over a short period at the beginning of September 1939, as war once again engulfed the nation. Bath was a designated 'receiving area' for evacuees, and during the first four days of the month over 4,000 people of all ages arrived by special trains, most of them from London's East End working-class communities.[39] Some were sent on to nearby towns and villages, but 2,296 (including about 1,700 schoolchildren) were billeted in Bath.[40] It has been estimated that

Table 7   General election results, Bath, 1918–1935

Election	Electors	Turnout (%)	Candidate	Party	Votes	%
1918	31,512	66.2	C. J. Foxcroft	C/Con	15,605	74.8
			A. J. Bethell	Lab	5,244	25.2
1922	33,023	82.4	C. T. Foxcroft	Con	13,666	50.2
			E. H. Spender	Lib	8,699	32.0
			H. H. Elvin	Lab	4,849	17.8
1923	33,520	79.1	F. W. Raffety	Lib	13,694	51.6
			C. J. Foxcroft	Con	12,830	48.4
1924	43,042	84.5	C. J. Foxcroft	Con	16,067	55.8
			F. W. Raffety	Lib	8,800	30.6
			W. B. Scobell	Lab	3,914	13.6
1929*	35,373	70.1	Hon C. W. Baille-Hamilton	Con	11,171	45.0
			S. R. Daniels	Lib	7,255	29.3
			G. G. Desmond	Lab	6,359	25.7
1929	46,877	81.3	Hon C. W. Baille-Hamilton	Con	17,845	46.9
			S. R. Daniels	Lib	11,486	30.1
			G. G. Desmond	Lab	8,769	23.0
1931	47,932	80.6	T. L. E. B. Guinness	Con	24,696	64.0
			S. R. Daniels	Lib	8,241	21.3
			G. G. Desmond	Lab	5,680	14.7
1935	49,022	74.5	T. L. E. B. Guinness	Con	20,670	56.6
			S. R. Daniels	Lib	8,650	23.7
			G. G. Desmond	Lab	7,185	19.7

* By-election, 21 March, as a result of the death of Foxcroft.

Source: F. W. S. Craig, *British Parliamentary Election Results 1918–1949* (Surrey: 1969; 3rd edn, 1983).

between the beginning of September and the end of December 1939 the resident population of Bath rose by some 10,000, and mid-year estimates during the war show that the city's civilian population reached a peak of 83,000 in 1942.[41] Official evacuees were, however, only a small part of those who came to the city as a direct result of the war. A large number of private individuals who could afford to move to what was perceived to be a place of relative safety also sought accommodation in Bath. Their presence made it a target for sustained criticism in some sections of the national press, as a 'city of old crocks' living out the war in complacent

30. The bombing of the Francis Hotel in Queen Square during the Bath blitz,
April 1942. (Guildhall Archives, Bath)

comfort.[42] Such attacks largely ignored the fact that several government
departments and their staffs had been moved to south-west England,
and that Bath had been virtually taken over by the Admiralty. The Pump
Room, the Pulteney, the Spa and the Empire Hotels were all requisitioned, together with many schools, colleges and other large buildings.
Temporary accommodation was erected at Foxhill to house some per-
sonnel, but the main offices of the Admiralty were in central locations.

The arrival of the Admiralty probably enlivened the social life of war-
time Bath, for, as one writer has commented, 'uniformed naval officers
paced her streets as they had not done since the days of Nelson'.[43]
However, they numbered several thousands and added to the pressure
on housing. Moreover, their presence was no protection to the city, and
any idea that Bath was exempt from the impact of total war vanished in
the Baedeker bombing raids of April 1942, which reduced the recently
restored Assembly Rooms to a pile of rubble.[44] Churches, chapels, and
Georgian buildings in Queen Square, the Royal Crescent and the Circus
were flattened or structurally damaged. The working-class residential
areas of Kingsmead, Twerton and Oldfield were also hit. At least 400
people were killed and as many more seriously injured. Some 19,147
buildings were damaged. Out of a total of fewer than 20,000 houses, 1,000
were virtually destroyed and nearly 4,000 more were badly damaged.[45]

As before, war ushered in occupational change. In addition to the
armaments factories established nearby in the late 1930s, some of Bath's

31. The bomb damage in Kingsmead Street during the Bath blitz, April 1942. (Guildhall Archives, Bath)

industries were later converted to the production of war materials. The engineering firm of Stothert and Pitt (which chiefly manufactured components for tanks) was the key firm involved during 1939–1945, as it had been in the First World War. Munitions workers from Corsham in Wiltshire were organized by the Amalgamated Engineering Union, and the branch was represented at the Trades and Labour Council by four delegates, which suggests a substantial labour force and a high rate of union membership. Similarly, by the period 1941–2, the Fire Brigades' Union had eight representatives listed on the Trades Council delegates roll. The affiliation of the Association of Engineering and Shipbuilding Draughtsmen to the Council in September 1942 can be accounted for by the presence of the Admiralty.[46] This marked a lasting change in the occupational structure, for when the war ended in 1945 central government decided that the Admiralty department should stay on in Bath. Some forty years later the Ministry of Defence was the largest single employer in the city, with a workforce of just over 5,600.[47]

Change and continuity in postwar Bath: 1945 to the 1980s

Bath was caught up in the rapid and extensive changes that affected all aspects of life in Britain in the decades after 1945, but continuity with some aspects of its past was also a feature of the recent history of the city.[48] National trends were reflected at local level in the structure of the population and in overall patterns of employment, for instance. Yet, viewed within an historical context, it is apparent that well-established traditional features of Bath in earlier times have had some influence on the processes of socio-economic change.

In Bath, as elsewhere, the 1950s and 1960s were decades of confidence in the future, based on the expectation of continuous economic growth and full employment. It was then anticipated that the city would expand to a population of some 100,000 by the mid-1980s, and most local employers assumed that their workforces would also rise over the same period. By the 1970s, however, attitudes and economic circumstances where changing. Plans for the minimal growth of Bath were in place by the end of that decade, and the ideal of full employment seemed an increasingly unrealistic dream. The boom years of the 1980s witnessed considerable investment in retail and office property in the city, but the later recession brought with it a rise in unemployment. The tourist trade has remained of importance to Bath's prosperity, but the vitality of this sector is dependent on factors other than the efforts of the council to maintain the character of the city and to capitalize on its assets. These efforts range from attention to such details as the sort of shop frontages and types of advertising that retailers may use, to imaginative ventures such as the Bath Film Office, which provides a range of media production services that have been used by many well-known companies over the years. Nonetheless, however effectively the city is promoted, the state of the national and international economy is bound to affect the tourist trade in Bath.

The population of the city in mid-1945 was estimated at 76,000 and thereafter it rose over thirty years to reach more than 84,500 in 1971. However, in the following decade it fell to just under the level of twenty years earlier (see Table 8).

Table 8   Population of Bath, 1951–1981

Census	Total population
1951	79,294
1961	80,901
1971	84,670
1981	80,771

Sources: Census (England and Wales) County Reports (Somerset), 1951 and 1961; The City Plan, mid-stage report, Bath City Council, November 1982, p. 17.

Most of the increase to 1971 can be accounted for by the in-migration of new residents, although boundary changes in the mid-1960s brought the whole of Combe Down within the city limits, as well as an area extending almost to the village of Batheaston. Falling numbers over the decade to 1981 were attributable mainly to a movement of population out of the city, which may have been caused in part by a sharp decline in house building within the borough from around the mid-1970s. With a minimal growth policy in place from 1978, it is likely that Bath will remain for the foreseeable future a small city, with a population in the 80–85,000 range.

Despite its sometime image as 'a city of old crocks', in the immediate postwar years Bath did not have an exceptionally high proportion of residents aged 65 and over. In census reports from 1951 the seaside resorts of Clevedon, Weston-super-Mare and Minehead were identified as the urban districts of Somerset with the most elderly populations. The demographic profile of modern Bath does not differ significantly from that of the total UK population: women outnumber men because of their longer life expectancy, and a rising life expectancy for both sexes (coupled with a falling birth rate) explains the fact that the population as a whole is an ageing one. However, Bath's popularity as a place for retirement seems to have persisted: in 1981 people aged 60-plus made up 22.6 per cent of the population, compared with 18.4 per cent and 17.7 per cent in that category within the County of Avon and Great Britain respectively. The contemporary function of the city as a medical centre, and a proliferation of private residential nursing homes, have perhaps added to Bath's attraction for the elderly. Another change, more clearly in line with national trends, is that as average family and household sizes have fallen, the actual number of households has increased, because more people are living on their own.

Structural changes in UK employment patterns since the war are also reflected in Bath. The primary and secondary manufacturing sectors have declined, and service industries have come to dominate the national economy. Employment in the manufacturing industries of Bath was increasing by almost 3 per cent per annum during the late 1950s and 1960s, while postwar reconstruction and development ensured that the local construction industry remained buoyant. The building of the University of Bath on a greenfield site at Claverton Down was one major project that provided many skilled and unskilled manual jobs for several years from the late 1960s into the early 1970s.

Growth in the manufacturing sector centred on the traditional industries of Bath. The Horstmann Gear Company and Bath Cabinet Makers were representative of established firms that expanded old premises or built new ones, and the shoemakers Clarks of Street opened a factory in Bath.[49] In the early 1970s engineering accounted for 5,000 jobs; 2,000 workers were employed in printing and publishing, and a further 800

Table 9   Industrial characteristics of employment in the 1970s

| | Bath | | | | Great Britain | |
| | 1971 | | 1978 | | 1971 | 1978 |
Industry	No.	%	No.	%	%	%
Primary	*412	0.9	279	0.63	4.32	3.25
Manufacturing	7,745	18.6	7,245	16.42	34.12	31.98
Construction	2,780	6.7	2,516	5.17	7.12	5.50
Service	30,686	73.8	34,058	77.20	53.64	59.26

* Agriculture, forestry and fishing, mining and quarrying.

Source: The City Plan, mid-stage report, Bath City Council, November 1982.

were occupied in the manufacture of clothing. Mechanical engineering accounted for the largest number of workers in the manufacturing sector of the early 1980s (5.9 per cent of the total), most of them employed by Stothert and Pitt, a company whose origins could be traced back to an eighteenth-century iron-foundry. The scale of industry in modern Bath remained relatively small: over half of the manufacturing firms employed fewer than ten people. During the 1980s some 'high-tech' companies were attracted to the city's industrial estates, but the data set out in Table 9 is indicative of long-term trends in local employment. As early as 1965, service employment in the city predominated over manufacturing by a ratio of 3:1. At the beginning of the 1980s almost 78 per cent of employees worked in the service sector.

Within the service category the two most important occupational orders were professional and scientific services, and public administration and defence. These subgroups accounted respectively for 22.7 per cent and 17 per cent of employment in services. Growth in these areas reflected both postwar change and some continuity with the past. Once the 'Hospital of the Nation', modern Bath had become a medical centre. The Royal United Hospital complex at Combe Park provided 2,400 jobs in 1980, while the District Health Authority employed 4,000 people in the city. In addition, there were several other NHS (later 'Trust') hospitals in Bath, as well as numerous private nursing homes and the Bath Clinic. The expansion of higher education, particularly since the 1960s, gave the city a new role as an education centre. The presence of the University of Bath and Bath College of Higher Education made some impact on the locality beyond the occupational structure.

The influx of a student population of several thousands intensified the competition for scarce and increasingly expensive rented accommodation. It also created a demand for more 'youth-orientated' entertainment.

As with higher education, public administration became a growth area as a result of central government policies, associated with the expanding role of the state in postwar Britain. However, from the late 1970s government endeavours were made to 'roll back' the public sector, and in a council report of the early 1980s it was noted that privatization policies might ultimately lead to a fall in local employment in public administration. The continued presence of the Ministry of Defence was also uncertain by the end of the 1980s. The MOD moved out of the Empire Hotel after almost fifty years, in 1988, but it remained the largest single employer in the city, with a workforce of over 5,000. Relocation of some or all of the Bath labour force was under review thereafter. The likely consequences caused concern about direct job losses, and the possible knock-on effect on the hotel trade, the housing market, and the retail sector. Moreover, the MOD had made a vital contribution to Bath's prosperity by attracting defence-related companies to the city.

A persistently important strand in the economy has been retailing. This too was subject to radical change from the 1950s, when small shops owned by independent traders were commonplace and there were few department or chain stores in the city. The trend moved towards larger shops, staffed by fewer employees, as self-service or 'cash and wrap' replaced old-style selling, and multiple chain stores increasingly replaced independent traders in many British towns. In Bath the distributive trades accounted for 13.4 per cent of all employment around 1980. The Southgate shopping area in the lower town was developed as part of the postwar reconstruction programme, but by the late 1980s the northern part of the city centre was becoming the prime shopping area. There was considerable investment in the retail sector during that decade. Green Park Station, which had stood empty and increasingly derelict for many years, was redeveloped by Sainsburys, in a scheme that incorporated meeting rooms, offices, small retail units and extensive car parking, as well as the superstore itself, which opened in 1983. The Colonnades shopping mall (on Bath Street) was completed in 1986, and the Podium (linking New Bond Street to Pulteney Bridge) was developed between 1987 and the early 1990s. Smaller developments were also undertaken, at Abbey Gate Street, Upper Borough Walls and elsewhere. Modern Bath had become a regional shopping centre for a population of over 300,000, in a catchment area extending to Stroud (Gloucestershire) in the north and including much of west Wiltshire. Visitors to the city, however, continued to make a significant contribution to the prosperity of retailers: it was estimated in 1986 that 50 per cent of the total annual influx into Bath of some 3 million tourists used the shopping facilities.[50]

Bath today has its share of familiar chain stores, such as Boots, Marks and Spencer, W. H. Smith and McDonald's, and high-quality retailers like Habitat, Laura Ashley and Liberty, but it did not become an 'anywhere town' of the 1980s. The central shopping area retained much of its character. Large out-of-town shopping centres were not developed, in part because of the city and county authorities' policies aimed at maintaining the dominance of central Bath. Another factor was the lack of sites sufficiently large to be considered suitable, except on land designated for industrial purposes. Moreover, small traders remained relatively numerous in Bath. In among the premises of multiple stores, the wine bars and gift shops, there could be found greengrocers, newsagents, bakeries, specialist booksellers, antique dealers, snuff- and tobacco-sellers. Some 50 per cent of those employed in retailing worked in small shop businesses. Independent traders, however, were under pressure from high rents and business rates during the recession of the later 1980s, and, as trade declined, many were forced out of business.

The recession also made a wider impact on the local level of unemployment, but modern Bath and the surrounding region remained one of the relatively prosperous areas of the country. The unemployment rate remained low until the mid-1970s, and, although a steady upward trend developed thereafter, the rise was at a slower rate than that in County Avon or Great Britain as a whole. The ratio of numbers registered as unemployed to job vacancies in 1981 (when 8.7 per cent of the occupied population was out of work) was particularly high for unskilled manual workers and for skilled men such as carpenters, electricians, bricklayers, and machine-tool setters. This was not unique to Bath. As the primary and secondary manufacturing sectors declined nationally, there was a falling demand for labour based on muscular strength and for the skills of craftsmen-artisans, trained in their work through traditional apprenticeships. Nonetheless, it was the policy of the local authorities to retain manufacturing and a varied economy although, as in the past, prosperity was regarded as inextricably linked to dependence on visitors to the city. It was argued by those who administered Bath that the tourist trade generated trade and employment in businesses other than those directly serving the needs of the visitors. The transport and service industries and the manufacturing sector were said to benefit indirectly from tourism. Moreover, the ability to maintain and develop services for the benefit of the city's resident population was also considered to be dependent on the tourist industry, and on the prosperity of the shops in the city.

It was pointed out in the City Plan report of 1982 that Bath was perhaps unique among local authorities, in that less than 10 per cent of its gross rate expenditure was actually met from the rates. Bath ratepayers enjoyed almost the lowest district rate in the entire country. The city attracted a high level of rate support grant from central government at that time, but it also benefited from events in its past, and the policies of earlier custodians of its heritage. It will be recalled that after the dissolution of the monasteries in the sixteenth century, lands and property were transferred to the corporation. As owners of virtually all of the walled city, the eighteenth-century corporation shrewdly retained its chief assets, and the freehold of land developed as Bath became the resort of fashion. Consequently, the city of the 1980s derived considerable income from council-owned tourist attractions such as the Pump Room and the Roman Baths, as well as from modern facilities such as car parks and leisure centres. The city's investment estate as a whole contributed the equivalent of a 9.45p rate to the council in 1982–3, about 60 per cent of which derived from commercial rents on shop property in the central area.

Tourism, widely regarded as the mainstay of Bath's prosperity, directly employed only an estimated 14 per cent of the working population in 1980. Nonetheless, successive councils in the postwar era placed great emphasis on the benefits of tourism in terms of trade and business. The Roman Baths, the Pump Room, and the delights of shopping in Bath were promoted as vigorously as they had been in guide books of the nineteenth century, but the function of the city as a spa, on which it built its reputation, has been – somewhat surprisingly – in abeyance for many years, after temporary closure in the late 1970s. The council retained ownership of the spa after legislation in the late 1940s created the National Health Service, but it became little more than an outpatient department of the old Mineral Water Hospital. Interest in the hot springs as a unique asset revived over the years, and a development plan issued in 1966 included proposals for improvements to the spa, with a more commercial approach to the waters. It seemed likely then that the spa might again became one of the major tourist attractions. But within ten years, Bath ceased to be a spa at all: the waters were turned off in December 1976 for an investigation into their purity and for repairs to a leaking conduit in Stall Street. Within months of the repairs being completed in 1978, an amoebic contamination was discovered in the waters. Bath without its spa was unthinkable to some people, and letters to the press and complaints to the council soon followed.[51] Following this, for more than fifteen years, while hydrotherapy treatments were carried on with heated tap water in place of that from Bladud's healing springs, the future of the spa was a recurring theme in local debate about the development of Bath. Research undertaken in that period led to a greater understanding of the hot spring and its waters, and long-term development plans envisage the city becoming a spa resort of fame equal to its reputation in centuries past.

Whether or not the sick in search of cure will come to be a part of the modern tourist trade remains to be seen, but some visitors of the late twentieth century have been attracted by other traditional features of

Bath. A survey of their intentions taken in the winter of 1981–2 revealed that most of those interviewed were particularly interested in shopping. Over 50 per cent of participants intended to 'enjoy the shops', compared with just under 22 per cent who looked forward to enjoying the renowned architecture and general sightseeing. This suggests that the authorities were justified in emphasizing the economic links between the tourist and retailing sectors. The modern visitor, however, was increasingly likely to be a 'day-tripper' rather than a long-stay holiday-maker. Bath has become ever more accessible from London (107 miles to the east), the Midlands and South Wales. Indeed, the city of today is easily reached from all parts of Britain: by intercity rail service it is only 80 minutes journey time from London, and it is located on the M4 corridor, while also being within a relatively short distance of the M5. It was estimated that between August 1972 and July 1973 some 340,000 day-trippers visited Bath, arriving chiefly by coach or train.[52] In addition, the demand for holiday accommodation or 'bed spaces' rose over the decade from 1971 and 1981, and persuading visitors to stay longer (to the ulti-mate benefit of the residents) was a key part of the City Plan, prepared in the early 1980s to determine policies over the following ten years.

The modern city remained best known for its image as a tourist cen-tre, and the visitor of the 1980s could be forgiven if he or she made the same assumptions as many of those who came to Bath in the eighteenth and nineteenth centuries. The long-established tradition of Bath as a place without general trade or industry, entirely dependent on serving the needs of the visitors, was perhaps perpetuated by the layout of the city and the concentration on the interests of the tourists. In the 1980s the industrial manufacturing strand employed 20 per cent of the total working population, but modern industry was located in the western riverside area, which had been the industrial district of the city since the late eighteenth century. Moreover, the main locations of the most important sectors of the service industries were also sited way beyond the tourist trail: the Royal United Hospital at Combe Park, the Uni-versity at Claverton Down, the MOD departments at Foxhill, Ensleigh and the Warminster Road, are all in districts peripheral to the central area. The average tourist was likely to arrive by train at Bath Spa station, or by coach or by car, to visit the major attractions in the central area and perhaps trek up through Georgian Bath to the Costume Museum in the Assembly Rooms. At least half of them would also visit the shops. They might well leave Bath with an image of the city as little more than a monument to the architecture of the eighteenth century, its earlier history represented solely by the Roman Baths and its contemporary functions encapsulated in the shops and the Tourist Information Centre.

Another continuity with the past was apparent in the attitudes of per-manent residents towards the tourists and, more particularly, to council policies perceived as being in the interests primarily of visitors. While

Table 10   Numbers of visitors to tourist attractions, selected sites, 1978–1980

Site	1978	1979	1980
Roman Baths/Pump Room	793,664	709,364	679,891
Abbey	250,000*	—	—
Museum of Costume	207,287	120,168	174,194
Victoria Art Gallery	30,742	29,374	36,750
Holborne Menstrie Museum	—	20,374	21,205
Bath Postal Museum	—	5,000*	5,750
Bath Bookbinding Museum	3,232*	3,000*	2,000*

* Estimated numbers.

Source: Data from English Tourist Board 1981, Table 1, p. 74, City Plan, mid-stage report, Bath City Council, November 1982.

many local people liked the 'variety and bustle', others believed that the city was 'tourist dominated', and unpleasantly crowded in July and August. Moreover, some residents questioned the amount of money that the council deemed necessary to spend in order to sustain the 'tourist city', and the large proportion of the local budget (as well as outside investment) that was spent on the central area of Bath. Such debates are reminiscent of similar conflicts of interest in the nineteenth century: those who administer modern Bath face the same difficult task in seeking to balance the needs of residents and tourists to the benefit of all.

Chapter 8

Heritage City:
Images of Modern Bath

The role of successive corporations and councils in developing Bath has been controversial from the days of John Wood's complaints in the early eighteenth century about the corporation's failure to implement some of his ambitious plans. There is also a well-established tradition of ambivalence towards the leisure function of the city, and of conflicts of interest arising between residents and visitors. Long before 'town planning' in the modern sense existed, the corporation was able to exercise considerable influence on the built environment because of its ownership of land and property within the city limits. As the power of the local authority increased over time, so it often became the focus of resentment or protest whenever it was perceived to be favouring the interests of the tourist trade over the needs of the permanent population. Moreover, residents themselves could disagree over the pattern of local authority expenditure in different parts of the city.

None of this was unique to Bath, but it does seem that the special character of the city, and its role in the life of the nation, fostered both an awareness of its 'heritage' value and a sensitivity over its image that was somewhat exceptional in early twentieth-century Britain. In this chapter we identify some key policy and planning issues from the 1920s onward, before considering the views of preservationists and others about the future of postwar Bath, and commenting on the various images of the city revealed by a public consultation exercise carried out by the council in the early 1980s. In conclusion, we note some of the discrepancies between the image and reality of Bath in the 1990s.

Whose city? Planners, preservationists and the people of Bath [1]

During the interwar period the council pursued initiatives which increased its powers of control over development in and around the city. Local Acts of 1925 and 1937 empowered the council to regulate the design of new buildings and the materials used in their construction. In the first

32. Sir Patrick Abercrombie's Plan for Bath, 1945. A Utopian postwar reconstruction was proposed, including the development of an embankment for the River Avon. (Guildhall Archives, Bath)

of these, the use of Bath stone was insisted upon at the expense of Victorian red brick. The Act of 1937 also provided for the listing of all buildings erected before 1820, and required planning permission to be granted for any alterations to listed properties. Moreover, in 1929 the local authorities of Bath, Bristol and the surrounding areas took the unusual step of commissioning an outline regional plan for the district. This was undertaken by Patrick Abercrombie and B. F. Brenton, who, in their report in 1930, identified Bath as 'a compact city in a setting of beautiful country specially to be preserved'.[2] The novel 'green belt' measures put forward in this regional plan were incorporated into the Bath and District Planning Scheme of 1933, which was way ahead of national legislation on planning typical of the 1950s and 1960s. There was a further examination towards the end of the war. Abercrombie, working with the city engineer and the planning officer, prepared a specific 'Plan for Bath' which was published in February 1945.

This was a bold scheme for postwar reconstruction, expansion and development of the city. The suburbs were envisaged as fourteen neighbourhoods. There were to be shopping precincts, open plazas, five more bridges over the Avon, a new hospital and technical college, modern hotels, a recreation ground and lidos, a grand concert hall and a major development of the riverside in Walcot. Vision and optimism were not in short supply in the mid-1940s, but money and materials were. Repairing bomb damage and increasing the housing stock took priority over plazas and recreation grounds in the immediate postwar years, and

33. Postwar council housing: council flats in Combe Down in the 1950s.
(Guildhall Archives, Bath)

Abercrombie's 1945 plan was overtaken by national legislation. Only some modest parts of it, such as the technical college, were incorporated in the twenty-year development proposals that the city authority was required to submit to central government under the terms of the Town and Country Planning Act of 1947, which also established statutory protection for listed buildings. It led to the designation of nearly 2,000 buildings in Bath as Grade I or Grade II, and a further 1,000 or so were listed as Grade III. There were, in addition, many hundreds of other buildings that would probably have been listed as worthy of preservation if they had been in a city with a less rich architectural history than that of Bath.[3]

In Bath, as elsewhere, the pace of redevelopment and new building gathered momentum from around the mid-1950s, but by then concern was growing about the adverse impact on towns of increasing motor traffic and the extent of demolition. Concern for the historic urban centres, in particular, grew stronger in the 1960s. In 1966 the Minister of Housing and Local Government announced an investigation aimed at discovering 'how to reconcile our old towns with the twentieth century, without actually knocking them down'. Bath, Chester, Chichester and York were chosen as case studies for this enquiry, because all four were recognized as cultural assets, but also – with the growth of mass tourism – as economic assets to the nation.[4]

At local level, the council had commissioned Colin Buchanan and Partners in 1964 to carry out a planning and transport study of Bath. The principal feature of the report (published in 1965) was what came to be known as 'Buchanan's tunnel', which was proposed to run under the north-central part of the city to take east–west traffic. Publication of Buchanan's Plan intensified the debate over preservation, but the slow processes of government meant that its implementation was not an immediate prospect. It was not debated by council until the summer of 1971.[5] Meanwhile, virtually wholesale demolition was underway in those parts of Bath which the council had designated as comprehensive development areas. Local controversy over planning policies in the city led to the setting up of a public enquiry in 1972, but this was cancelled before the hearing began, and in its place the Secretary of State for the Environment instigated joint consultations between Bath City Council, Bath Preservation Trust, and the County Council.

The powers of the local council had, however, been eroded by increasing centralization since the 1940s and they were diminished further when the Local Government Act of 1972 was fully implemented two years later. Thereafter, Bath was merely a 'district' within the new county of Avon. It retained the right to use its coat of arms, to call itself a city and to have a mayor, but control of education and highways passed to the county. Moreover, the city's hospitals were now controlled by the West Wiltshire Health Authority, and the council was no longer wholly responsible for water supply or sewage and refuse disposal.[6] Bath's future was henceforth to be determined primarily by the Avon county structure plan. Since the late 1970s a policy of minimal growth for the city has been in place, and preservation has been integral to subsequent plans and proposals for the city. The city council has nevertheless remained the focal point of criticism from residents. The debate over conservation and development has a long history in Bath, but the emergence of an organized preservation movement in the early twentieth century almost certainly owed something to the growing popularity of the city in the Victorian and Edwardian eras as a place of genteel residence. The wealthy or comfortably-off newcomers, with the advantages of education and a leisured life style, were a potentially articulate pressure group and many of them were likely to be more sympathetic to conservation than to radical change. The first organization dedicated to preserving the city's architectural heritage, the Society for the Preservation of Old Bath, was established as early as 1908.

'Old Bath' apparently meant Georgian Bath, to conservationists and councillors alike. Public consultation by means of a local referendum preceded the local Acts of the interwar years, and the powers that the council obtained related to new buildings and to those pre-dating 1820. A neo-Georgian style was approved for the new premises of the Royal Literary and Scientific Institute in Queen Square in 1932. The council undertook some improvements which modified Georgian Bath between the wars, including rebuilding the corners of Kingsmead Square and making a new thoroughfare from St James Street to Southgate Street. The eighteenth-century Kingston baths, south of the abbey, were levelled and the area was paved over to form the present courtyard. No controversy over these measures has been recorded, but proposals by the council (under the 1937 Act) for substantial changes to Walcot Street and to move the Royal National Hospital for Rheumatic Diseases to a new site generated some heated debate and public opposition.[7] A local referendum would have taken place had it not been for the outbreak of war in 1939, which put an end to development for the duration.

The 1945 Abercrombie Plan is said to have been received by the public in general with moderate enthusiasm, although the scale of demolition that it would have entailed and the impact of a proposed ring road (following the lines of the old city walls) brought some opposition. Until the early 1960s, however, reconstruction and the repair of war damage took priority over long-term development. Buildings in the Paragon, the Circus, the Crescent, and in Queen Square were made good. The Abbey churchyard was substantially rebuilt, the Assembly Rooms were again restored and opened to the public in 1963. Publication of the Planning and Transport Study in 1965 marked the beginning of some fifteen years of intense debate over Buchanan's tunnel. It was regarded by the Ministry of Housing and Local Government as an acceptable solution to Bath's traffic problem, and it was supported by the majority of councillors and also the architectural correspondent of the *Bath Chronicle*. But public opinion was sharply divided over the road plan. The debate broadened to encompass the consequences of council policy in the comprehensive development areas, and conservation in general, and in the 1960s the council altered some of its policies in response to public opposition. Beaufort Square (*c.*1730), Kingsmead Square (1730s) and New Bond Street (1806–10), for example, were all saved from demolition or radical modification by the campaigning conservationists. Buchanan's tunnel and accompanying plans were officially abandoned in 1979, on the grounds of escalating estimated costs, but the issue had attracted attention in the national press and the outcome could be claimed as a victory for the conservation lobby.[8]

Changing attitudes in the country as a whole, as well as local events and circumstances, contributed to the growing strength of the preservation movement in Bath. In the first postwar decades an either/or attitude to conservation and development was commonplace. In the climate of the times, restoration, renovation and redevelopment for new uses were rarely considered as viable alternatives to rebuilding. Those who shared the view that redevelopment was a welcome sign of progress would no doubt have agreed with the comment attributed to the city architect of Bath, that 'If you want to keep Georgian artisans' houses, then you will have to find Georgian artisans to live in them.'[9] To others it seemed an act of cultural vandalism to clear away aesthetically pleasing

34. The bus station built on the site of bomb damage incurred in 1942, a serious candidate for the ugliest postwar building in the city. Note the installation of the security camera as part of the fight against crime and disorder. (Fotek, Bath)

35. The Hilton Hotel, Walcot Street, built in 1973. An example of insensitive, modern architecture on an important site close to the River Avon and to the rear of the Pulteney Bridge. (Fotek, Bath)

36. A picture postcard view of the front of Pulteney Bridge, designed by
Robert Adam and built between 1769 and 1774. (Fotek, Bath)

old buildings, particularly when they were replaced by what some regarded
as the depressingly utilitarian bus station, the Snow Hill high-rise flats,
the 'hen coops' of Holloway, and what has been described as the 'vulgar
mass-produced monotony of the Marks and Spencers and Woolworths
building'.[10] Concern for the built and natural environment has increasingly come to be shared by growing numbers of people from all social
classes, as better education and rising living standards have raised the
general level of awareness of cultural and aesthetic values. Consequently,
the either/or attitude was gradually superseded by concepts of sympathetic development, good modern architecture and the conversion of
old buildings for new uses.

   In Bath the conservation issue was given added weight by the
publication in 1973 of *The Sack of Bath*, in association with the Bath
Preservation Trust, which was formed in 1934 following the demise of
the earlier Society for the Preservation of Old Bath. It was further
strengthened by a proliferation of new organizations, including the Bath
Action Group, the Bath Environmental Campaign and the Bath Amenity
and Transport Association, which represented between them a wide
spectrum of opinion in the debate about Bath's future. Such groups, and
many other sympathizers, took part in the 'Save Bath' campaign of the

37. The rear of Pulteney Bridge, located in a prime site in Bath, yet continuing to appear mean and shabby in contrast with the front of the bridge. (Fotek, Bath)

1970s, which culminated in the council adopting the main proposals of the campaigners in the 'Saving Bath' plan of 1978. *The Sack of Bath* became something of a key text, an influential book in which the authors vehemently condemned the consequences of planning in Bath:

> Today artisan Bath is largely rubble. Acres upon acres of the Georgian City's minor architecture have been flattened in the course of a decade and a half … The set pieces – Royal Crescent, the Circus, Milsom Street, the Pump Room, and so on – stand glorious and glistening (some have been restored and cleaned) for tourists to come and see in their thousands every year. But now they have become like mountains without foothills, like Old Masters without frames. The Bath of the working classes, the Bath which made Beau Nash's fashionable resort possible has been swept away … In few places has the notion of 'urban renewal' been applied with such destructive vigour as here, or with such callous disregard for the finer subtleties of urban charm.[11]

Those who actively participated in the campaign to 'Save Bath' – by lobbying MPs and government ministers, by organizing public meetings and marches, and other strategies of protest – were an articulate minority. They came from diverse backgrounds, including students and house-wives, businessmen and professional people, bodies such as the Young Liberals, and at least one former city councillor, as well as the retired city engineer who had been part-author of the Buchanan Plan of the mid-1960s. The majority of Bath's citizens were silent in the great debate over its future.[12] An attempt to canvass their opinion was made, however, in an exercise in public consultation during the early 1980s, as part of the preliminary work on preparing a city plan setting out the council's policies and proposals for Bath in the decade from the mid-1980s to the mid-1990s. A number of organizations were invited to comment on what should be included in the plan, and local papers pub-lished the text of a publicity brochure about the project. A wide range of interests was represented by the organizations consulted, which included conservation and environmental groups, charities, housing associations, women's groups, and such diverse bodies as the Rotary Club and the University of Bath. In total, 194 replies were received by the council, of which 140 were letters or comments submitted by individuals.

The good intentions of the authorities were stated in the prologue to the mid-stage report on the City Plan (November 1982), in which it was acknowledged that planning for the future of Bath entailed recognizing the expectations placed upon the city by a wide spectrum of people. The fundamental question, familiar to corporations and councils of earlier centuries, was also set out: 'Do we preserve Bath at the expense of the needs of the residents?' Some conservationists might reply by agreeing with Adam Fergusson (co-author of the *Sack of Bath – and After*) that 'those who live in and enjoy the beauties of an eighteenth-century town should not expect the amenities of Harlow New Town or Hemel Hemp-stead',[13] but it is highly likely that the majority of Bath's residents would concur with the council's assumption that they expect 'the same oppor-tunities and facilities as those in any similarly sized town in Britain'.

In trying to satisfy the conservationists, while also seeking to meet the needs of the resident population, the business community, and the tourists, those who administer Bath are subject to certain restraints and influences. Physical expansion is curtailed by the minimal growth policy and the green belt around the urban boundaries. What little land there is available for development is concentrated at the periphery, and is designated primarily for industrial use. There are now 5,000 listed buildings in Bath and the whole of the city centre is a conservation area, constituting the largest single such area in the whole country. As in the past, there is a widespread belief that tourism and the retail sector with which it is closely associated are vital to the prosperity of Bath.

These factors have direct consequences in several interrelated ways. The council is reluctant to release land set aside for industrial usage, as this would affect its efforts to maintain economic diversity and provide local jobs by attracting manufacturers and small businesses to its industrial estates. Coupled with the minimal growth policy, this accounts in part for the unmet demand for housing in Bath – particularly for relatively cheap 'starter homes'.[14] The former mining village of Peasedown St John is currently being developed as a dormitory town to house the 'overspill' of Bath's population. The council's concern to maintain the character of Georgian Bath can lead to disputes between home-owners and the planning department over such matters as the colour of external paintwork. There is also tight control over shop frontages, advertising, and street furniture. In general, retail projects likely to draw trade away from the centre are opposed by the council. Pedestrianization and park-and-ride schemes have been introduced to make the central shopping area more attractive, but traffic restrictions on some streets have not been universally welcomed by traders.

Decisions made by the council clearly affect the perceptions that Bathonians have of their city and, as in the nineteenth century, there are those who believe that the official concerns of the council do not coincide with the requirements of the residents. Many of the respondents to the consultation exercise of the early 1980s considered that there was 'a difference in the care and direction of resources to the affluent Georgian Bath and the city centre compared to the outer areas'. Moreover, there existed a strong feeling that if many of the suburban problems were to occur centrally, they would be dealt with promptly and effectively. Allied to these views there was also a conviction among some of the respondents that 'a snob element tends to linger in Bath', exemplified by a professional couple living off the Lower Bristol Road who recalled being told: 'Of course, nobody who is anybody lives south of the river.'

In reality, social segregation is probably not as marked in central Bath and the inner suburbs as it was in the past. Some Georgian houses in the upper town are in multiple occupation, let out to students and young working people. Victorian artisan dwellings, however, have become desirable residences, beyond the means of the contemporary equivalent of an artisan, and are now likely to be lived in by middle-class home-owners. The central Abbey ward remains one of sharp contrasts, encompassing both the Circus and the council flats off Kingsmead Square, but the most extreme social divide in modern Bath is between the central conservation area and the council estates rarely seen by visitors to Georgian Bath. In the early 1980s more than a quarter of the population lived in council-housing estates, located mainly in the south-west sector of the city some three kilometres from the centre. One aim of the City Plan was to consider the needs of residents in outer Bath, for when it was being prepared community centres, branch libraries, banks and other facilities were conspicuously few in outlying neighbourhoods. People living in such places had to travel into the centre not only to enjoy the general amenities of the city, but also to obtain some essential services.

There was clearly a class dimension involved in local perceptions of Bath as 'two cities', but the underlying conflict was seen as the competing interests of residents and tourists. A number of residents held the view that 'the balance ... at present, veers too much towards the tourists', and it was suggested that: 'The people of Bath are turning against the tourists because the powers that be appear to think more of the tourists than the residents.' Comments on visitors to the city ranged from 'tourists are our life blood' to 'the ordinary people of Bath do not benefit from tourists'. The question of tourism evoked some muddled images of the city. While some people saw Bath as 'a Tourist Centre first and foremost', others spoke of it as primarily residential ('one of the pleasanter towns in which to live') and there were those who feared that tourism might destroy the 'special character' of Bath. One conclusion drawn in the report published in November 1982 was that the comments of respondents suggested the possibility of having a clear image of Bath, and that the management of the city would be 'effective, efficient and economic' if it was conducted in accordance with that image. The acknowledged difficulty with that suggestion, however, would be in deciding 'whose image of the city to pursue'. The diversity of the city was obscured in earlier times, by its dominant image as the resort of fashion or a place of genteel residence, and the differing images evoked by modern Bath seem to imply that its complexities were still not fully recognized in the 1980s. In that decade Bath was, in reality, a provincial city with a historic past and a variety of functions. Twentieth-century day-trippers had succeeded 'the quality' and the seasonal visitors, but Bath was widely known as a major international tourist resort. Yet it could also be accurately defined as any one of the following: a residential city, home to a population of some 80,000; a subregional shopping centre serving upward of a quarter of a million people; a subregional medical centre with extensive hospital facilities; a centre for further and higher education; a principal administrative base for the Ministry of Defence. In seeking to understand Bath, diversity remains a more useful concept than any dominant image.

A postscript for the 1990s

Some 3 million tourists visit Bath each year. What brings them to the city, and accounts for it being one of the most popular tourist locations outside London, is set out in a recent official guide:

> For almost two millennia, the city of Bath has welcomed visitors of all kinds: the sick, seeking a cure from the healing waters, the wealthy seeking entertainment, and today's visitors, drawn by the legacy of that past. This includes some of the most spectacular Roman remains

in Britain and a city unique in being almost exclusively Georgian. Bath is one of the best-preserved Georgian cities in the world. Such is its importance that in 1988 the whole city was designated a World Heritage site, the only one in Britain … Today the city attracts visitors from all over the globe and the atmosphere sparkles with cosmopolitan life. Some of the world's greatest actors and musicians perform here and even the streets are alive with entertainers. Bath has become an international cultural centre, as well as a world heritage city.[15]

The tourist who strays beyond the central area might question the description of Bath as being 'almost exclusively Georgian', and few who visited the city in the early 1990s could fail to notice that its streets were alive with beggars as well as buskers. As in the past, the guides present a selective image of Bath with which to attract potential visitors. Similarly, today's residents can feel harassed by the sheer numbers of visitors, in ways that are reminiscent of nineteenth-century encounters.

For some permanent residents of the World Heritage City, the compensations of living in a particularly beautiful architectural environment are offset by the inconveniences of making one's home in a major tourist resort. During the season, life in Bath can take on the quality of a film set, when groups of camera-clicking visitors crowd the streets. Tourism makes a particular impact on those who live in Georgian Bath, such as residents of the Royal Crescent, who are typical of others in their uneasy relationship with the visitors. A voluntary agreement between bus operators and the council theoretically limits the number of guided tours along the Crescent to nine per hour, but the agreement is often breached at peak times, when as many as twelve tourist buses an hour – or one every five minutes – may rumble along the street. The chairman of the Royal Crescent Society has expressed concern about the deteriorating condition of the road, and the volume of traffic causes damage to the stonework of the Grade I listed buildings. Some residents accept that 'If you choose to live in the Royal Crescent you should expect to have your house used as a tourist attraction', but most would like the buses to be limited to five an hour, if not banned completely.[16]

The Crescent has also been the focal point for another clash of interests in the city. As part of the Bath Festival, open-air concerts were held in the Victoria Park in 1992 and 1993, when the international stars José Carreras and Dame Kiri Te Kanawa performed. The lawn in front of the Royal Crescent was used as seating space for the concerts, but this prestige event was modified in 1994 when four residents used an ancient power of veto to refuse to allow the same arrangement as in previous years. The chairman of the Royal Crescent Society told the local press that the majority of residents were happy to share their 'front garden' with others once a year, and the minority of objectors were castigated by one householder as 'selfish snobs'.[17] It is somewhat ironical that one

38. A City Tour bus taking visitors around the Royal Crescent. Controversy surrounds the frequency of the buses and the intrusion of privacy for residents. (Fotek, Bath)

Royal Crescent resident should call others 'snobs', and particularly so in this context, for the festival is an annual event that brings with it evidence of latent class hostility in Bath. The International Festival of Music and the Arts brings top-quality performers to the city, much good publicity, and many 'cultural tourists'. Its organizers (Bath Festivals' Trust) make efforts to appeal to a wide range of tastes, and 'fringe' events are intended to bring entertainments within the reach of all. Yet every year the onset of the festival is accompanied by what has became another annual event, a spate of letters to the press complaining about high ticket prices and élitism. The nineteenth-century social divide between upper-town gentry and the lower-town working classes persists and is given expression in diatribes like the following, written by a resident of Twerton: 'Bath Festival is mainly for the upper class, who want to listen to morbid chamber music, and the likes of it. The festival is run at a loss each year, and they still carry on with it. We must please the snobs in Royal Crescent, Circus and Lansdown.'[18] Moreover, the best intentions of the organizers can be regarded as patronisingly offensive. The idea of setting up a 'soapbox' in the Abbey churchyard (as part of the Festival in 1994) was intended to add something destinctively local to an event acknowledged to be 'full of imported culture', but, instead of turning Bath's town square into a Hyde Park Corner, the soapbox provided a forum for councillors, businessmen, and clergymen.[19] One incensed resident, particularly put out by a 'sermon' from the soapbox, wrote to the *Bath Chronicle* to complain that setting the day, the time, the agenda, the speakers and the order of the speakers was 'more akin to an annual congress of a totalitarian regime, than anything symbolising free speech'.[20]

Another persistent feature from the nineteenth century and earlier is the extremes of wealth and relative deprivation, if not absolute poverty, that co-exist in Bath. These are particularly evident in the housing sector. The recession of the late 1980s stemmed the influx of wealthy new residents, but in the early 1990s the housing market showed signs of a slight recovery. Grade I listed houses are costly to purchase and expensive to maintain. Consequently, few complete period town houses come on the market (only five of the thirty houses in the Royal Crescent remain in single occupation) but, nonetheless, local estate agents were reporting renewed interest by the summer of 1994 from London commuters and by investors from Hong Kong, South Africa, North America and Europe. Houses in the Crescent were selling for some £850,000 to £975,000 in 1993 and 1994. The asking price for a five-bedroomed town house in Lansdown in 1994 was £290,000, and £245,000 for a Grade I listed house in St James Square. A Bath purchasing agent described his clients as 'well-heeled thirty-somethings looking for a permanent home in the £400,000 plus range',[21] but such prices are well beyond the reach of most of Bath's residents. Moreover, substandard homes, lacking basic amenities or in a state of severe disrepair, co-exist with listed buildings in the World Heritage City. Housing reports issued in 1994 revealed that some 3,500 homes in Bath were unfit for habitation and a further 3,400 were in need of essential repairs.[22] Out of a total of 34,100 households surveyed, 10,007 were defined as 'in housing need'. Of these households, 117 lacked basic amenities such as a bath, inside toilet or hot-water supply. A further 1,845 had to share facilities with another household, and 2,688 were in accommodation that was overcrowded.[23] In the report of Avon County Council's Social Stress Study (published in 1994) two parts of the city – Abbey Ward and Twerton Ward – were classified as areas of social and economic deprivation. The criteria by which social stress was measured were criticized in the press by a councillor, photographed in the Circus, who declared: 'I think it is an insult to the people who live in the Abbey ward.' The city centre, however, is not a homogeneous district of Georgian architecture and contemporary affluence. As in the nineteenth century, it remains one where the extremes of both wealth and poverty are particularly apparent. The classification of working-class Twerton as deprived was accepted by the local press as 'perhaps more predictable': 'Families are used to the description. They are also used to seeing little done.'[24] The council estates in and around the city are benefiting from improvement schemes, and the council has powers to issue orders for repairs to private landlords, but the age of the city's housing stock means that poor housing is likely to be a feature of Bath for some time to come. About 40 per cent of houses in the city were built before 1891, and a further 16 per cent date from before 1850.[25]

In addition to those of its population living in substandard accommodation, Bath has a number of homeless people. Precise figures are not available, but in the early 1990s the problem was of sufficient scale to prompt action by the council, the churches, and various charities. A night shelter (initially funded by a £100,000 capital grant from the council) was established, and voluntary bodies organized 'soup runs' to those sleeping rough. During National Housing Week of 6–12 June 1994 the press gave publicity to a proposal to launch a 'deposit bond scheme', with the aim of helping 100 people a year to move into privately-rented accommodation. Another organization, the Bath Resettlement Service, was also active in helping the homeless. The reappearance of beggars on the streets of Bath was a feature of the early 1990s, closely associated with the rise in the numbers of the homeless caused by the effects of recession and government policies, which restricted the right of young people to state benefits. The authorities' response to this phenomenon evokes reminders of past efforts to clear the streets of beggars, for fear of frightening away trade. Genuine humanitarian concern undoubtedly exists for the 'deserving poor' of today, and this was reflected in the response of some councillors, clergymen, the local MP, and several local residents to Prime Minister John Major's remarks in May 1994 about 'offensive and unjustified' beggars. Indeed, a police inspector commented on the liberal tendencies of 'a substantial proportion of people' in Bath, and recalled some members of the public giving money to beggars even as the 'offender' was being cautioned by a policeman.[26] Nonetheless, a complaint that has echoed down the centuries was reiterated in a letter to the *Bath Chronicle* in June 1994, in which the writer expressed the view that 'a lot of the begging here is a con trick' and went on to ask 'why do beggars only appear in the honey-pot areas?' The affluence of Bath, with its comfortably-off residents and its numerous wealthy visitors, has traditionally been a 'honey-pot', attracting the poor in search of charity. Alarmist news reports of beggars making easy money on the streets are nothing new either, and similarities with the past are also discernible in the efforts of the authorities to regulate street life, and to discriminate between the 'deserving' and 'undeserving' poor.

By the summer of 1994, aggressive begging had been stamped out by the 'strenuous efforts' of the council and the police. The activities of some of Bath's beggars in the early 1990s (most of them young, often accompanied by large dogs, and not always sober) did undoubtedly amount

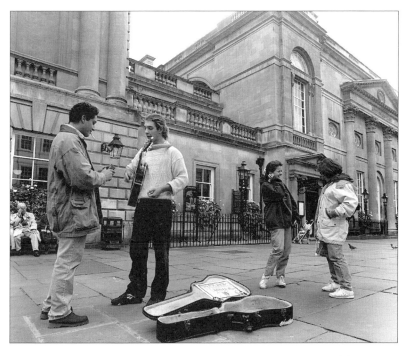

39. A Bath busker performing in the Abbey Churchyard in front of the Pump Room. Buskers represent a popular form of modern beggar, forming a historical continuity with the legendary Bath beggars. (Fotek, Bath)

to harassment, and their presence was an irritation, if nothing more, to many residents and visitors. For retailers and those involved in the tourist trade, they also posed a genuine threat to business by directly intimidating some passers-by and deterring others from frequenting the central areas. However, the available evidence suggests that the numbers of aggressive beggars were few, but that somewhat extreme measures were taken to suppress them. The combined efforts of the council and the police included a more rigorous enforcement of existing laws and the introduction of a by-law prohibiting the consumption of alcohol in public places. As part of this initiative the *Big Issue* magazine for the homeless came to Bath. Those who sell *Big Issue* (and who earn money by retaining a proportion of their takings) are issued with an official badge, which is withdrawn if complaints are made against the vendor: it clearly identifies them as the new 'deserving poor'.

The regulation of street life has been a perennial concern of the authorities throughout Bath's history, and today the buskers as well as the beggars are subject to social control. They operate under an agreed code of practice, and in 1993 the Guild of Buskers was formed to give a voice to the street entertainers of Bath. They seem to be popular with the tourists, and they feature in much of the publicity that advertises the city, but complaints from city-centre residents and shopkeepers about noise levels and affronts to public decency led to greater restrictions on their activities in the summer of 1994. Thereafter, performing in the streets after 10 p.m. was banned, and the press reported that the police would be given powers to 'crack down on any dress, actions or words by buskers which are likely to cause alarm or distress to the public'.[27]

Criminal activity in the city is another perennial feature, with modern overtones. Bath has its share of petty crime and urban disorder, but violent events such as murder are rare. Vehicle-related offences were the predominant problem during 1990, when theft of and from motor vehicles accounted for a third of the city's total crime.[28] The court reports in the local press are a catalogue of vandalism, shoplifting, benefit fraud, drink- and drug-related offences, and prosecutions for using televisions without a licence. Inner-city rioting is unknown in Bath, although in 1992 an incident on one of the suburban council estates escalated into a major disturbance, during which some forty youths stoned a bus, set fire to a car, and smashed windows in houses and shops, before the police gained control of the situation.[29] (This took place in Twerton, which has a reputation reinforced by repetition: the disturbances of 1992 were recalled in a press report of 1994, about planned improvements to the estate.) A few shops in Bath have been burgled by ram-raiders, but the metal blinds that protect retail premises in many towns have not been allowed to disfigure the Georgian city. The installation of roller shutters requires planning permission, and the view of the planning authority is that such shutters could 'destroy the appearance of the street to the detriment of both the residents and the tourists, who like to window-shop in the evenings and at weekends'.[30]

The retail sector of the economy, however, was badly affected by a decline in trade as the recession deepened. High rents and business rates forced out many retailers from the shopping complexes built in the 1980s. About 6 per cent of the city's shops were empty in May 1993. In the Colonnades complex shop after shop closed down, until by June 1994 only one tenant, the Tourist Information Centre, remained in the development.[31] The recession also deterred investors from redeveloping various sites in the city, including the Empire Hotel besides the Guildhall.

In the mid-1990s future prospects are improving. Plans to rejuvenate the spa are in hand, the Empire Hotel is to be converted into expensive accommodation for the elderly, and an Ideas for Bath exhibition at the Hot Bath Gallery attracted much interest. On the other hand, the Ministry of Defence decision, finally made in June 1995, to close its Foxhill site and relocate some 1,600 jobs, is a cause for concern, because of its consequences for local employment. The city also faces uncertainties in other areas. Political change is underway in Bath, after some fifty years of Conservative dominance. The city consistently returned a Conservative MP at every general election from 1945 until 1992, when the electorate rejected Chris Patten in favour of a Liberal Democrat. The revival of Liberalism in Bath has also given the city a Liberal Democrat council, which has already made some controversial decisions and thereby prompted a long-overdue renewal of public interest in municipal politics. The reorganization of local government, in order to create a few unitary authorities, will sweep away Avon County Council, and the Bath and Wansdyke councils will combine to become Bath and North East Somerset, thus posing problems of identity. The position of mayor is again under threat – but tradition has a powerful appeal in Bath and the council is considering how it may preserve its heritage in changed circumstances.[32]

Alongside local reorganization, Bath's civic leaders need to think on a more international scale, making full use of the city's rich diversity and history to create a more sophisticated appeal to visitors from around the world. Many tourists make a depressingly brief visit to the Pump Room and the Roman Baths, purchase a cheap souvenir in Bath Mementos and then depart quickly on the coach to Oxford or Stratford. This produces little cultural or commercial gain for the city, at the heavy price of more annoyance to residents. Bath has always had to respond to changing circumstances and will do so again, albeit reluctantly in the future. A positive way forward would come from harnessing the most important visions of past centuries as models for developing the city into the next century. Remembering the architectural and aesthetic vision of John Wood (father and son) in the eighteenth century, recognizing the unifying purpose of Jerom Murch's civic gospel of the Victorian period and drawing on the Utopian planning of Patrick Abercrombie after World War II, would set the precedents. What is required is a new vision for the twenty-first century that draws on the rich legacy of the city's past for the benefit of its present and future citizens – a difficult task, as earlier historic attempts have shown. What is certain is that commercial imperatives will continue to foster images of Bath that support the generation of tourist money, images that can sit uneasily alongside the realities for people who live in the city.

Notes

Chapter 1

1. Paul Cresswell (ed.), *Bath in Quotes. A Literary View from Saxon Times Onwards* (Bath: 1985), p. 19.
2. Barry Cunliffe, *The City of Bath* (Gloucester: 1986), Chs. 1–6, pp. 1–146. Bryan Little, *Bath Portrait* (Bristol: 1961), Chs. I–VII, pp. 1–92.
3. J. Bulley, 'To Mendip for coal', *Proceedings* of the *Somerset Natural History and Archaeological Society*, Part I, 97 (1952), pp. 48–78; Part II, 98 (1953), pp. 17–45.
4. John Haddon, *Portrait of Bath* (London: 1982), p. 19.
5. Jane Austen, *Persuasion*, first pub. 1818 (Ware, Herts.: 1993), p. 36.
6. Daniel Defoe, *A Tour Through the Whole Island of Great Britain (1724–1726)* (Harmondsworth: 1971), p. 359.
7. Cunliffe, *City of Bath*, p. 89.
8. R. W. Dunning, *A History of Somerset* (Bridgwater: 1987), p. 17.
9. Cunliffe, *City of Bath*, p. 91.
10. Quoted in Cunliffe, *City of Bath*, p. 90.
11. Sylvia McIntyre, 'Bath: The Rise of a Resort Town, 1660–1800', in Peter Clark (ed.), *Country Towns in Pre-Industrial England* (Leicester: 1981), p. 222.
12. John Wroughton, *The Civil War in Bath and North Somerset* (Bath: 1973), pp. 58–84.
13. Wroughton, *Civil War*; Little, *Bath Portrait*, pp. 30–1. See also Robert Dunning, *The Monmouth Rebellion, A Complete Guide to the Rebellion and Bloody Assizes* (Wimborne, Dorset: 1984).
14. Copies of the original warrant (16 November 1685) are held at Bath Library, copy dated July 1786, AL 374 A; copy made *c.*1800, AL 374 B.
15. McIntyre, 'Bath', p. 201.
16. Christopher Morris (ed.), *The Journeys of Celia Fiennes* (London: 1947), p. 21.
17. McIntyre 'Bath', pp. 202–3.
18. *Ibid.*
19. *Ibid.*, pp. 203–4.
20. Little, *Bath Portrait*, p. 31.
21. R. S. Neale, *Bath: A Social History 1680–1850 or A Valley of Pleasure, Yet a*

Sink of Iniquity (London: 1981). See also Roger Rolls, *The Hospital of the Nation: The Story of Spa Medicine and the Mineral Water Hospital at Bath* (Bath: 1988), p. 2.

Chapter 2

1.   R. S. Neale, *Bath: A Social History 1680–1850, or A Valley of Pleasure, Yet a Sink of Iniquity* (London: 1981); David Gadd, *Georgian Summer. The Rise and Development of Bath* (Newbury: 1987).
2.   Princess Amelia's journey is described in Benjamin Price, *The Benevolent Man, A Life of Ralph Allen of Bath* (Harvard University Press, Cambridge, Mass., USA: 1967); information on boat services between Bath and Bristol is taken from the same source, p. 25.
3.   Neale, *Bath*, p. 118.
4.   C. W. Chalklin, *The Provincial Towns of Georgian England. A Study of the Building Process, 1740–1820* (London: 1974), pp. 182–6. The role of international and national credit is emphasized by Neale, but see Chalklin for detailed analysis of regional and local investment in urban development in Bath and other towns between 1740 and 1820. On investment in the Bath Turnpike Trust and other information about capital investment in the Bath region, see B. J. Buchanan, 'The evolution of the English turnpike trusts: lessons from a case study,' *Economic History Review*, 2nd series, XXXIX, 2 (1986), pp. 223–43; 'Aspects of capital formation: some insights from North Somerset, 1750–1830', *Southern History* 8 (1986), pp. 73–93.
5.   Neale, *Bath*, p. 151.
6.   *Ibid.*, pp. 185–209.
7.   Tobias Smollett, *The Expedition of Humphry Clinker* (1771; repr., Harmondsworth: 1983), p. 63.
8.   Anon, 'Bath – A Simile' (1779), quoted in Neale, *Bath*, p. 205.
9.   Sylvia McIntyre, 'Bath: The Rise of a Resort Town, 1660–1800', in Peter Clark (ed.), *Country Towns in Pre-Industrial England* (Leicester: 1981), Table 22, p. 226.
10. Neale, *Bath*, p. 180.
11. McIntyre, 'Bath', p. 225.
12. *Ibid.*, p. 226.
13. Chalklin, *Provincial Towns*, pp. 182–3.
14. Neale, *Bath*, p. 148.
15. Buchanan, 'The evolution of the English turnpike trusts', pp. 231–2.
16. Bryan Little, *Bath Portrait* (Bristol: 1961), p. 80.
17. McIntyre, 'Bath', pp. 208–10.
18. R. W. Dunning, *A History of Somerset* (Bridgwater: 1987), p. 80.
19. Daniel Defoe, *A Tour Through the Whole Island of Great Britain (1724–1726)* (Hammondsworth: 1971) p. 360.
20. From Christopher Anstey, 'A Farewell to Bath', in *The New Bath Guide* (London: 1767), in Paul Cresswell, *Bath in Quotes. A Literary View from Saxon Times Onwards* (Bath: 1985), p. 69.
21. Roger Rolls, *The Hospital of the Nation: The Story of Spa Medicine and the Mineral Water Hospital at Bath* (Bath: 1988), p. 80.

22. McIntyre, 'Bath', pp. 204–6.
23. Smollett, *Humphry Clinker*, p. 68.
24. Graham Davis, 'Entertainments in Georgian Bath: gambling and vice', *Bath History* 1 (1986), pp. 1–26.
25. Smollett, *Humphry Clinker*, pp. 78–9.
26. Chalklin, *Provincial Towns*, pp. 52–3.
27. Jane Austen, *Persuasion* (Ware, Herts.: 1993), p. 19.
28. Anon., 'A Step to the Bath with a Character of the Place', 1700, quoted in Neale, *Bath*, p. 12.

Chapter 3

1. R. S. Neale, *Bath: A Social History 1680–1850, or A Valley of Pleasure, Yet a Sink of Iniquity* (London: 1981), Ch. 3; Sylvia McIntyre, 'Bath: The Rise of a Resort Town, 1660–1800' in Peter Clark (ed.), *Country Towns in Pre-Industrial England* (Leicester: 1981).
2. *The Fussletons in Bath: A series of poetical letters*, (Bath: 1836), letter VIII from Sir Hector Stormer to Admiral Tornado. Bath Library.
3. R. Rolls, *The Hospital of the Nation: The Story of Spa Medicine and the Mineral Water Hospital at Bath* (Bath: 1988), p. 9.
4. Rolls, *Hospital of the Nation*, p. 77.
5. Neale, *Bath*, pp. 70–9.
6. M. Brown and J. Samuel, 'The Jews in Bath', *Bath History* 1 (1986), pp. 150–72.
7. Trevor Fawcett, 'Black people in Georgian Bath', *Avon Past* 16 (Spring 1993), pp. 3–9.
8. McIntyre, 'Bath', p. 215.
9. Trevor Fawcett, 'Eighteenth-century shops and the luxury trade', *Bath History* III (1990), p. 49.
10. McIntyre, 'Bath', p. 238.
11. Louis Simond, *Journal of a Tour and Residence in Great Britain* (1810–11), in Paul Cresswell (ed.), *Bath in Quotes. A Literary View from Saxon Times Onwards* (Bath: 1985), p. 83.
12. Steve Pool, 'Radicalism loyalism and the "Reign of Terror" in Bath, 1792–1804', *Bath History* III (1990), p. 120.
13. *Ibid.*, pp. 114–37, from which information in the following section is chiefly drawn. See also Neale, *Bath*, pp. 310–15.
14. Neale, *Bath*, pp. 50–6, 63–9.
15. John Cam Hobhouse, 'Snug Lying', from *Wonders of a Week at Bath* (1811), in Cresswell, *Bath in Quotes*, pp. 80–1.

Chapter 4

1. R. Mainwaring, *Annals of Bath* (Bath: 1838), p. 262.
2. 'Bodies and Souls: a discursive paper with Glimpses of the City of Bath' (1864), Bath Library.
3. A letter to the mayor of Bath on the causes of the present declining condition of the city, LUD HUDIBRAS (Bath: 1840), Bath Library.

4. S. Gibbs, *The Bath Visitant* (Bath: 1844), pp. 56–7.
5. E. Yates, 'A Week at Bath', *The World*, 8 April 1891.
6. Yates, 'Week at Bath'.
7. *The Guide Through and Round Bath* (1900), p. 10.
8. Bryan Little, *Bath Portrait* (Bristol: 1961), pp. 92–3.
9. Little, *Bath Portrait*, p. 99.
10. *Bath Chronicle*, 4 December 1890.
11. R. Warner, *A History of Bath* (Bath: 1801), p. 344.
12. *Bath Guide* (1900), p. 7.
13. Bruce Crofts, *Forgotten Year: News from Bath in 1882* (Bath: 1982), pp. 4–5.
14. R. Mainwaring, *Narrative of the Progress of an epidemic disease which appeared in Bath in the autumn of 1832* (Bath: 1833).
15. *The Denunciad up to Date*, by Cynic, dedicated to the Bath Corporation, in 2 parts (1898; 1902), p. 7, Bath Library.
16. *The Original Bath Guide* (1830), p. 51.
17. Bath Redivivus, *St Stephen's Review*, 29 October 1887.
18. John Wroughton (ed.), *Bath in the Age of Reform 1830–1841* (Bath: 1972), pp. 59–66.
19. *Ibid.*, pp. 67–9.
20. *Ibid.*, pp. 74–7.
21. Barry Cunliffe, *The City of Bath* (Gloucester: 1986), pp. 157–60.
22. *Ibid.*, p. 160.
23. *Ibid.*
24. Crofts, *Forgotten Year*, p. 4.
25. Cunliffe, *City of Bath*, pp. 160–2.
26. Roger Rolls, *The Hospital of the Nation: The Story of Spa Medicine and the Mineral Water Hospital at Bath* (Bath: 1988), p. 84.
27. Cunliffe, *City of Bath*, pp. 163–5.
28. Visit to Bath (London Doctors), 18 January 1913, pamphlet B914.238 VIS, Bath Library.
29. *Bath and District Shilling Guide Books* (London: c.1916), p. 60.
30. *Ibid.*
31. *The World*, reprinted in *Bath Chronicle*, 20 April 1876.
32. G. P. Davis, 'Image and reality in a Victorian provincial city: a working class area of Bath, 1830–1900', unpublished Ph.D. thesis, University of Bath (1981), pp. 83–4; see also Elizabeth Trotman, 'The employment of female domestic servants, 1851–1881, with special reference to the City of Bath', B.Ed. Hons. dissertation, Bath College of Higher Education (1984).
33. Armistead Cay, *The Mayoralty of George Woodiwiss, Esq., JP, DL, Mayor of Bath November 1897* (Bath: 1898), p. 65.
34. *Bath Chronicle*, 11 November 1869.
35. 'Penelope's Diary', *Bath and County Graphic*, 7 June 1897.
36. *Ibid.*, 27 October 1897.
37. *Shilling Guide Books*, pp. 48–59.

Chapter 5

1. R. S. Neale, 'The standard of living, 1780–1844: a regional and class study', *Economic History Review* 19 (1966), p. 592.

2. Neale, 'The standard of living', p. 593.
3. Duncan Harper, *Bath at Work* (Bath: 1989), p. 7.
4. Mary Ede, 'Bath and the Great Exhibition of 1851', *Bath History* III (1990), pp. 138–58.
5. Harper, *Bath at Work*, p. 91.
6. Hugh Torrens, *The Evolution of a Family Firm. Stothert and Pitt of Bath* (Bath: 1978).
7. R. S. Neale, *Bath: A Social History 1680–1850, or A Valley of Pleasure, Yet a Sink of Iniquity* (London: 181), p. 271.
8. Torrens, *Stothert and Pitt*, pp. 55–6.
9. Harper, *Bath at Work*, pp. 70; 91–2.
10. Elizabeth Trotman, 'The employment of female domestic servants, 1851–1881, with special reference to the City of Bath', unpublished B.Ed. Hons dissertation, Bath College of Higher Education (1984), pp. 39–40.
11. Trotman, 'Employment of female domestic servants', p. 10.
12. J. S. Bartrum, *The Personal Reminiscences of an Old Bath Boy* (Bath: 1910), p. 46, Bath Library.
13. Kenneth R. Clew, *The Kennet and Avon Canal* (Newton Abbot: 1968).
14. Martin Hemmings, 'Bath and its Communications', in J. Wroughton (ed.), *Bath in the Age of Reform 1830–1841* (Bath: 1972), pp. 67–78.
15. Hemmings, 'Communications', p. 72.
16. The Somerset Coal Canal was also bought by the GWR, in 1904, and a new GWR branch line was constructed over most of its course. See Clew, *Kennet and Avon*, and *The Somersetshire Coal Canal and Railways* (Newton Abbot: 1970).
17. Census Enumerators' books, St Michael's Parish, Bath, 1861 (Public Record Office, London).
18. Bath Directory, 1893, Bath Library.
19. Annual Reports of the Chief Constable (1885–1894), Guildhall Archives.
20. Neale, *Bath*, p. 269.
21. R. S. Neale, 'Economic conditions and working class movements in the City of Bath, 1800–1850', unpublished MA dissertation, University of Bristol (1963), p. 6. Neale is inclined to make generalizations in distinguishing between the city's parishes, thus obscuring their complexities. He defines Lyncombe and Widcombe as 'poor' and emphasized its industrial aspects, when in reality it was both industrial and suburban. Similarly, Neale sees Walcot as a suburb of the wealthy, but the size and socio-economic diversity of the parish meant that it did not match entirely either category of 'inner-city' or 'suburban' parish.
22. *Bath and Cheltenham Gazette*, 20 November 1821.
23. *Ibid.*, 19 August 1820; 5 September 1821.
24. *Bath Chronicle*, 22 January 1852.
25. Trotman, 'Employment of female domestic servants', pp. 29–30.
26. See Jay Winter (ed.), *The Working Class in Modern British History* (Cambridge: 1983), pp. 171–9.
27. G. Sanger, *Seventy Years a Showman* (1910), quoted in Kellow Chesney, *The Victorian Underworld* (London: 1970), p. 33.
28. Bath Watch Committee Minutes, 6 volumes, 1836–1900, Guildhall Archives. Evidence, drawn specifically from Minutes 1861–99, in G. P. Davis,

'Image and reality in a Victorian provincial city: a working class area of Bath, 1830–1900', unpublished Ph.D. thesis, University of Bath (1981), p. 48.

29. Davis, 'Image and reality', p. 301.
30. Louie Stride, *Memoirs of a Street Urchin*, ed. Graham Davis (Bath: 1984), pp. 7–8.
31. Neale, *Bath*, p. 271.
32. Walcot Parish Valuation List (1862), Guildhall Archives.
33. *Bath Chronicle*, 2 April 1863.
34. *Ibid.*, 6 November 1876.
35. *Ibid.*, 22 August 1867.
36. Medical Officer of Health Report (1907), p. 25.
37. R. B. Hope, 'Educational developments in the city of Bath, 1830–1902, with special reference to its inter-relations with social and economic change', unpublished Ph.D. thesis, University of Bristol (1970), p. 143.
38. Hope, 'Educational developments', p. 166.
39. Board of Education Report (1902), pp. 11–12, in Hope, 'Educational developments', p. 166.
40. Report of the Interdepartmental Committee on the Employment of Children Act 1903, Parliamentary Papers, 1910, Volume XXVIII, Bath Tabular Statements, Appendix (pp. 534–41), pp. 502–9.
41. Neale, 'The standard of living', pp. 590–606, and *Bath*, pp. 77–81, 282. His main sources were the Account Books of Overseers of Highways (Walcot) for the period 1809–32 (Bath Library), and retail price lists published in the *Bath and Cheltenham Gazette* from 1812 to 1844. The average number of labourers employed by the Highway Surveyors in the first weeks of January, May and September from 1780 to 1851 was only 11.3, although the actual numbers ranged from nil to 89.
42. P. Mathias, *The First Industrial Nation: An Economic History of Britain 1700–1914* (London: 1969), p. 378.
43. Neale, *Bath*, pp. 289–91.
44. Neale, *Bath*, p. 291.
45. Davis, 'Image and reality', pp. 379–448.
46. Medical Officer of Health Annual Reports (1910), pp. 14–15.
47. *Ibid.*
48. *Ibid.*, pp. 56–7.

Chapter 6

1. John Wroughton (ed.), *Bath in the Age of Reform 1830–1841* (Bath: 1972).
2. R. B. Hope, 'Educational development in the city of Bath, 1830–1902, with special reference to its inter-relations with social and economic change', unpublished Ph.D. thesis, University of Bristol (1970), p. 91.
3. The main source for this section is R. S. Neale, *Bath: A Social History, 1680–1850, or A Valley of Pleasure, Yet a Sink of Iniquity* (London: 1981) particularly Ch. 10. Quotations in the text are those used by Neale (unless otherwise indicated) and his references to sources are given in the notes.
4. *Bath and Cheltenham Gazette*, 16 March 1820.
5. *Bath Journal*, 12 June 1829.

6. Wroughton, *Bath in the Age of Reform*, pp. 21–3.
7. *Bath and Cheltenham Gazette*, 18 October 1831.
8. *Ibid.*, 8 November 1831.
9. Wroughton, *Bath in the Age of Reform*, p. 24.
10. For a full account of Roebuck's career in Bath see Neale, *Bath*, pp. 346–83.
11. Wroughton, *Bath in the Age of Reform*, p. 25.
12. Neale, *Bath*, p. 348.
13. For more information on local Chartism see Asa Briggs (ed.), *Chartist Studies* (London, 1959; repr. 1972), Ch. VI.
14. *Bath Guardian*, 9 June 1838, quoted in D. Nicholls, 'Chartism: a local study', unpublished BA Combined Studies dissertation, Bath College of Higher Education (1986), p. 85.
15. *Bath and Cheltenham Gazette*, 19 December 1837.
16. Briggs, *Chartist Studies*, pp. 187–8, 190.
17. Wroughton, *Bath in the Age of Reform*, pp. 105–6.
18. On the Anti-Corn Law League, see J. T. Ward (ed.), *Popular Movements c. 1830–1850* (London: 1970).
19. Briggs, *Chartist Studies*, pp. 342–3; Wroughton, *Bath in the Age of Reform*, pp. 18–19.
20. *Bath Chronicle*, 8 July 1841.
21. Parliamentary election results for the city of Bath (Guildhall Archives).
22. *Bath Chronicle*, 9 January 1902.
23. Wroughton, *Bath in the Age of Reform*, pp. 82–4.
24. Neale, *Bath*, p. 364.
25. *The Fussletons in Bath: A series of poetical letters* (Bath: 1836), p. 4, quoted in Alexander E. Kolaczkowski, 'The Politics of Civic Improvement: Bath 1835–1879, with special reference to the career of Sir Jerom Murch', unpublished Ph.D. thesis, University of Bath (1995), p. 109.
26. Neale, *Bath*, pp. 378–9.
27. G. P. Davis, 'Image and reality in a Victorian provincial city: a working class area of Bath, 1830–1900', unpublished Ph.D. thesis, University of Bath (1981), p. 297 and footnote 82.
28. A. M. Press, *Liberal Leaders of Somerset* (1890), pp. 125–8, Bath Library.
29. Davis, 'Image and reality', Ch. 8, pp. 503–92.
30. *Bath Chronicle*, 11 August 1864.
31. Letter from J. Murch, *Bath Chronicle*, 26 April 1866.
32. C. S. Barter, 'Report on the Sanitary Condition of the City and Borough of Bath during the years 1867 and 1868' (1869), p. 14, Bath Library.
33. *Bath Chronicle*, 24 March 1864.
34. *History of the Bath Waterworks*, published by order of the Council (Bath: 1878) (authorship attributed to the Revd C. W. Shickle), Bath Library.
35. *Bath Chronicle*, 16 May 1895; *Bath Year Book* (1896), Bath Library.
36. See Chapter Four, footnote 33.
37. *Bath Chronicle*, 13 December 1890.
38. See Derek Fraser (ed.), *The New Poor Law in the Nineteenth Century* (London, 1976); for Bath, see Davis, 'Image and reality', pp. 264–71; also Revd Spencer, 'The Working of the New Poor Law in the Bath Union, or a Peep into the Board Room at Walcot', *Bath Tracts* (1836), and Augustus G. Barretté, 'A Few Plain Facts', *Bath Tracts* (1837), Bath Library.

39. Spencer, 'The Working of the New Poor Law', p. 12.

40. British Parliamentary Papers, 1851 Census, Great Britain. Report and Tables on Religious Worship, England and Wales. Table F, p. cclii: Religious Accommodation and Attendance in Large Towns.

41. All information on the school board taken, unless otherwise indicated, from Hope 'Educational development'.

42. Minutes, Church School Managers' Union, 23 March 1876; 20 April 1876; quoted in Hope, 'Educational developments', p. 128.

43. School Board Chronicle, vol LVIII, 1897, p. 320, quoted in Hope, 'Educational developments', p. 161.

Chapter 7

1. A. J. P. Taylor, English History 1914–1945 (Oxford: 1977), p. 2.

2. In replies to a questionnaire on Bath's war effort, the total number of recruits was given as 'direct enlistment 2,969; grouped men 6,813; Military Service Act 1,431'. The first two categories were probably all volunteers, and the remaining 1,431 were conscripts. World War I, Mayor's Business Papers, File CL 10/2, Guildhall Archives.

3. Louie Stride, Memoirs of a Street Urchin, ed. Graham Davis (Bath: 1985), p. 15.

4. Lord and Lady Temple gave over Newton Park House to the military for the duration. It was described in magazine articles as 'Lady Temple's Hospital', to which she donated two Ford ambulances. See Graham Davis, The Langtons at Newton Park, Bath (Bath: 1985).

5. 'Bath War Hospital 1914–1929', copy of talk given by Kate Clarke to Weston History Group (1993), Ref. PP 626, Guildhall Archives.

6. World War I, Mayor's Business, File CL 10/2, Guildhall Archives.

7. Ibid. No figures given for women employed in occupations other than munitions production. For some experiences of one of Bath's nurses, see 'Letters of a VAD' (photocopies) written by Kathleen Ainsworth (1892–1982) to her parents in Swindon, Bath War Hospital, 1916–17, PP 627, Guildhall Archives.

8. World War I, Mayor's Business, File CL 10/2, Guildhall Archives.

9. Stride, Memoirs of a Street Urchin, p. 15.

10. Anne Part, 'The development of the school medical service: a case study of Bath, 1913–1939', History Papers III (Bath College of Higher Education, 1980–1), p. 23. The article is based on Part's unpublished B.Ed. dissertation (1980) of the same title.

11. John Haddon, Portrait of Bath (London: 1982), p. 25.

12. Stride, Memoirs of a Street Urchin, p. 38.

13. The restored Assembly Rooms were reopened by the Duchess of Kent in 1938, only to be gutted by fire in the bombing raids of 1942. Haddon, Portrait of Bath, p. 25.

14. John K. Walton and Cliff O'Neill, 'Numbering the holidaymakers: the problems and possibilities of the June census of 1921 for historians of resorts', The Local Historian 23, 4 (November 1993), p. 20.

15. Barry Cunliffe, The City of Bath (Gloucester: 1986), p. 168.

16.   Stride, *Memoirs of a Street Urchin*, pp. 38–9.

17.   In his Annual Reports, 1919–39, the MOH consistently estimated that 10 per cent of the population were employed in the industrial sector.

18.   For example, in the 1921 census, hotel-, inn- and lodging-house keepers, publicans and beer-sellers, were assigned to the 'Food, Drink and Tobacco' category, but they were included in the 'Personal Service' category at the 1931 census.

19.   *Somerset Guardian*, 29 January 1937.

20.   Dr J. Blackett (MOH for Bath 1919–45), 'Fifty years of public health and social welfare in a county borough, Bath, 1895–1944', unpublished MA dissertation (1949), p. 186, no awarding institution identified: copy held at Bath Library is stamped 'Degree conferred 5 July 1949'.

21.   Bryan Little, *Bath Portrait* (Bristol: 1961), p. 109.

22.   Annual Report, MOH (Bath), 1934, p. 10.

23.   Part, 'Case Study of Bath', p. 22.

24.   Part, 'Case Study of Bath', pp. 7-8 and appendix 1, p. 240; for York see B. S. Rowntree, *Poverty and Progress* (London: 1941).

25.   Annual Reports, MOH (Bath), 1919–39.

26.   Blackett, 'Fifty years of public health and social welfare', p. 13.

27.   *Ibid.*, p. 193.

28.   For a brief account of interwar housing see Stephen Constantine, *Social Conditions in Britain 1918–1939* (London: 1983), pp. 23–32.

29.   Annual Report, MOH (Bath), 1919, p. 24.

30.   Part, 'Case Study of Bath', p. 23.

31.   Blackett, 'Fifty years of public health and social welfare', pp. 186–7.

32.   In 1918–19, 28 unions were affiliated to the Trades and Labour Council.

33.   *Bath Chronicle*, 15 May 1926. Reports from *Bath Chronicle*, 4–15 May, on the strike.

34.   Bath Trades and Labour Council, Minute Books, University of Bath Library, Special Collections: Coop Archive.

35.   *Ibid.*, Delegate Rolls, 1918–19; 1930, University of Bath Library, Special Collections.

36.   Miscellaneous papers found in the Trades and Labour Council archive (not catalogued) include a letter from the Bath Unemployed Association, dated 10 February 1936, and a press cutting of the editorial column of the *Bath and Wiltshire Chronicle and Herald*, 14 February 1936. The BUA wrote to urge the Trades Council to exclude the press from its meetings, apparently because of critical newspaper comments on the role of the BUA in raising the issue of 'underpayment' to some railway workers. The charges were proved to be without foundation.

37.   Letter from Bath Labour Party to Bath Trades Council, 20 September 1932. The Coop Archive (Bath Trades and Labour Council), University of Bath Library, Special Collections.

38.   Blackett, 'Fifty years of public health and social welfare', p. 186.

39.   Niall Rothnie, *The Bombing of Bath* (Bath: 1983), p. 10.

40.   Blackett, 'Fifty years of public health and social welfare', p. 186.

41.   Census (England and Wales), County Reports, Somerset (1951), Table A, Population Change mid-1931–mid-1951, p. XIV.

42.   Rothnie, *Bombing of Bath*, p. 10.

43. Little, *Bath Portrait*, p. 109.
44. See Rothnie, *Bombing of Bath*, and M. Wainwright, *The Bath Blitz* (Bath: 1992).
45. Blackett, 'Fifty years of public health and social welfare', p. 189.
46. Bath Trades and Labour Council, delegate rolls, Coop Archive, University of Bath Library, Special Collections.
47. The City Plan, mid-stage report (November 1982), Bath City Council, p. 37.
48. Unless otherwise acknowledged, all information in this section is taken from the City Plan (November 1982).
49. Little, *Bath Portrait*, pp. 108–21.
50. GOAD Shopping Report (1986), Bath Library.
51. Roger Rolls, *The Hospital of the Nation, The Story of Spa Medicine and the Mineral Water Hospital at Bath* (Bath: 1988), pp. 162–3.
52. The City Plan (November 1982), p. 73: evidence based on data from survey conducted by South Western Industrial Research Limited in 1972–3.

Chapter 8

1. 'Whose city' was asked rhetorically in the prologue to the City Plan (3), mid-stage report (November 1982), Bath City Council.
2. Christopher Pound, *Genius of Bath. The City and the Landscape* (Bath: 1986), pp. 93–4.
3. Adam Fergusson and Tim Mowl, *The Sack of Bath – and After* (first published Bath: 1973; extended edn: 1989).
4. Barry Cunliffe, *The City of Bath* (Gloucester: 1986), p. 173.
5. John Haddon, *Portrait of Bath* (London: 1982), pp. 168–75.
6. *Ibid.*, pp. 33–74.
7. *Ibid.*, p. 25.
8. *Ibid.*, p. 29.
9. *Ibid.*
10. Cunliffe, *The City of Bath*, p. 12.
11. Fergusson and Mowl, *The Sack of Bath*, p. 62.
12. Haddon, *Portrait of Bath*, p. 29.
13. Fergusson and Mowl, *The Sack of Bath*, p. 62.
14. A recent housing report stated that 1,200 new homes were needed to meet housing demand in Bath, *Bath Chronicle*, 19 October 1994.
15. *Official Visitor Guide*, 1993.
16. *Bath Chronicle*, 9 June 1994.
17. *Ibid.*
18. *Ibid.*, 12 June 1994.
19. *Ibid.*, 3 June 1994.
20. *Ibid.*, 9 June 1994.
21. *The Guardian*, 'Weekend', Property Section, 21 May 1994.
22. *Bath Chronicle*, 24 May 1994.
23. *Ibid.*, 19 October 1994.
24. *Ibid.*, 9 September 1994.
25. *Ibid.*, 24 May 1994.

26. *The Guardian*, 'Society' (article by Tim King, 'Those who pass by', on begging and homelessness in Bath), 14 September 1994.
27. *Bath Chronicle*, 24 May 1994.
28. Avon and Somerset Constabulary, Annual Report of the Chief Constable (1990), Bath Library.
29. *Bath Chronicle*, 24 May 1994.
30. *Ibid.*, 9 August 1993.
31. *The Guardian*, 'Weekend', 21 May 1994.
32. *Bath Chronicle*, 10 June 1994.

Further Reading

A. Books and Reports

Patrick Abercrombie *et al.*, *A Plan for Bath* (Bath: 1945)

Christopher Anstey, *The New Bath Guide* (London: 1767)

A. Barbeau, *Life and Letters at Bath in the XVIII Century* (London: 1904)

C. S. Barter, *Report on the Sanitary Condition of the City and Borough of Bath during the years 1867 and 1868* (1869), Bath Library

B. S. Bartrum, *The Personal Reminiscences of an Old Bath Boy* (1910), Bath Library

Asa Briggs (ed.), *Chartist Studies* (London: 1959; repr. 1972)

C. W. Chalklin, *The Provincial Towns of Georgian England. A Study of the Building Process, 1740–1820* (London: 1974)

Paul Cresswell (ed.), *Bath in Quotes. A Literary View from Saxon Times Onwards* (Bath: 1985)

Bruce Crofts, *Forgotten Year. News from Bath in 1882* (Bath: 1982)

Barry Cunliffe, *Roman Bath Discovered* (London: 1971; 2nd edn 1984); *The City of Bath* (Gloucester: 1986)

Graham Davis, *The Langtons at Newton Park, Bath* (Bath: 1980; 2nd edn 1985); *Bath Beyond the Guide Book. Scenes From Victorian Life* (Bristol: 1988); 'The Scum of Bath: The Victorian Poor', in Barry Stapleton (ed.), *Conflict and Community in Southern England* (Stroud: 1992), pp. 183–98.

Daniel Defoe, *A Tour Through the Whole Island of Great Britain (1724–1726)* (Harmondsworth: 1971)

Robert Dunning, *The Monmouth Rebellion, a Complete Guide to the Rebellion and Bloody Assizes* (Wimbourne, Dorset: 1984)

Trevor Fawcett and Stephen Bird, *Bath: History and Guide* (Stroud: 1994)

Adam Fergusson and Tim Mowl, *The Sack of Bath – and After* (first published Bath: 1973; extended edn: 1989)

Derek Fraser, *The New Poor Law in the Nineteenth Century* (1976)

David Gadd, *Georgian Summer. The Rise and Development of Bath* (Newbury: 1987)

S. Gibbs, *The Bath Visitant* (Bath: 1884), Bath Library

John Haddon, *Portrait of Bath* (London: 1982)

Duncan Harper, *Bath at Work* (Bath: 1989)

Walter Ison, *The Georgian Buildings of Bath* (London: 1948; 2nd edn, Bath: 1980)

J. Lees-Milne and D. Ford, *Images of Bath* (Richmond-upon-Thames: 1982)

Bryan Little, *The Building of Bath* (London: 1947); *Bath Portrait* (Bristol: 1961)

R. Mainwaring, *Annals of Bath* (Bath: 1838); *Narrative of the Progress of an epidemic disease which appeared in Bath in the autumn of 1832* (Bath: 1833)

Sylvia McIntyre, 'Bath: The Rise of a Resort Town, 1660–1800', in Peter Clark (ed.), *Country Towns in Pre-Industrial England* (Leicester: 1981), pp. 198–244

L. Melville, *Bath under Beau Nash – and after* (London: 1926).

Tim Mowl and Brian Earnshaw, *John Wood: Architect of Obsession* (Bath: 1988)

R. S. Neale, *Bath: A Social History 1680–1850, or A Valley of Pleasure, Yet a Sink of Iniquity* (London: 1981)

Benjamin Price, *The Benevolent Man, A Life of Ralph Allen of Bath* (Cambridge, Mass.: 1967)

Christopher Pound, *Genius of Bath. The City and the Landscape* (Bath: 1986)

Roger Rolls, *The Hospital of the Nation: The Story of Spa Medicine and the Mineral Water Hospital at Bath* (Bath: 1988)

Niall Rothnie, *The Bombing of Bath* (Bath: 1983)

R. A. L. Smith, *Bath* (London: 1944)

Tobias Smollett, *The Expedition of Humphry Clinker* (Harmondsworth: 1983)

Louie Stride, *Memoirs of a Street Urchin*, ed. Graham Davis (Bath: 1984)

Hugh Torrens, *The Evolution of a Family Firm. Stothert and Pitt of Bath* (Bath: 1984)

M. Wainwright, *The Bath Blitz* (Bath: 1975; Bath: 1992)

J. T. Ward (ed.), *Popular Movements c.1830–1850* (London: 1970).

John Wood, *A description of Bath* (2nd edn, corrected and enlarged, London: 1765)

B. Wriston, *Rare Doings at Bath* (Chicago, USA: 1978)

John Wroughton (ed.), *Bath in the Age of Reform 1830–1841* (Bath: 1972); *The Civil War in Bath and North Somerset* (Bath: 1973)

B   Journals

Mick Aston, 'The Bath region from late prehistory to the middle ages', *Bath History* I (1986), pp. 61–89

Stephen Bird, 'The earliest map of Bath', *Bath History* I (1986), pp. 128–49

M. Brown and J. Samuel, 'The Jews in Bath', *Bath History* I (1986), pp. 150–72

Brenda Buchanan, 'Aspects of capital formation: some insights from North Somerset, 1750–1830', *Southern History* 8 (1986), pp. 73–93; 'The evolution of the English turnpike trusts: lessons from a case study', *Economic History Review*, 2nd series, XXXIX, 2 (1986), pp. 223–43

R. Angus Buchanan, 'The bridges of Bath', *Bath History* III (1990), pp. 1–21

Barry Cunliffe, 'Major Davis: architect and antiquarian', *Bath History* I (1986), pp. 27–60

Peter Davenport, 'Bath Abbey', *Bath History* II (1988), pp. 1–26

Graham Davis, 'Entertainments in Georgian Bath: gambling and vice', *Bath History* 1 (1986), pp. 1–26

Mary Ede, 'Bath and the Great Exhibition of 1851', *Bath History* III (1990), pp. 138–58

Trevor Fawcett, 'Eighteenth-century shops and the luxury trade', *Bath History* III (1990), pp. 49–75; 'Black people in Georgian Bath', *Avon Past* 16 (1993), pp. 3–9

Mac Hopkins-Clark, 'A change of style at the Theatre Royal, 1805–1820', *Bath History* IV (1992), pp. 124–35

John Kite, '"A Good Bargain": the struggle for a Public Library, 1850–1924', *Bath History* IV (1992), pp. 136–54

Briggitte Mitchell, 'English spas', *Bath History* I (1986), pp. 189–204

Tim Mowl, 'A trial-run for Regent's Park: Repton and Nash at Bath, 1796', *Bath History* III (1990), pp. 76–89

R. S. Neale, 'The standard of living, 1780–1844: a regional and class study', *Economic History Review* (1966), pp. 590–608

Steve Pool, 'Radicalism, loyalism and the "Reign of Terror" in Bath, 1792–1804', *Bath History* III (1990), pp. 114–37

Robin Whalley, 'The Royal Victoria Park', *Bath History* V (1994), pp. 147–69

C Unpublished dissertations and theses

J. Blackett, 'Fifty years of public health and social welfare in a county borough, Bath, 1895–1944', MA dissertation, no awarding institution identified (1949). Copy held at Bath Library

G. P. Davis, 'Image and reality in a Victorian provincial city: a working class area of Bath, 1830–1900', Ph.D. thesis, University of Bath (1981)

R. B. Hope, 'Educational developments in the city of Bath, 1830–1902, with special reference to its inter-relations with social and economic change', Ph.D. thesis, University of Bristol (1970)

V. J. Kite, 'Libraries in Bath, 1618–1964', thesis presented for the Fellowship of the Library Association (1966)

Alexandra E. Kolaczkowski, 'The Politics of Civic Improvement: Bath 1835–1879, with special reference to the career of Sir Jerom Murch', Ph.D. thesis, University of Bath (1995)

R. S. Neale, 'Economic conditions and working class movements in the City of Bath, 1800–1850', MA dissertation, University of Bristol (1963)

D. Nicholls, 'Chartism: a local study', BA Hons. Combined Studies dissertation, Bath College of Higher Education (1986)

Anne Part, 'The development of the school medical service: a case study of Bath, 1913–1939', B.Ed. Hons. dissertation, Bath College of Higher Education (1980)

Ann Partridge, 'The Dolemeads: a study of early municipal housing in Bath', B.Ed. Hons. dissertation, Bath College of Higher Education (1980)

J. Saunders, 'Hotel provision in Bath, 1851–1891', B.Ed. Hons. dissertation, Bath College of Higher Education (1980)

Elizabeth Trotman, 'The employment of female domestic servants, 1851–1881, with special reference to the City of Bath', B.Ed. Hons. dissertation, Bath College of Higher Education (1984)

P. M. Wadsworth, 'Leisure in nineteenth century Bath', MA dissertation, University of Kent (1977)

Index

Figures in bold indicate illustrations.